WHAT PEOPLE
ARE SAYING ABOUT
WHEN NATIONS DIE .

D0401941

Brilliant. . . . Thoroughly documented and persuasively pre-sented, the message of *When Nations Die* is one that is needed now.
> **D. James Kennedy**

Black writes with a rich sense of history and a deft treatment of modern issues. Thought provoking and powerful.
> **Os Guinness**
> author, *The American Hour*

A lucid and revealing analysis of how great civilizations have died, and a practical prescription for avoiding their fate. Timely, provocative, and essential reading.
> **William Kilpatrick**
> author, *Why Johnny Can't Tell Right from Wrong*

The analogy between the decadence of ancient civilization and the decadence of our own culture is striking and dreadfully true.
> **Russell Kirk**
> author, *The Roots of American Order*

WHEN NATIONS DIE

Ten Warning Signs of a Culture in Crisis

JIM NELSON BLACK

Tyndale House Publishers, Inc.
WHEATON, ILLINOIS

Published in association with the literary agency of Alive Communications, 1465 Kelly Johnson Blvd., Suite 320, Colorado Springs, CO 80920.

Cover illustration © 1994 by Loren Baker. Portrait of Henry VIII provided courtesy of the Board of Trustees of the National Museum & Galleries on Merseyside (Walker Art Gallery).

Scripture quotations marked NKJV are taken from The New King James Version. Copyright © 1979, 1980, 1982, Thomas Nelson Inc., Publishers.

Scripture verses marked TLB are taken from *The Living Bible,* copyright © 1971 owned by assignment by KNT Charitable Trust. All rights reserved.

Library of Congress Cataloging-in-Publication Data

Black, Jim Nelson.
    When nations die : ten warning signs of a culture in crisis / Jim Nelson Black.
       p.   cm.
    Includes bibliographical references and index.
    ISBN 0-8423-8007-8 / (softcover) :
    1. History (Theology) 2. Christianity and culture.
  3. Civilization—Philosophy. 4. Civilization, Modern—20th century.
  5. United States—Moral conditions. I. Title.
    BR115.H5B47   1994
    261—dc20   94-30406

Printed in the United States of America

00 99 98 97 96 95
7   6   5   4   3   2   1

To my wife, CONNEE,
not only for her assistance
with ideas and research,
but for her love
and companionship;
and to my daughter,
ALISON,
and my son, GAVIN,
who have championed
this study from the first.

BECAUSE Roman civilization perished through barbarian invasions, we are perhaps too much inclined to think that that is the only way a civilization can die.

If the lights that guide us ever go out, they will fade little by little, as if of their own accord. . . .

We therefore should not console ourselves by thinking that the barbarians are still a long way off. Some peoples may let the torch be snatched from their hands, but others stamp it out themselves.

Alexis de Tocqueville
Democracy in America

Contents

Acknowledgments *xi*

Introduction: The Temper of the Times *xiii*
    Chapter 1 America on the Brink 1

Part 1 *SOCIAL DECAY*
    Chapter 2 The Crisis of Lawlessness 19
    Chapter 3 Loss of Economic Discipline 41
    Chapter 4 Rising Bureaucracy 59

Part 2 *CULTURAL DECAY*
    Chapter 5 The Decline of Education 73
    Chapter 6 Weakening of Cultural Foundations 101
    Chapter 7 Loss of Respect for Tradition 125
    Chapter 8 Increase in Materialism 149

Part 3 *MORAL DECAY*
    Chapter 9 The Rise in Immorality 173
    Chapter 10 Decay of Religious Belief 199
    Chapter 11 Devaluing of Human Life 211

Conclusion
    Chapter 12 The Enduring Challenge 229

Appendix: Classical Studies on the Fate of Nations 255
Notes 265
Bibliography 271
Index 277

ACKNOWLEDGMENTS

I WOULD like to express my deep gratitude for the suggestions and comments of Dr. Russell Kirk, made shortly before his untimely death in the spring of 1994. As one of the most illustrious historians and thinkers of our day, Dr. Kirk was an authority on the parallels between modern culture and the past. His insight and advice have been of immense value to me in preparing the final draft of this work. As a longtime disciple of Kirk's writings on democracy and the history of ideas, it gives me immense pleasure to be able to include many of his observations in these pages.

In a letter to me about this book, written shortly before his death, Russell Kirk acknowledged the undeniable dangers ahead for American society, saying, "I perceive that we are agreed on the present state of our culture." And he added, "Aye, the analogy between the decadence of ancient civilization and the decadence of our own culture is striking and dreadfully true." In his remarks, Dr. Kirk indicated that he hoped to review the book in his literary journal. Though he did not live to see its publication, I have been challenged by his perspectives and research in these subjects; and I trust that each reader may grasp some sense of the great man's own passion for these matters.

In addition, I would like to thank my esteemed friend Dr. Os Guinness for his review and comments; and a word of thanks to Blesson Oborokumo of Washington, D.C., for his candid remarks on conditions in the nation's capital. I am grateful to Dr. Ken Taylor, Mark Taylor, Ron Beers, and Ken Petersen at Tyndale

House for their interest in and support of this project, and to Dan Elliott, Kathy Stinnette, and their colleagues who have labored with me in its preparation. I would like to express my gratitude to my agents, Rick Christian and Greg Johnson of Alive Communications, and especially to my friend Michal Mardock, who helped shape the project at the outset.

INTRODUCTION

The Temper of the Times

LOOKING out across the wastes of ancient Carthage, it is hard to imagine the wealth and power that once existed here. Six hundred years before the birth of Christ, this was the political and commercial center of the Western world. Legions anchored here; fortunes beyond imagination were won and lost in these very streets. On any given day, a hundred seagoing merchant vessels crowded into the huge crescent-shaped outer harbor while as many as two hundred fighting ships stood at arms in the inner lagoon.

Today there is nothing but desolation and ruin as far as the eye can see. Even scruffy trees and weeds find it hard to exist on this barren soil. The hollowed-out stone coffins of infants sacrificed to the pagan gods of the Carthaginians and the pillaged ruins of the Roman baths of Julius Caesar offer scant evidence today of the empire that once thrived in this place.

When I lived and taught here for a short time in the city of Tunis—the modern capital that now occupies a promontory of land where Carthage once stood—I was constantly aware of the incredible paradox of history. Today a thriving city of modern Tunisians—neither Arab nor Greek nor Roman, but a mixture of all of them, plus a handful of other races—lives and works here in the shadows of a once great empire. The memory of former glory survives: It is never entirely out of mind. But the reality today is far different. The empire is dead.

Across the Mediterranean and six hundred miles to the west are the ancient ports of Spain—Cádiz, Málaga, Almería, Cartagena, Alicante, and Barcelona—from which the Carthaginians, the Moors, the Romans, the Jews, and later the ethnic Spaniards dispatched their galleons and merchant fleets to open up the West. In cities such as Sevilla, Granada, Córdoba, and Valencia, the signature of great empires is still visible in a cacophony of architecture, language, and traditions. But the glory is gone.

The pride and the power of ancient Spain are all but invisible today. In cities like Marbella on the Costa del Sol, where I spent a year of my youth, there is now wealth and opulence, but it is the wealth of Arab, French, Italian, German, and American entrepreneurs. It is the wealth of jet-setters who discovered a playground on the shores of a faded empire. The castles of Spain no longer inspire fantasy or terror.

History is littered with the remains of ancient empires. Prowling among the ruins provides employment for legions of scientists, archaeologists, and tour guides—and it even makes for some rousing Hollywood scripts, as the Indiana Jones films will attest. But when we are confronted by signs of decay within our own culture and when so many resonant parallels with the fallen giants ring out from the pages of history, we have to wonder: How can such great nations die? How can such vast wealth simply disappear? And what does all this say about the chances for our own civilization?

The collapse of the Soviet Union, which has been constantly in the headlines since the fall of 1989, is clearly the most recent example of the fate of nations. But it is not the only one. In this century alone we have seen the fall of the German Reich, the Austro-Hungarian Empire, the Italian Empire of Benito Mussolini, the Japanese Empire of Hirohito, and not least, the British Empire. So what is the force that brings great nations to their knees? Obviously, war is often a factor in the final dissolution of empires, but what causes certain societies to rise so high and then collapse so suddenly? That will be the concern of this book.

Ten Symptoms of Decline

In his important study of "decadence" in modern society, the British scholar C. E. M. Joad said that luxury, skepticism, weariness, superstition, and a preoccupation with self are unmistakable signs of decline. In a similar study, C. Northcote Parkinson offered six symptoms of decline. They included overcentralized government, inordinate growth in taxation, a top-heavy system of administration, promotion of the wrong people, the urge to overspend, and a rise of "liberal opinion"—that is, the popularization of attitudes and policies controlled by sentiment rather than sound moral judgment.

Do these symptoms sound familiar today? Could our own culture already be in the latter stages of decline? Is it possible that America—once universally acknowledged as the foremost economic and military power in the world—may one day, perhaps very soon, go the way of Greece and Rome?

In these pages it is my intention to examine these and other questions and to review the symptoms of decline that may be found in the literature of the great civilizations—conditions that demonstrate the weakening of society. In particular, I would like to review, in context, the unmistakable evidence of decay that heralds the death of great nations.

Among the social symptoms we should recognize are a general increase in lawlessness throughout the culture; the loss of economic discipline and self-restraint; rising bureaucracy, government regulation, and taxes; and a decline in the quality and relevance of education. Among cultural factors, we see a weakening of the foundational principles that contributed to the greatness of the nation, a loss of respect for established religions, and an increase in materialism. Important spiritual indicators include a rise in immorality, the lure of alien gods, and a decline in the value of human life. These ten symptoms of cultural dysfunction are unmistakable signs of decay that may be discovered in great societies from antiquity to the present—symptoms that, in sufficient combination, indicate the impending demise of any culture.

When nations die, they do not simply disappear. Obviously, certain elements of Greek and Roman culture survive to this day. Babylonian, Egyptian, and Sumerian artifacts remain as indicators of the forms of cultures that once dominated the ancient world. And clearly many ideas from the age of exploration and enlightenment have come down to us from the empires of Spain and France. While the people of those lands are still struggling with their loss of power and esteem, many of their monuments and achievements have passed into our own hands. Today we hold the mantle of history, but for how long?

From recent experience we can see that the collapse of Communism did not cause the Russian people to vanish; and the fall of the British Empire in the first half of this century did not lead to the disappearance of the nations of Great Britain. But the loss of creative vitality in each of these cultures and the fundamental shift from one system of belief to another, in each instance, signaled the beginning of enormous social and political changes.

By all reports, the people of Russia are now marching in a new direction. For the moment at least, we are still hearing good news of the restoration of personal liberties, of freedom of speech and freedom of worship. Britain, on the other hand, has turned even further away from its moral and political heritage in pursuit of a socialist utopia. And short of some miracle or a great spiritual awakening, even greater despair and some final collapse may be in the picture for Great Britain in the years just ahead.

The lesson for us is that, even if we fear that America has turned its back on its foundational beliefs and its civic virtues, we certainly cannot afford to give up on this country or to lose hope of a spiritual renewal. We are under tremendous pressures; we are confronted by a level of social disintegration that exceeds anything we have ever experienced in this nation. But one of the greatest reasons for the decline of American society over the past century has been the tendency of Christians who have practical solutions to abandon the forum at the first sign of resistance. Evangelicals in particular have been quick to run and slow to stand by their beliefs. In reality, most Christians had already vacated the "public square" of moral and political debate by their own free will, long before civil libertarians and others came forth to drive us back into the churches.

Our challenge today is not to run from conflict but to engage in it. Our "fight or flight" reactions should propel us forward into the center of the controversy. We should also remember that in the parable of the talents, as spoken by Jesus in the Gospel of

Luke, the landowner tells his servants to go forth into the vineyard and "occupy till I come." That should be a vital lesson for every Christian today. Jesus Christ did not warn us to run away, to flee to the hills, or to hide our eyes, but to go into the fields and bring forth the harvest. We are to occupy as faithful soldiers of a loving God until the Commander himself returns.

It is my hope that the book will be instructive and eye-opening and that it may cause each reader to feel closer to those who went before us and laid the foundations of our culture. We are not really all that different from those men and women of the past, and we can profit a great deal from their achievements and their failures if we are willing to listen and learn from them. But most important of all, it is my prayer that we will recommit ourselves to the values from which American society was born, that we will return to the very Source of our strength—to the one and only Truth that sets us free.

1

America on the Brink

EVENTS surrounding the D-day celebrations of June 1994 caused many people in the United States and Europe to pause briefly to reflect upon the enormous changes in Western society over the past fifty years. Whenever you stop to consider all that has happened since the end of the Second World War, you immediately recognize the incredible transformations that have taken place in the world around us. Science and technology have altered all our perceptions about the dimensions of time and space. The fall of the Iron Curtain has shifted political boundaries. And the emergence of new economic forces in Europe and the Far East has created a whole new chapter in diplomatic affairs.

Unfortunately, none of these changes has enhanced our sense of peace or security. We seem to be threatened by chaos as never before. We are facing social collapse in the cities of this nation, and our fears are only complicated by feelings of uncertainty about the coming century and the new millennium. Even as we applaud the innovations that have brought us a half century of "progress" and a host of new technical marvels, we have to admit that most things have not changed for the better in the decades since 1944.

Thanks to the shocking growth of government, we face an avalanche of new taxes, increased regulation, and more interference in every aspect of our daily lives. Public education is on shaky ground, and job security is no longer very secure for anyone, male or female. These and other concerns are testing the limits of our emotional and spiritual resolve. Yet many people are trying to deal with their problems without the support of traditional values or the moral foundations our predecessors once took for granted.

Earthquakes, floods, fires, hurricanes, deadly winter storms, and a record number of tornadoes over the past two years have aroused even deeper fears and concerns. Suddenly we wonder if the earth itself has turned against us. And in the background the threat of armed conflict has not gone away. At this moment more than forty wars are being waged somewhere in the world. Which of these might escalate to the magnitude of a Sarajevo, a Kuwait, or another Vietnam? What are we to make of so much strife and tension in the modern world? How are we to deal with the growing polarization of the Right and the Left in political and cultural affairs? And how do we deal with the problems caused by the obvious decline in morals, the rising crime and violence in our cities, and the genuine threats posed by personal debt and an out-of-control federal deficit?

Warnings from History

The tensions in the world today are only an indication of the deep turmoil in our souls. The American people have come to a moment of crisis like no other in our history. We are being pressured by educators, intellectuals, and political elites into experimenting with new ideologies that are not only revolutionary but alien to our fundamental beliefs. We have every reason to worry about things such as multiculturalism, diversity, and political correctness. We should be concerned about rising immorality and the signs of a growing disrespect for human life. It is high time we expressed concern for the collapse of law and order. Conditions like these have contributed to the demise of nations throughout history.

As I have looked back across the ruins and landmarks of antiquity, I have been stunned by the parallels between those societies and our own. For most of us the destruction of Carthage, the rise of the Greek city-states, and the Fall of Rome are mere ghosts of the past, history lessons long forgotten. And such things as the capture of Constantinople, the dissolution of the Holy Roman Empire, the collapse of the kingdoms of France and Spain, and the slow withering decline of the British Empire are much less clear and less memorable. Most of us do not remember much from our history lessons about the French Enlightenment or, for that matter, the issues that led to the American Revolution. But this is the legitimate background of our culture. If we are to grasp the importance of our own place in history, it is vital that we reconsider the nature of life in those earlier times. For within those eras and movements are the seeds of the troubles we face today.

In an influential book written nearly thirty years ago, Harold F. Blum said that we are implicated in an experiment as old as time, building in one direction—toward bigger, bolder, more fully developed life. He used the phrase "time's arrow"—an expression first employed by Sir Arthur Eddington—claiming that societies are instruments for improving the fortunes of mankind. It is the attitude that, in time, all adversities may be overcome. Great ideas are rewarded with great success, and tyrants always fall. But is it really that simple?

When you begin to align the events of history with the wars and international events of our day, you will discover a startling portrait. In the great empires of history we see a picture of our own world; and in the fatal decisions that have led time after time to catastrophe, we have a stark warning of the consequences of cultural and moral decay. To ignore such lessons is to court disaster; but, if heeded, they may yet save us from collapse.

When nations die, millions of lives are affected. The innocent and the wicked suffer much the same defeat. Of the twenty-one great civilizations studied by Arnold Toynbee in his monumental work *A Study of History,* ours alone survives intact; but we are facing incredible pressures. Virtually every one of the symptoms of decline that can be detected from history is present in this nation today. So we must ask: What happens in Washington or Moscow or Rome when science and scholarship come up empty? And what happens when history and ideas collapse? Is there any hope for saving a society once decay sets in? Are there any lessons to be learned from the failures of all the ancient civilizations? And is there still hope for America? These are some of the questions to be discussed in this book.

Pressures from Within

The lesson of history is that nations die from a lethal combination of internal and external pressures. Moral decay, combined with rising violence, lawlessness, and intellectual apathy, leads invariably to the disintegration of the structures that make civilization possible. War, natural disasters, and social deterioration wreak havoc upon society. From ancient times to the present, the pathology of decadence is unmistakable, and in times of trouble it is imperative that we heed these warnings.

Once, America was a beacon of integrity and virtue. We were a nation dedicated to life, liberty, and the pursuit of happiness, and our example of moral and material prosperity made us the envy of the entire world. But things are changing. Today America is more of an object lesson to the world—an example of what happens to great nations when they lose their vision and moral restraint. Even tiny Singapore recently proved to be morally superior. To most of the world, the dispute over the caning of Michael Fay in early 1994 was a dramatic statement of the decline of American character. We were simply too weak and undisciplined to see the practical realities of the situation.

In an address I attended at the Heritage Foundation in December 1993, former secretary of education William Bennett recounted a conversation with a well-known Asian writer who offered a grim assessment of this country. He said, "While the world still regards the United States as the leading economic and military power on earth, this same world no longer holds us in moral respect as it once did. When the rest of the world looks at America now, they no longer see a 'shining city on a hill.' Instead, they see a society in decline, with exploding rates of crime and social pathologies."

Bennett said, "We all know that foreigners come to America with fear, and once they are here they travel in fear. It is our shame to realize that they have good reason to fear: A record number of them get killed here. Today many who come to America believe they are visiting a degraded society." There are still plenty of jobs. We have enormous opportunities and unmatched material comforts. "But," Bennett added, "there is a growing sense among

many that when they come here they are slumming." Then he
went on:

> Intellectual honesty demands that we accept facts that we would
> sometimes like to wish away. Hard truths are truths nonetheless,
> and the hard truth is that something has gone wrong with us.
> America is not in danger of becoming a Third World country. We
> are too rich, we are too proud, we are too strong to allow that to
> happen. It is not that we live in a society completely devoid of
> virtue. Many people live well, decently, even honorably. There
> are families; there are schools, churches, and neighborhoods, and
> even entire communities of virtue that work. There are places
> where virtue is taught, but there is a lot less of this than there
> ought to be.

Evidence of this nation's social and moral decline can also be
found in the *Index of Leading Cultural Indicators,* published in
1993 by the Heritage Foundation and Empower America, a
research group headed by Bennett and Jack Kemp. Since 1960,
the population of the United States has increased 41 percent. The
Gross Domestic Product has nearly tripled. Total social spending
at all levels of government, measured in constant 1990 dollars,
has risen from 142 billion to 787 billion—more than a fivefold
increase.

But according to Bennett's study, during that same thirty-year
period, there was a 560 percent increase in violent crime and a
400 percent increase in illegitimate births. Despite massive levels
of public assistance and unprecedented welfare spending, we
witnessed a quadrupling of the divorce rate, a tripling of the
number of children in single-parent homes, a 200 percent increase in teenage suicides, and a drop of 75 points in the average
SAT scores of high school students.

The Decivilization of America

These are shocking statistics, but how does the United States compare with other industrialized nations? Surely conditions must be worse in other places. The index shows that the United States is at or near the top of all nations in the industrialized world in the rates of abortion, divorce, and births to unwed mothers. We lead the industrialized world in murder, rape, and violent crime. But in elementary and secondary education, we are at or near the bottom in achievement scores.

What all this reveals is that the spiritual and intellectual qualities of American life are seriously degraded, and the soul of the nation is in jeopardy. William Bennett says, "There is a coarseness, callousness, and cynicism, a banality and a vulgarity to our time. There are just too many signs of decivilization: that is, civilization gone rotten." And we have to agree. We can no longer deny that we are a nation in peril. Under the rubric of change, this nation is being systematically stripped of its historic democratic values and transformed into a socialist state, bound to the very policies and values that led to the collapse of the Soviet Union and others before that.

As Russell Kirk has said, the roots of "culture" come from the "cult"—that is, the religious beliefs upon which societies are founded. Every society is based on some kind of cult-ure and upon some form of religious and spiritual worldview. Ancient Egypt was, first and foremost, a religious society founded upon the worship of the nature gods and goddesses. Greece and Rome were founded upon belief in a whole pantheon of pagan deities that exemplified the spiritual values and customs of the people. Love, virtue, courage, industry, and even pride and deceit were personified by the gods and goddesses of the ancient world. And to the degree that the men of Athens and Rome turned away

7

from their devotion to the "cult," their culture declined and eventually collapsed.

No matter how far back or how long you look, you will find that religion was always foundational to the great societies. Whether in India, China, Palestine, Greece, Carthage, Africa, or the civilizations of South and Central America, the story is always the same. Civilization arises from religion, and when the traditional religious beliefs of a nation are eroded, the nation dies.

Many people would argue that the ascendancy and might of the Soviet Union disprove such a view. But now that the Soviet Empire is dead, we understand better than ever the degree to which atheism and state socialism had become not just the political system but the official religion of the Soviet people.

The people worshiped at the shrine of Vladimir Lenin. In fact, Russian scientists created a special research institute dedicated to the study of Lenin's brain. Portraits and statues of him were everywhere in the Communist nations, and adoring citizens marched through his tomb day and night to venerate the memory of the father of the Leninist ideology. But as the fraud and hypocrisy behind the theory became unmistakable during the 1970s and 1980s, the Soviet people lost faith in their false gods.

Communism did not bring prosperity but starvation; it did not bring health but disease; it did not save them from crime or violence or other dangerous emotions. And finally it was the full flowering of all their doubts and fears that led to the debacle of 1989.

America's Loss of Faith

A world away, the United States has been struggling over its own convictions for most of the past century. Institutional religion remains visible and reasonably strong in many places, but secular society has been doing its best to strip away the dignity of devotion, trying to disparage the fundamental beliefs of Christianity and to discredit everyone who claims to live by Christian principles.

Remember that when Friedrich Nietzsche declared that "God is dead," he added, "and we have killed him." God did not simply fade away. Science did not disprove the reality of God. No, men who were hostile to God and his laws set about deliberately to kill God and to rob him of the worship and veneration he deserves. And our own society seems intent on laying God to rest once and for all.

As only one example, in November 1980, the Supreme Court of the United States ruled that the Ten Commandments could not be posted on the wall of a schoolroom in Kentucky because seeing the words of the Mosaic law on the wall "may induce children to read, meditate upon, perhaps to venerate and to obey the commandments." The distinguished justices of this nation declared that the posting of religious principles was tantamount to establishment of a state-sponsored religion, and they worried that the mere presence of such insidious ideas as fidelity, self-restraint, respect for parents, honesty, and faith might influence the minds of impressionable children, and modern justice could not tolerate such a possibility.

Never in the history of man has any society been able to establish standards of decency, cooperation, and social order without a code of moral values. The historian Will Durant said, "There is no significant example in history, before our time, of a society successfully maintaining moral life without the aid of religion." Yet the modern code of the humanists who dominate the culture today tells us that the Christian principles upon which this nation was founded are dangerous, destructive, and divisive.

Even as we are being confronted by a siege of violence that ranks

9

the United States as the most dangerous nation on the planet, judges and lawyers across this nation maintain that Christianity and traditional religious values are the most dangerous threats to our national security. What an irony, but what a tragedy.

Obviously the legal system of this nation is in trouble. We have no system of rights for the victims of crime, yet we have the most sophisticated (and dangerous) code of rights to protect the accused of any nation in history. But science has also contributed to the growing moral disintegration of our culture. British scientists of the late nineteenth and early twentieth centuries—including Huxley and Haldane—taught that Creation could occur without a Creator, and they argued that science proved the irrelevance and absurdity of traditional religious beliefs.

But today, just 140 years after the publication of Darwin's *Origin of the Species,* the nations of Europe and North America are lost in a sea of doubt and confusion. Millions have seemingly lost their moral compass, and to fulfill their innate spiritual longings, they are turning to a witch's brew of New Age beliefs, paganism, environmental pantheism, humanistic egoism, and even devil worship.

Deprived of faith in the one true God, men and women will worship anything, even foreign ideologies and destructive beliefs that will destroy society. The pagan beliefs and false ideologies of our day have robbed millions of people of the meaning and value of life. And the tortured humanistic philosophies of America's social reformers have contributed to a deep inner sickness that is destroying the soul of the nation.

The Reality of Decline

It is no longer a very original claim to say that the nations of Europe and America are in an advanced state of decline today. Scores of books and essays have been written on the subject in recent years.

In the appendix to this book I offer a brief summary of several of those works, beginning with a review of some of the great historical studies dealing with these issues. But the indicators of stress and strain within contemporary culture are all around us today. Over the past half century many of the most secure values and beliefs of Western culture have come under attack. Every day, it seems, we discover that another fortress of the culture is under assault. Yet no one has offered anything of equal value.

Along with all the frontier skirmishes of the "culture wars," the economies of the United States, Europe, and Japan are in tatters. Government has turned predator, pouring the wealth of the nation down the rat hole of debt; and our social resources are being depleted at an astonishing pace. Crime, abuse, and racial violence are exploding, and the law seems powerless to stop the siege of vandalism that is destroying our cities.

Science, education, and law, once heralded as pillars of the earthly kingdom, have not saved us. Instead, they have brought even gloomier vistas of apocalypse. Our beliefs about population, the environment, and the welfare of the state have never seemed so fragile, and the rapid advances in technology over the past half century have complicated our lives enormously without offering even the slightest relief from our fears.

In addition to the technological and political changes, educators and social theorists have been telling us forcefully and often that the age of Christian influence in the world is past, and the "faith of our fathers" is merely a relic of an unhappy past. Like Germany, France, Great Britain, Canada, and Australia before us, the United States has finally entered the post-Christian age. Thus divested of faith and values, we drift between litanies of vain musings upon the past and the sacrament of a new but disturbing vision of the future.

Journalist and author <u>Thomas Hine</u>, in a book about the coming millennium, writes, "Our lives are inevitably the wrong shape. They are too short to allow us to do what we want to do. They are too long, and as values change and verities disappear, we become embittered living in a world in which we cannot believe. Life's rewards are not distributed fairly. There is always less luck then we deserve." When we try to step back and get some perspective on our place in time and space, Hine says, we run up against the dislocations of science. Then he adds:

> *At least since Copernicus, science has been revealing human beings as ever more peripheral phenomena in the universe. Humans are passengers on a mote in the universe; individual lives span a time little more significant than the one-day maturity of the mayfly. People are chance events, temporary aggregations of matter and energy, effective carriers of an almost willful chemical called DNA. Because the nervous system settles for an approximation of reality, most of what is important happens on a scale either far larger or far smaller than anything we can perceive. And when we talk about the future, we are dealing with time, a phenomenon that our nervous systems allow us to experience in only a simplistic and distorted way.*

This is the dispassionate view of modern science. Instead of the transcendence once provided by religious beliefs, science gives us raw, empirical data. In place of the hope and allure of the prophetic vision, the consumer theology of modernism advances a catechism of greed, intellectual arrogance, and unrestrained ambition. Like ancient Ozymandias, the grimace of modern civilization glares silently and enigmatically toward heaven, while its arrogant boast, engraved forever on the sarcophagus of our own culture, pronounces the most damning epitaph upon the moral failure of the age.

The Human Factor

According to the popular beliefs being promoted in the universities and the media, the ethical behavior of citizens in an enlightened society is no longer a moral issue but a matter of personal choice. Attitudes and behaviors, we are told, are political concerns that fall more naturally under the umbrella of government. Even charity, once the duty of the church, has become the responsibility of the state. Obviously a welfare system that fosters ever greater levels of dependency upon government cannot be left to goodwill, mercy, or philanthropy. The state demands absolute control, which is clearly the point of government's sudden interest in the economy and health-care reform.

Public assistance demonstrates the symbiotic relationship between government and a dependent electorate. It attests to government's attachment to the weak and the indebtedness of the poor. Naturally in its eagerness to maintain this relationship, the welfare state will allow no interference. Through the efforts of its armies of experts, advisers, and bureaucrats, the state deliberately limits and discredits all rivals to its own authority.

It is because of this historic tension that there has been a forced separation of church and state in recent years, just as there was a separation of church and school a generation ago. And in supporting the state's domination of our society, the courts have handed down a vast corpus of inferential rulings to ensure that the clergy and other advocates of religious or moral suasion are effectively barred from the arenas of public debate. As in eighteenth-century France, the war with the church is not so much a matter of doctrine as of power. In the eyes of government, theology promotes another kingdom and another truth, while the secular state promotes the kingdom of man and the truth of the here and now.

In the process of deconstructing the older, more traditional view of society in which church and state shared an interest and concern for the common good, the values of Western civilization are being reinterpreted daily in our public schools. The arts and humanities are undergoing fundamental redefinition, along with the entire canon of great literature and Anglo-European studies. And the social sciences are being retooled to conform more closely to a modern social code of moral relativism.

Neither law nor government nor the universities have yet put forth any sort of moral alternative to help elicit our feelings of public spiritedness or generosity. Nor is there any evidence of ethical insight capable of informing what the philosopher Edmund Burke once identified as "the moral imagination." Instead, the idea of "change for the sake of change" has become the dominant ideology of our day.

There is not even a consensus on what our culture might have aspired to become; yet many segments of American society have apparently accepted the notion that our cultural traditions were flawed from the start. Our nation's achievements were a colossal myth, and its former glory was one of history's most conspicuous lies. At least, this is the lesson being taught to our children in the schools and universities of this nation.

They are being told that Western culture is exploitative and imperialistic by nature, and that the idea that there was ever a noble purpose and meaning to our way of life is merely a fraud perpetrated by a self-serving patriarchy. The myth of a code of morality was a lie of even greater perversity because it led to social exploitation, misogyny, and greed. At best, traditional Western values have lost their significance. At worst, they still interfere with the richness and diversity of life on the planet.

All across the nation, intellectuals and progressives are systematically undermining the legacy of our Founding Fathers. In place of the old ways they offer a new concept for a new age—a global ecological sensitivity, a radiant vision of a new world order, and a radical political system only waiting to be born. All this represents a concerted effort to change the world through various kinds of "expert systems" being devised by the elites in government, the judicial system, higher education, and the media. But can this nation hope to endure such a radical agenda? Can any civilization survive such fundamental changes?

Redeeming the Time

"Redeem the time," wrote T. S. Eliot. "Redeem the unread vision in the higher dream." And that truly is our challenge as we assess the damage being done to America's cultural heritage by socialist politics and other foreign ideologies. Much good still remains, but things will not get better on their own. You and I must become engaged in the struggle. We must determine that we will not allow our heritage of faith and freedom to be dismantled and revised by liberal dreamers with visions of a man-made utopia. We must redeem the time and reclaim the higher vision.

In these pages we will witness many dark and disturbing moments. We will see how nations have succumbed to terrible perversions and how they have been subverted by their own failed ideologies. Touching upon nearly three thousand years of history, we will witness the patterns of decline, insurrection, anarchy, and collapse, and in these conditions we will no doubt recognize many aspects of our own situation. We will also see how the United States of America is racing mindlessly down many of the same blind alleys that have led the great empires of the past to oblivion. But we will also examine the sources of hope.

In the *Study of History* Toynbee shows that the advances and failures of society follow a predictable pattern of "challenge and response." Whenever a people are presented with a formidable challenge—whether by nature, by the terrain, by internal conflict, or by foreign invasions—the character of the response determines the future of the nation. A timely and appropriate response can lead to great victory and a higher level of civilization; however, a poor or inadequate response leads to decline. Clearly we are a nation on the brink, but there is a way back to sanity and to prosperity if we are willing to take it. Two roads stretch before us. One way lies the road to renewal and regeneration; the other way lies the well-worn path to disaster.

In succeeding chapters, we will explore the ten symptoms of dysfunction that recur in mature societies and attempt to determine the prospects for overcoming the various threats to our own security. We begin with the social issues—the crisis of lawlessness, the loss of economic discipline, a rising bureaucracy, and the decline of public education. From there we will turn to the cultural and moral concerns and the challenges before us as we approach the beginning of the new millennium.

PART ONE

SOCIAL DECAY

2

The Crisis of Lawlessness

IN DALLAS a sixty-nine-year-old veteran of the Korean War is shot to death in a suburban parking lot while putting groceries into his car. Teenage gang members say they picked their victim at random. It was just "something to do." A few miles away, a young father picking up his two-and-a-half-year-old son from nursery school is targeted by another gang. Five males and a female, all in their teens, follow the man home, then stomp and beat him unconscious in front of the child, who is left screaming in terror.

While leaving the scene, the punks wreck their stolen van and flee on foot into an upper-income neighborhood, where they are easy to spot and apprehend when the police arrive. Again, the gang members say they targeted the man at random, and when arraigned in a Dallas courtroom, the young hoodlums—accompanied by their lawyers, parents, and girlfriends—laugh and snicker throughout the brief proceedings, knowing there is little chance they will ever go to trial.

Both these incidents happened within the past few weeks in my own neighborhood; but crimes just like them, and much worse, happen every day in America. Dark and terrible episodes like these are coming to be seen as normal in the United States. But can we even claim to be a civilized people when an entire nation can be held captive by thugs? This country is in the midst of an unprecedented crisis of law and order. Once the model of peace, prosperity, and responsible citizenship to the entire world, the United States today is obviously a nation in chaos, a broken and humiliated empire apparently on the verge of collapse. There seems to be no sign of hope or relief on the horizon.

On one hand, crime is out of control and ravaging the streets of our cities. On the other, politically correct rulings without legal precedent are being handed down by the nation's courts, granting unheard-of rights for a wide range of newly minted minorities and apparently guaranteeing protection from prosecution for criminals. America is being held hostage by violence and by the out-of-touch social agenda that allows it to thrive.

The Pathology of Disorder

Wherever you look today, it is clear that the American legal system is in serious trouble. All too often the idea of "justice" has become a pathetic joke. Police are unable to enforce the law. And jails, which are already overcrowded, often serve as little more than temporary holding tanks for offenders who are released within hours of arrest.

Is it any wonder that lawyers, judges, and police officers are no longer treated with respect in this nation? Judicial activism has made a joke of justice. Instead of being held in esteem, authority is scorned and ridiculed. The men and women who risk their lives to protect us have become an endangered species. And lawyers regularly become the objects of coarse jokes. But this is just one more sign that something is desperately wrong in America.

Even during the cold war, when the Soviet Union was our political adversary, the most serious dangers to America's security were all homegrown. "We can crane our necks and peer across the oceans for as long as we please in search of a threat to America," says a recent article in the *New York Times*, "but the gravest threat, without a doubt, is the epidemic of murderous violence here at home."[1]

The writer's statement is only too true and so obvious it hardly bears repeating. But the situation is not getting any better, and apparently no one in the government is listening. Instead, the president and the media talk about taking guns away from law-abiding citizens and about raising taxes for more prisons and more police officers—the cosmetic approach to crime—while the moral fabric of the nation goes unattended. And instead of stronger laws and more realistic punishment for crime, the solutions to the problems in our cities are left in the hands of the very social planners, behaviorists, and activists who created the problems in the first place.

So today the American culture stands at a pivotal crossroads. Which way will we turn? Will we turn to more "freedom of expression," more restraints on police authority, and more empathy for the violent offenders identified by progressives as "society's victims," or will we finally heed the demand for responsible behavior and genuine restraint?

We have become a nation obsessed with crime and violence,

21

yet all too often it is the criminals who go free while their victims are harassed and exploited. But the consequences of such moral blindness cannot be ignored. The constant and pernicious abuse of basic moral laws is bound to spill over into America's homes and businesses. Left unchecked, small problems grow into full-scale disasters.

In the decade of the 1980s, more than seventy-six hundred people were murdered on the job in this country. While the murder of tourists in Florida was making headlines in 1993, other people were being victimized in less publicized but perhaps even more perplexing crimes. In Miami, a Dade County commissioner and his wife, who was a state representative, were robbed at gunpoint. The thief took five hundred dollars in cash and stole the commissioner's car. Just one year earlier, the manager of Dade County was robbed in much the same way. Burglars even entered the homes of a former Miami police chief and the city's mayor. In both cases, the intruders only fled after they were fired upon by the homeowners.

Where will the violence end? Carjackings, random shootings, gang activity, muggings, and robberies are becoming commonplace. And purse snatchers kill their victims for the least provocation. And Dr. Joycelyn Elders, U.S. surgeon general, advocates legalizing narcotics nationwide, even as murder, robbery, vandalism, and other serious crimes are already being committed by junkies and drug dealers who recognize no legal or moral limits. What must happen to any nation when the defenders of truth and justice join sides with the criminals?

"Public anxiety about crime is rising," says the *New York Times*. "The toll that crime is taking on the American way of life is growing. But the Clinton administration, committed to other struggles, like health care reform and the North American Free Trade Agreement, is not yet paying close enough attention."[2]

Worst-Case Scenarios

Thanks to satellite communications and news services that span the globe, now America's problems can be seen around the world. And surely the entire world must be shocked by how dangerous America's cities have become. Imagine their horror, like our own, when an unemployed handyman used his 9 mm pistol to wound twenty-three passengers and kill six others on the subway from Manhattan to Hicksville, Long Island. In the pre-Christmas rush of December 1993, the angry gunman fired two clips into the crowd and was reaching for a third before he was finally subdued by passengers. But now spokesmen for the Nation of Islam have praised the gunman for his actions, and students from Howard University interviewed recently on the *MacNeil-Lehrer News Hour* said they understand exactly how the killer feels and why he would commit such a violent act.

From the other side of the country, we were shocked by the news of the kidnapping, rape, and murder of twelve-year-old Polly Klaas in Petaluma, California. And then we were outraged by the case of Lyle and Eric Menendez, kids from a posh Los Angeles suburb who confessed to brutally murdering their parents because they wanted more money and privileges. Despite their open confessions, two juries refused to convict the brothers. Mistrials had to be declared in both cases.

And as one more indication of the level to which morals and values have fallen, the rap singer Tupac Shakur, charged with sodomy and sexual abuse in New York City, was nominated for an NAACP Image Award as a role model for young blacks. His crimes were committed while he was already out on bail after being charged with the shooting of two off-duty police officers in Atlanta.

This is a long and disturbing litany, but it doesn't stop there. There is still the uniquely American phenomenon of serial killers and mass murderers. The names Ted Bundy, Henry Lee Lucas, John Wayne Gacy, Charles Manson, and many others have entered the American lexicon. Mass murderers gain instant notoriety in this country, along with what often seems to be hero status. In July 1993, Gian Luigi Ferri shot eight people in a San Francisco office building. In 1991, George Hennard killed twenty-two in a Killeen, Texas, cafeteria. James Pough killed eight in a loan office in Jacksonville, Florida, in 1990. And in 1989, Patrick Edward Purdy shot a teacher and thirty-four elementary students in Stockton, California, killing five of them.

The whole world was stunned in 1984 when James Huberty attacked and killed a dozen customers in a McDonald's restaurant in San Ysidro, California. And who can forget the moment John Hinckley, Jr., shot the president of the United States, Ronald Reagan, and his press liaison, James Brady, in 1981. For a moment the legacy of 1963 seemed all too real.

Such crimes were virtually unknown thirty years ago. When James Earl Ray and Sirhan Sirhan carried out the political assassinations of Martin Luther King, Jr., and Bobby Kennedy in 1968, the nation reacted with horror. And when Lee Harvey Oswald and/or his accomplices killed President John Kennedy in 1963, the whole world was paralyzed.

But of all these cases, only the political shootings offered any hint of a motive. The others were random outbursts by deranged sociopaths, almost all of whom were known offenders with criminal records and histories of emotional illness. Several were on parole for other crimes.

So what is the root of America's crime problem? What is the root of the sickness that is killing thousands of innocent citizens every year? Are there visible symptoms? In 1993, 375,000 babies born in U.S. hospitals—nearly 10 percent of all live births and an even greater number of those stillborn—were exposed to illegal drugs in the womb. Add to this the fact that 22 percent of all white births and 65 percent of all black births were to unwed mothers, and you have a portrait of a serious and pernicious social pathology in the land. One out of every three children born in America today is illegitimate, and current research shows that a frightening percentage of these children will become the sociopaths, criminals, and violent offenders of the future.

A Crisis of Conscience
Charles Murray, a fellow of the American Enterprise Institute, points out that the number of births to unwed mothers is rapidly approaching the critical mass among whites that marked the disintegration of the black community in the 1960s. Murray says that an illegitimacy rate of 26 percent is the point of no return for our society. When the rate of illegitimacy among whites passes that point, we can expect the rise of a "new white under-class" that may very well bring about the end of civilization as we know it.

The problem, he says, is welfare; and the solution is to elimi-nate welfare entirely, immediately. Murray says we have to go cold turkey on government handouts. We must restore the im-portance of individual initiative and personal responsibility, and bring an end to the "politics of resentment" that has split society and turned rich against poor, white against black, and nonpro-ductive citizens against the productive.[3] Here again we come face-to-face with issues that will determine the future of Ameri-can society. Can the nation survive without some kind of radical turnaround? Can we respond to all these challenges in time? The answers to such questions are still uncertain.

Writing in *U.S. News & World Report*, columnist John Leo has called the problems facing this nation a "crisis of conscience." What we see today is open warfare between honest Americans, who are outmanned and outgunned, and the thugs, who own the streets in many of our major cities. Suddenly we are engaged in a street war that is rapidly escalating into a life-and-death struggle for the future of this nation. It is a confrontation that is changing the context of American culture and daily redefining our hopes for the future.[4]

The culture war in America is no longer merely a war over personal preferences or religious beliefs. Rather, it has become a battle with real guns and bullets. It is a blood-soaked battle between honest citizens and a generation of hoodlums who have been born and raised under the policies established by liberal politicians. The American people are saying over and over again that they are fed up with crime and violence and the lack of self-restraint. But it hardly seems to matter anymore. Law, public policy, and social engineering have aided and abetted the under-class for so long and the pathology of disorder has become so deeply ingrained that we may already be powerless today to make constructive changes.

At this very moment, federal and local government agencies are trying to disarm law-abiding citizens, knowing very well that criminals have no intention of giving up their weapons. For the first time in living memory, no place in this country is safe. No town, no neighborhood, no public or private establishment is safe. Millions of Americans have become captives in their own homes. Our neighborhoods have become war zones. And the commercial centers of our largest cities are no longer secure at any hour of the day.

A Call for Reform

Legislators in both political parties are under intense pressure from the voters to do something about these situations. They are being challenged to pass tough crime bills and ensure swift and appropriate punishment for offenders. But we have all seen the way government works, and we fear that no amount of business as usual will stem the rising tide of blood and violence. We want hard-hitting reforms, but government is notoriously soft on crime.

A few radio stations around the country have said that they will not play certain rap songs that glamorize rape, violence, and abuse. There has been a public outcry against lyrics that incite "cop killers." But the problems go far deeper. Neither bans nor boycotts will have much effect until these public remedies begin to penetrate the culture and change the way people think about crime, violence, rape, and robbery.

Even the media liberals who blasted former vice president Dan Quayle for his outspoken pro-family position are beginning to speak out for family values. But talk will not solve our problems. Welfare politics in this country has already created a vast "constituency of dependency" that is empowered by at least three generations of welfare recipients. The promise of cradle-to-grave support has removed the desire and the prospect of self-reliance or family integrity. Individual initiative is no longer considered to be the way to achieve prosperity. Rather, government largesse is considered to be the source of wealth.

By looting the treasury, by constantly increasing the burden on the declining number of taxpayers, and by entering into disastrous levels of debt through deficit spending, politicians have bought off the votes of the underclass. This nation desperately needs a complete refocusing of its views and values, a complete turnaround in its morals and behavior. If the nation is to be spared imminent disaster, the welfare addiction of government must be abandoned and the failed policies of the sixties must be discarded.

Charles Murray has said that as destructive as the current wave of lawlessness has become, the greater problem by far is *family*

27

formation. Crime and violence must be stopped. Criminals must be taken out of circulation, and changes must be made in our social and fiscal policies. But until we solve the problems in American families, the other problems will continue to be unmanageable. Murray says, "Illegitimacy is the single most important social problem of our time," and family instability and single-parent families are direct contributors to the sociological problems of our day.

New research shows that children without fathers are more likely to get involved in crime and other antisocial behaviors. According to a recent report from the Washington-based Family Research Council, it is "children without fathers who commit the crimes." Citing Bureau of Justice Statistics (BJS), the report shows that more than 70 percent of juveniles in reform institutions grew up in single-parent or no-parent families. "Attacking the crime problem," they say, "is disproportionately a problem of young unsupervised males." [5]

The editors of this study then conclude that the problem of crime in this country will never be solved until balance and order are restored in the home. Government can continue to throw money at these problems forever, but until our dysfunctional families are healed, there is little hope for the future.

The End of Civilization
The dangers of crime and violence already reach from the top to the bottom of our culture. More than 3 million crimes are committed in or near the nation's schools each year. The murder rate among adolescents is 700 percent higher in this country than it is in Japan or any European country. Writing in the *American Spectator,* Emmett Tyrrell insists that "it is about time that the intellectual and moral authorities of our society properly abominate criminals and come to the defense of society. Deride

the fanciful violence that suffuses our entertainments. Denounce violence, whether it is found in the street, in the pop music, or in sports. Advocate manners and law-abidingness. In other words, it is time our progressive intellectuals break with their time-honored rhapsody on a theme of perversity."[6]

But the authorities themselves do not seem to be listening. No less a jurist than Justice Sandra Day O'Connor, who delivered the United States Supreme Court's decision in the case of *Hudson v. Macmillan,* spoke of the "evolving standards of decency that mark the progress of a maturing society." With these words, Justice O'Connor betrayed the sentiments of the activist Court: that they are authorized to interpret the laws of the land beyond the scope of the United States Constitution. The phrase, which actually originated in an earlier ruling, implies that Supreme Court justices are free to venture into uncharted ethical territory and to determine on their own how Americans should think and act. Whatever happened to the idea of checks and balances on the Court?

Throughout American history, we have believed that responsible behavior is based on traditions of honor, mutual respect, and duty. The Christian tradition calls for inner controls and moral sanctions that come through religious instruction in the home, the church, and the school. The traditional safeguards of civilized society were the principles of self-control, deferred gratification, fear of detection, and fear of God. But we should be able to see now that when those guides of civilized behavior are removed—whether by secular educators or progressive reformers—civilization is placed in grave danger. That is the situation we are facing today.

In a time of deep distress, the Old Testament writers said, "Every man did that which was right in his own eyes." Today we face a similar situation, and the entire nation must pay the price for the arrogant defiance of divine authority. The law of the land is no longer an inviolable standard. American justice is often unjust, and too many judges no longer subscribe to even commonsense principles.

Consider these examples of American justice. In Florida, a forty-eight-year-old man sentenced to life in prison for raping a thirteen-year-old girl with muscular dystrophy was released when the Second District Court of Appeals ruled that the rapist had been convicted with the wrong charge. The charge, "sexual battery of a helpless person," was deemed unfair in the court's opinion since the girl wasn't completely helpless. After all, the judge ruled, she had screamed for help and tried to push the man away. So instead of life, the rapist served a few months for battery.

A Philadelphia mother was cleared of murder charges in the smothering death of her infant daughter. The judge cleared the woman because, as she explained, the child had lingered in a coma before she eventually died and the court was not convinced the mother was guilty of "murder." Later the mother told detectives she was glad to be rid of her kids, saying, "Now I can go out and do what I want. It's all about freedom."

Unfortunately, such cases of judicial blindness are no longer rare, and they reach from the bottom to the top of the justice system. In New Jersey, the supreme court decided that a robber convicted of purse snatching had been wrongly sentenced, since he slipped the purse off the victim's arm quietly and did not actually "snatch" it. Even more shocking, the Pennsylvania Supreme Court vacated the death sentence of a convicted murderer because a deputy district attorney had cited the Bible in the closing arguments. The prosecutor was severely admonished by the justices, and a new sentencing was ordered.

A Crisis of Justice
Evidence of a legal system in serious trouble is everywhere. Judicial misconduct is on the rise, and judicial activism—using

the bench as a political soapbox—has become the rule rather than the exception. Justices subscribing to their own arbitrary and independent interpretation of law are rewriting tradition and legal precedent daily in our courts. Crime has reached epidemic proportions, much of it perpetrated by repeat offenders, and the urban ghetto has become a breeding ground for destructive behaviors. As we know only too well, criminals with shrewd lawyers can be back on the streets within minutes of arrest while in many cases their victims may never recover.

Until modern times, the foundations of law rested on the Judeo-Christian concept of right and wrong. Everyone, regardless of age, race, religion, or national origin, understood that this was a Christian nation. While there was to be absolute freedom of religion, there was nevertheless a code of laws based upon Judeo-Christian principles. The concept of original sin was essential because the knowledge that man is inherently corrupt helped us to understand that men and women are capable of wrongdoing by nature. Restraint and discipline were necessary to keep people working together for the common good.

Without apology, the law prescribed and exacted appropriate punishment for those who chose to break the law. We believed that without suitable social and moral restraints and without a strong legal code, society would degenerate into chaos and anarchy. Good citizenship was based on agreement to abide by a pact of good behavior. To violate that pact was to submit to the judgment of the law.

But a new wave of liberal thinkers had another vision for America. They set about to dismantle the old ways and to challenge the notion that we are born sinners. They wanted to inculcate a new theology—the theology of humanism. Consequently, modern secular sociology turned away from the Bible as an inviolable standard in favor of a new evolutionary hypothesis derived from the theories of Darwin, Freud, Einstein, and others. And using language and ideas borrowed from Voltaire, Rousseau, and other Enlightenment idealists, they assumed the view that man is a "noble savage." Their task was to free man from his chains, and in so doing they subscribed to the idea that man had evolved from the slime and that with time and ever greater freedoms we would someday ascend to the stars.

Suddenly, students in our public schools and universities were being taught to be sensitive to the suffering, the oppressed, and the downtrodden. Those who committed crimes were not sinners, they were told, but "victims of society." Extenuations from these basic principles have helped to create an entire "society of victims" today. As a result, every sort of deviant behavior and every pathology is excused as "diversity" or an "alternative lifestyle."

Because of liberal notions of defendants' rights and the rights of the accused, we now have a situation that encourages litigation, name-calling, and a dangerous splintering of society. Society has been splintered and divided into dozens of warring factions—black against white, young against old, poor against rich, women against men, and on and on. And since crime is the result of poor socialization, not sin, even criminals are demanding their rights. Many demand equality and protected rights for all persuasions, and *civil rights* has now become an umbrella term for any liberal cause designed to challenge the general will and efficiency of American democracy. Does anyone still believe that this nation can survive such dangerous conditions?

32

Judicial Activism

The true flowering of these ideas did not come about until the 1960s, but the legacy of the sixties is very much with us today. The free-love, antiwar, psychedelic, drug-crazed hippie generation proclaimed not only their right to dissent but the right to protest against and defame even the most sacred institutions of society. The symbols of honor and tradition that millions had died for were suddenly rendered meaningless.

Today people are free to burn the American flag, to desecrate national shrines and emblems, to disavow allegiance to God and country, and to assault all the moral foundations of our culture. Sexual deviance and open promiscuity have become commonplace. Cohabitation is accepted as normal. Despite a 40 percent increase in population, there are 25 percent fewer marriages in this country today than there were during the 1960s.

In addition, we are seeing the rise of new cults, witchcraft, goddess worship, and many other expressions of the New Age movement, along with bizarre beliefs and behaviors that thrive in this atmosphere of defiance. And perhaps the greatest holocaust in history—the proabortion movement—is one of the most sinister expressions of the new permissiveness. The courts have not impeded crime. They have not restricted murder. As in ancient Rome, they have actually licensed and encouraged it.

The founders of this nation anticipated a time when one branch of government might attempt to gain control of the others. That is why the United States Constitution specifically established a balance of powers between the executive, legislative, and judicial branches. However, not to be restrained by a mere document, today's judges and lawyers have attempted to change the laws of the nation to suit their own political ideologies.

Supreme Court Justice Antonin Scalia once wrote, "We live in an age of hair-trigger unconstitutionality." And Appeals Court Justice Alex Kozinski wrote in the *Wall Street Journal,* "Judges who get into the habit of playing legislator find it tempting to start treating all laws—including the Constitution—as merely a springboard for implementing their own sense of right and wrong." The principle that justice must be impartial and equal for all people is no longer applied, and there are lawyers and judges at every level who know just how to twist and bend the law to accomplish their own purposes.

The result of all this manipulation of justice has been to encourage incredible abuse of the system not only in criminal cases but in tort law and damage claims as well. There has been a shocking rise in civil litigation in recent years, and the trend is sharply upward. Instead of the "crisp and specific interpretation" prescribed by judicial precedent, today's legal specialists are instituting what legal scholar Walter Olson calls "fuzzy new standards" that virtually guarantee that *everything* will end up in court. As with Justice O'Connor's "evolving standards," greed and exploitation thrive in such an environment.

In Dubious Battle

You don't have to look very far to see the results of these things. Practically everything ends up in court these days, and the more outrageous the claims, the more likely they are to be taken seriously by judge and jury. In his book *The Litigation Explosion,* Walter K. Olson writes, "For all the many successes of American society, our system of civil litigation is a grotesque failure, a byword around the world for expense, rancor, and irrationality. America's litigation explosion has squandered immense fortunes, sent the cream of a nation's intellectual talent into dubious battle, reduced valuable enterprises to ruin, made miserable the practice of honorable professions, and brought needless pain to broken families. It has been a spiral of destructive recrimination, with no end in sight."[7]

The truth is that the situation is equally desperate on both sides—in both civil and criminal cases. And despite the attempts of a few individuals and groups to regulate the legal profession, the lawyers themselves have consistently defied the efforts of regulators. From inside the system, attorneys have effectively frustrated even the executive and legislative branches of government. When Vice President Dan Quayle announced his plan to introduce judicial reforms in 1991, members of the American Bar Association reacted immediately and succeeded in disarming the administration's plans. Since that time, almost nothing of substance has been attempted.

Big government, the media, educators, and university and law school professors have an agenda that is oblivious to the wishes of the American people. Tradition and standards no longer seem to apply in that arena since these people are convinced that their task is to discredit the past and to redesign the future according to their own idealistic beliefs. Among other things, they believe that Christians and conservatives are the real problem in society, which accounts for at least a portion of the bitterness of their attacks on the "religious right." According to these doctrines, citizens who uphold "traditional values" must be silenced. A "silent majority" suits them just fine. Silence allows the proponents of "change" to wage their covert war on the mainstream culture.

In light of all these various threats, can we hold out any hope for saving this country from imminent collapse? Can we continue to stand against the growing number of activists and reformers who are dismantling the American value system? And with a generation-long drop in the quality of education in this country, will there be anyone left to care about such matters in the coming decades?

Historical Models
The lessons of history tell us what disastrous consequences come from the collapse of law and order. In ancient Greece, the first

symptoms of disorder were a general loss of respect for tradition and the degradation of the young. Among the early symptoms was the decline of art and entertainment. The medium of communication was distorted by the philosophers and pundits. Rhetoric became combative and intolerant; intellectuals began to deride and attack all the traditional institutions of Hellenic society.

Especially notable, art, music, and the theater became increasingly coarse and vulgar over time, and the "new thinkers" of the age argued that "fundamental change" was needed. They proclaimed, "The young must have a voice in society." "The young are the future," they said. "We must listen to them." But without traditional moral guidelines, the young men grew wild and undisciplined, and when they grew to be adults, they turned against the elders and patriarchs and worked to destroy the old order. The changes these people introduced led to the weakening and the final dissolution of that great society.

From being the very model of balance, beauty, and moral discipline—known throughout the ancient world for their great achievements in science, philosophy, and art—the Greeks slowly devolved into the most disreputable and lawless nation of the day. When the Romans conquered Greece in 146 B.C., they took the city-states under the protection of the Roman Empire. By placing everything under Roman military authority, they were able to restore order and bring back the rule of law. Not only were the young radicals discomfited, but the sovereignty and independence of Greece were lost forever. Little evils, unchecked, destroyed Greek society and led to their final conquest by Rome. Lawlessness, anarchy, and a doctrine of "change" subverted what may have been the greatest culture of the ancient world.

In a study of the French Revolution, José Ortega y Gasset remarks, "Order is not pressure which is imposed on society from without, but an equilibrium which is set up from within."[8] All the great empires of antiquity understood this principle, and none more so than the Romans. The success of the Roman Empire was based on a very simple formula. They believed that discipline and custom were essential to stability, and wherever they marched, the legions of Rome established strict principles of law and order.

The Peace of Rome

A similar story may be told of ancient Egypt. In the fourth century before Christ, the kingdom of Egypt had erupted into lawlessness and violence, which crippled the economy and made government impossible. Every level of society was divided against all the others—farmers against merchants, the young against the old, and the people who observed the traditional religions against the occultists and a growing number of atheists. Anarchy, chaos, and violence pervaded the land.

When Alexander the Great invaded the country in 333 B.C., his first task was to restore order, to quell violence, and to institute martial law under his legions. Alexander was ruthless, but order was restored, and for a brief time Egypt was once again a major force in the world—but under Macedonian control. After the death of Alexander, the old dangers and old corruptions returned. But, once again, the Roman Empire brought peace to the region through conquest, harsh penalties, and the imposition of martial law.

The Phoenician state of Carthage, midway across the north coast of Africa, offers yet another example of a great empire brought to its knees by lawlessness. Once called "the eternal rival of Rome" by Salvian of Marseilles, Carthage had, for at least four centuries, even greater military muscle and commercial vitality than Rome. Carthage was the trading empire par excellence, the dominant maritime culture of the ancient world, and the nation that did more to spread civilization than any other while Greece and Rome were still young and reckless. But in time Carthage also sank into debauchery and dissipation as a result of great wealth and luxury. And as they sank into greed and idolatry, bloodthirsty cults sprang up. Little by little, their traditional, elegant way of life was destroyed from within.

The rich young men of Carthage no longer wanted to serve in the armed forces, so they hired mercenaries to take their places. But these foreigners lacked deep attachment to the empire, and when the army came into fierce conflict with Rome or other adversaries, the mercenaries would run, leaving their comrades and the nation itself defenseless.

At the same time, the growing number of foreigners in the cities detracted from the unity and discipline of the state. The aliens felt no special allegiance to Carthage; instead, they contributed to the growth of a large underclass and a spirit of rebellion. When Carthage fell to Rome in 146 B.C., the first act of the legions was to restore law and order and to make the people of Carthage obey the customs and rules of the *Pax Romana*—the peace of Rome.

Eventually, Rome itself fell prey to the very lawlessness that it had exploited in conquering so many other nations. In the latter days of the Roman Empire, the law had little effect. Even the imposition of tyranny in the last years could not stop the collapse of law and order. When the Roman peace was no longer possible, the nation fell.

The Dark Ages, which spread over Europe for the next thousand years, was the result of the loss of order and balance in the world. No single nation and no empire could offer any transcendent system of authority. Only the Christian church was positioned to give meaning and purpose to the lives of the people.

And during the Middle Ages, this is precisely what happened. Rulers, such as Constantine the Great, Charlemagne, and Otto the Great, set out to implement godly discipline and ecclesiastical order over the world of that day.

Restoring the Moral Order

When we look back at the lessons of history, we cannot help but see the similarities between the collapse of the ancient empires and the dangerous conditions in our own. In assessing the precipitous fall of American culture in this century, Russell Kirk has said, "It appears to me that our culture labors in an advanced state of decadence; that what many people mistake for the triumph of our civilization actually consists of powers that are disintegrating our culture; that the vaunted 'democratic freedom' of liberal society in reality is servitude to appetites and illusions which attack religious belief; which destroy community through excessive centralization and urbanization; which efface life-giving tradition and custom."[9] And when we see what these same conditions accomplished in Egypt, Greece, Carthage, and Rome, the scholar's words should emphasize the urgency of our own situation.

The public outcry against crime, criminals, and abuse of the legal system in our own time is growing louder by the day. Americans are demanding change; but do we really want more liberal laws?

What we need are more checks and balances, stronger restraints on judicial practice to prevent manipulation of the courts, more realistic sentencing for criminals, and the certainty that punishment will be carried out in full without parole or limitation. We must stop putting recidivists and prison-hardened thugs back onto our streets, and we need to take another look at the importance of capital punishment for murder and other brutal offenses. Swift and certain punishment must be the standard of law, regardless of the motives or circumstances of the crime, if law is to have any authority.

Today a growing number of citizen action committees are getting together to try to make changes in some of these practices. Lawyers are being challenged to police themselves and to behave more responsibly. Citizens groups are demanding that sentencing and parole standards be reviewed and revised. And a new level of attention is being given to the causes of crime and the need for persuasive disincentives.

Christians have a duty to pray for the nations and their leaders. We are to pray for peace, for self-control, and for a renewal of law and order. But along with our prayers, we must also take up the challenge and become an active part of the solution to these problems. When Rome fell, it was in part because no one remembered how things used to be and no one stood up for the traditional virtues.

We must not allow ourselves to be lulled into inactivity by the vain promises of legislators and political leaders. If we disregard the stark reality of the challenges before us, we will be guilty of our own self-destruction. Government will only make appropriate changes when "we the people" force them to do so. And to ignore the problems that are crippling this nation is to ensure that we *shall* be destroyed, both from within and from without, precisely like the empires of old.

In his important book *The American Hour,* Os Guinness says, "A generation that fails to read the signs of the times may be forced to read the writing on the wall."[10] That is an ominous warning, but a timely one. What we stand to lose is simply too great. We cannot afford to fail.

3

Loss of Economic Discipline

ON EASTER weekend 1994, the New York Stock Exchange teetered once again on the verge of disaster. After staging a dangerous balancing act on Friday, April 1, blue-chip stocks plunged precipitously on Monday morning as traders responded to fears that interest rates might be headed up again. By midday Monday, however, the market recovered slowly as "bargain hunters" began buying up some of the hardest-hit issues.

After an initial plunge of more than 83 points, the Dow-Jones industrial average rebounded to 34.83 points. But it was only after twice invoking the automatic collar on computer program trading that the exchange was able to slow the market's descent and restore order.

Even with the corrections, the general tone of trading remained negative, with two thousand issues down and only three hundred up and a very heavy volume of more than 340 million shares changing hands. Ever since the Dow set a record high close on January 31, topping 3,978.36 points, it had been backtracking under pressures created not only by general anxiety but by reports that the economy could expect stronger growth than originally projected.

According to some reports, the near fatal collapse was set off by the news that nonfarm payrolls in March 1994 were double the 234,000 originally forecast by economists. The jobless rate held steady at 6.5 percent, as expected, but monthly personal income and spending were showing unexpectedly strong gains. What these figures said to professional economists was that unexpected growth would increase the risk of inflation, changing the financial dynamics of the market and bringing about various kinds of technical manipulation that could threaten the security of their investments.

Government reports only heightened these fears and boosted the prospect that the Federal Reserve Board would tighten credit again to keep the economy from overheating. It had already tightened credit twice in the previous two months. So while the Christian world was celebrating the good news of the resurrection of the Savior, White House experts were on nationwide television trying to assure the investment community that the "good news" of a strong economy wasn't really all that good and that no one should panic.

Fear of Failure

As the average layman looks at sudden outbursts like this most recent Easter surprise, many of us have to wonder how mere speculation—or how some matter-of-fact government report—can cause such panic. How can a mere report provoke such a volatile response? But this is the nature of modern finance, and informed observers say that this sort of shock is just the tip of something much bigger on the economic horizon—and they say it is not just an iceberg but more like a glacier.

What they fear is a growing pattern of nervous market manipulations that could rock the security of the entire world in a matter of minutes. If some genuine life-and-death panic—some mysterious feeding frenzy—were to occur, the result could easily dwarf the disaster of the crash of 1929.

What are the probabilities of something like that actually happening? First of all, we must realize that the economies of all the industrialized nations of the world are already fragile and top-heavy. The New York Stock Exchange has been shaky ever since the near disaster of October 1987. Stocks and bonds are perpetually nervous and insecure, the price of oil is down, and after a brief but salutary dip, the level of consumer credit debt is rising once again. Interest rates are, indeed, creeping back up, with the constant threat of an "administrative adjustment." Inflation has returned, and serious investors are racing back to the desperation securities of gold and land—a sure sign of growing *in*security.

At the same time, investment in American industry is down while overseas stocks are surging. More and more American capital is going abroad, even though the economies of Britain, France, and Germany are very weak and unemployment throughout the European Community is monstrous. The Europeans are in the midst of their worst recession since the 1930s, but apparently the situation is shaky beyond Europe as well.

Japan's stock market has already fallen once, and as we read in the headlines more often today, many analysts sense that it may fall yet again—but with more dramatic results this time. Some economists feel that Japanese investors, plagued by rising debt, a devalued bond market, widespread insolvency, high unemployment, and unprecedented levels of civil unrest, will soon begin to dump their trophy properties in the United States. And then, in order to pump capital back into their own failing currency system, they may launch a massive sell-off of major holdings around the world. This would, of course, have a disastrous effect on the value of property worldwide.

On top of all this, the economic interests of the United States are suddenly counter not only to the "trickle down" principles of the Reagan-Bush era but to the entire pattern of the Western constitutional democracies. While Europe, Asia, Africa, and Latin America are looking to America for leadership in the principles of capitalism and wealth building, our own government is suddenly headed in precisely the opposite direction.

Amid so many distresses and with such profound uncertainties about the future, is it any wonder that our sense of hope is fading and that even the nation's top economists fear the system is failing? In light of the wars, natural disasters, and crises of every description that have pummeled the nation in recent years, the hope of holding on to any sort of confidence in our prospects for the future hardly seems realistic. Some dreadful menace, it seems, has been loosed upon society. And the specter of doom will not disappear.

Economics of Doom

In their provocative best-seller *The Great Reckoning*, James Dale Davidson and Lord William Rees-Mogg predict that we are in for a period of even greater panic. While the Clinton election of 1992 may have given the United States economy a temporary boost, they say, the apparently insoluble problems of the budget deficit, the government's lax monetary policy, credit guarantees, and make-work employment will simply continue to eat away at our national solvency until, sometime in the very near future, there will have to be some sort of massive correction.

What they then describe is a depression well beyond the monster of the 1930s. They foresee a panic, a sell-off, and a crash that could just as easily bring with it a "global meltdown" of apocalyptic proportions. Today the United States is in the best economic shape of the three major players on the global scene— North America, Japan, and the European Community—but Davidson and Rees-Mogg hasten to say that this is not the good news. If the North American economy collapses, all the others will come with it, and the implications for what follows are, at best, grim.

Since the incredible boom of the late 1980s, the Japanese real-estate market has gone completely stagnant. Land values have imploded, and huge fortunes have disappeared overnight. The Japanese stock market (the Nikkei) is down 60 percent, and the next shoe to drop in Japan will likely be a savings-and-loan collapse that some analysts believe may well dwarf the one that rocked the United States in 1990 and 1991.

For the first time in Japanese history, unemployment is suddenly a major issue. Factory jobs are no longer secure, and this has placed unexpected burdens on Japanese families, boosting the divorce rate and the incidence of crime and violence. These are immense and unfamiliar social problems for the Japanese. Davidson and Rees-Mogg go on to say that it was the impact of these unusual conditions that helped to provoke the grassroots political revolutions in Japan in 1993, which brought about the ouster of the entire liberal government.

In mid-1993, it was reported that Japanese industry had

45

decided to start building more factories overseas in order to take advantage of cheap labor. A sign of the magnitude of the economic changes taking place on both sides of the Pacific is that one of the principal sites chosen for expansion is southern California. This odd circumstance, in which Japanese industry is sending its work to America, indicates just how great the marketplace differential has become since the postwar period when Japan was humiliated, powerless, and the cheapest labor provider in the world. For the moment, international trade is the main thing keeping the Japanese economy afloat.

But what would happen to this source of industrial security if there were further dislocations of the economies of the United States, the European Community, or the other major players on the Pacific Rim? Unfortunately, the concept of trilateralism, which has been promoted by the United States government the past seventy years, mandates a net of global economic interdependence, and when one domino in such an alliance starts to fall, they all go. At present, the ripple effect has not begun, but none of the partners in the trilateral network is very secure.

A Period of Adjustment

The European Community is in a particularly vulnerable position due to the high cost of labor and the high value of its currency in relation to the rest of the world. Davidson and Rees-Mogg report that European labor costs in 1993 were approximately fifty times that of China, India, or Eastern Europe. High currency and interest rates, pumped up by the false economy of Germany, were certain to plunge, which would set off an inevitable cycle of unemployment, recession, and political chaos. Who can say how this might impact those fragile democracies?

These economists offer compelling evidence that we are headed into an era of profound economic and political upheaval.

46

By every historic measure, the condition of the United States economy in mid-1993 was precisely parallel to the period leading up to the Great Depression of the 1930s. But what would the implications be of a catastrophe of that proportion in today's more complex world?

The authors suggest that the patterns of history—which may be traced from the days of ancient Egypt to the present—show us precisely what will happen. The collapse of the Berlin Wall and the dislocations in Eastern Europe came on what Davidson and Rees-Mogg believe to be a predictable cycle, precisely fifty years after the start of World War II.

But even greater changes come in five-hundred-year cycles, and the examples the authors offer from history are compelling. The greatest flowering of the economy of Rome came at the time of Augustus Caesar, during the time of Christ; five hundred years later, the empire collapsed. In A.D. 1000, a newly consolidated Europe emerged from the Dark Ages; five hundred years later came the Renaissance and the birth of the modern age. Now, five hundred years after the Renaissance, we face another cycle. But will it be a time of consolidation or collapse? They say:

All the stunning changes that have occurred since the fall of the Berlin Wall in 1989, however unthinkable a decade ago, are merely first installments of a broader upheaval in human affairs. The 1990s could mark the climax of a major phase of history that began in the decade when Columbus sailed for America. Hints from a variety of sources suggest that the technological change and economic exhaustion that brought the Cold War to an end will also bring about a new world disorder.[1]

47

Among the not-so-subtle hints Davidson and Rees-Mogg refer to are, of course, the runaway spending of government and the drain on business and industry brought about by increased taxation and regulation, which will be discussed in the following chapter.

Imperial Overstretch

One of the best-known books dealing with these subjects is historian and author Paul Kennedy's book *The Rise and Fall of the Great Powers,* which originally appeared in 1986 and has been updated recently. Based on the economic theory that the United States can no longer afford to maintain military supremacy in the world, Kennedy calls for a system of "managed decline" by which American industry attempts to hold on to its markets and resources in the world (primarily to prevent the kind of holocaust that might ensue if the nation were suddenly plunged into poverty) while the government and the people concede gracefully to being something less than number one in the world.

The American people must learn to live more like the rest of the world, says Kennedy, since "it simply has not been given to any society to remain *permanently* ahead of all the others, because that would imply a freezing of the differential patterns of growth rates, technological advance, and military developments which has existed since time immemorial."[2] But, Kennedy goes on to say, "there exists a dynamic for change [in great societies], driven chiefly by economic and technological developments, which then impact upon social structures, political systems, military power, and the position of individual states and empires."[3]

Paul Kennedy calls upon the example of history when he says, "The United States now runs the risk, so familiar to historians of the rise and fall of previous Great Powers, of what might roughly be called 'imperial overstretch'; that is to say, decision-makers in Washington must face the awkward and enduring fact that the sum total of the United States' global interests and obligations is nowadays far larger than the country's power to defend them all simultaneously."

The historian's context is, of course, the military apparatus of empire and the economic burdens imposed by maintaining a global defense posture. But what he thus applies to foreign affairs and diplomacy must of necessity be applied to domestic policy as well. A government can only do so much. There are also legal limits.

With all of our internal and external commitments, can the United States preserve its current position of military and economic dominance in the world? Kennedy's answer, without hesitation, is no. What he then prescribes is his strategy for managed decline, by which he says the nation must voluntarily shrink its appetite, affluence, and consumption. In 1945, the United States consumed approximately 40 percent of the entire wealth and power of the world. Based on its actual geography and population, Kennedy says, a more realistic portion would be a 16 to 18 percent share.

What right, he argues, does America have to dominate the world? By what right does our military and ideology maintain a hegemony on world order? Kennedy obviously accepts the idea of the zero-sum hypothesis, which holds that there is only so much wealth to go around, and through arrogance and imperialism the United States is taking unfair advantage. This is a fatally flawed theory, which Nobel Prize–winning economist Milton Friedman has repeatedly disproved, but that is another issue.

Still, if Kennedy's assessment was correct, what should Americans believe about our prospects for the future? Can we continue to be big brother and defender of the world when we cannot keep peace at home? What does the mordant decline in our cities say about our attitudes of responsibility and resolve?

The Changing World Order

That such conditions contribute to the collapse of great nations seems to go without saying. The British Empire was chewed up by just such extremes of socialist policies run amok and by the waste of its national treasure. France in the eighteenth century and Spain in the sixteenth grew into bureaucratic monsters that plundered the wealth of the nations and destroyed their ambition and resolve. And, of course, taxation grew so oppressive in the latter years of the Roman Empire that wealthy landowners actually fled into barbarian territories to avoid the long arm of Roman law—an act of defiance punishable by death.

The old world had no concept of debt creation in the sense that we understand it today. Personal debt was strictly limited. Credit was virtually unknown, except among friends, immediate family, and close associates or in certain special situations. The idea of large-scale public debt was unthinkable.

The nations of the world operated on a free-market economic policy, which meant that buying and selling were based on cash transactions and the strength or weakness of the market could not be propped up by false figures, reports, or some notion of consumer confidence. Even in the city-states of Venice and Germany, where modern finance first appeared, national economy was affected primarily by sheer business acumen, the prospect of a good harvest, and the condition of the national character at any given moment.

The modern concept of welfare as an instrument of government certainly did not exist anywhere in the world until this century. The needy were left to the care of churches, private charities, and philanthropists. At the same time, government never became indebted to the people, but rather it operated with capital specifically made available for its limited programs by revenues generated through customs, duties, tariffs, and simple taxes on goods. Taxes in those times were assessed on things, not people.

And another fact that many Americans today no longer seem to remember is that there was no such thing as income tax in this country until the second decade of this century. The first income tax was initially proposed as a *voluntary* system in 1909. But soon enough, the voluntary tax levy became a permanent fixture. World War I provided the provocation for government confiscation of wealth, but World War II made it law, and Franklin D. Roosevelt came on to the scene with the New Deal and a virtual grab bag of social programs designed to take wealth away from individuals and give it to government.

The result has been a new level of state socialism in this country. The mechanism for creating this new economic order was initially the Bretton Woods Conference of July 1944—officially the United Nations Monetary and Financial Conference— attended by delegates from forty-four nations. That conference laid the foundations for the postwar monetary system. It led to the creation of the World Bank, the International Monetary Fund (IMF), and an all-new definition of debt, credit, and government spending. It may be argued that the Bretton Woods Conference was the real beginning of the so-called new world order.

The Power to Destroy

At the founding of this nation, Supreme Court Justice John Marshall said that "the power to tax involves the power to destroy." Like Franklin, Jefferson, Madison, and others, Marshall believed that the people had to be vigilant and perpetually on guard against the temptation of government to raid the public treasury. But during the mid–nineteenth century, state socialism began in earnest in Great Britain, and federal-minded Americans watched their experiment with great interest.

The idea of a broad-based income tax first became a reality in Britain in 1842. The liberal British economist John Maynard Keynes had taught that it was necessary for government to control economic policy and, when needed, to confiscate private wealth for the public interest. Keynes's socialist policies not only set the direction of fiscal policy in Britain—fiscal policies that have led to the utter ruin of the empire in our own time—but were to become the principal influence upon United States monetary policy from that time to this.

After introducing the principles of unlimited taxation and state control of finance, the financial wizards of Europe decided that it would be even more profitable to go still further and to create a privately owned central bank that could transact business on a global scale. Such a bank would play the decisive role in managing economic policy, interest rates, and other public-policy matters worldwide.

The Bank of England was their first venture, and they quickly found that a major land war in Europe was the very best vehicle for overcoming resistance to their plans. The First World War created such an emergency situation that the people could not resist the offers of the financial leaders to help bail them out of their difficulties.

Control of European economic policy, in turn, gave a handful of wealthy men the ideal opportunity to make loans to the nations of the world. Repayment of debts by these foreign powers were to be made by levying taxes on the people. This led to the creation of a new breed of "monopoly bankers" who had two basic goals: first, to gain control of previously unimaginable sums of wealth; and second, to influence the economic and political policies of the entire world. It should come as no surprise that large-scale deficit spending by government was the surest guarantee that both of these objectives would be realized.

The first limited-wages tax in the United States was levied in 1861. It was supposed to be a temporary measure to help finance the Civil War. This tax was repealed in 1871, but the idea that the wealth of the nation could be tapped by a mere act of Congress, and furthermore that the federal government could now cross state lines to satisfy its desire for cash, entered the imagination of legislators at that time.

Changing the Rules

Twenty years later, Congress tried once again to levy the income tax. On that occasion, the Supreme Court declared, in the case of *Pollock v. Farmer's Land and Trust Co.,* that the attempt to levy taxes from citizens in this way was unconstitutional. But twenty-five years later, Congress was back to the well one more time, and this time they simply changed the rules by passing the Sixteenth Amendment to the Constitution, which was ratified in 1913, making it legal for government to levy an income tax on the people of the nation.

The initial legislation for a wages tax exempted the first three thousand dollars of income from taxation but taxed the remainder at graduated rates ranging from one percent (for income up to twenty thousand dollars) to as high as 7 percent (for incomes over five hundred thousand dollars). These levels were set high enough in relation to the average personal income so that less than one percent of the population was actually subject to the income tax in any form.

At one point a measure was presented to Congress to limit taxation to no more than 6.5 percent. At that time, a 6.5 percent tax seemed so outrageously high that Congress simply refused to allow the measure to pass. They rejected the measure on the grounds that, first of all, the American people would never submit to such a high rate of tax, and, secondly, if the limit of 6.5 percent was included in the bill, some administration someday would be tempted to levy that exact amount. So they ditched the measure.

But once the policy of taxing the people was established, the idea of a progressive tax structure became a reality, and it was only a matter of time until the federal government began squeezing more and more citizens into the system. For a brief time, Congress considered the idea of a proportional tax that would affect all wage earners at the same level—at a fixed percentage rate. But that was a short-lived idea. What they eventually settled on was the system used today of a "progressive tax" structure, which taxes high-wage earners at disproportionately higher levels.

From the highest rate of 7 percent in 1913, the top tax rate escalated to 77 percent just five years later, during World War I. After the war, the top rate dropped back to 25 percent, but it shot up to 78 percent as World War II approached. The top rate has been as high as 97 percent on a few occasions, but in 1981 the top rate was lowered by an act of Congress to 50 percent, and the Tax Reform Act of 1986 pushed it down slightly.

Today the top tax rate is approaching 35 percent once again, and it is certain to go even higher in coming months, especially if even a portion of the Clinton administration's promised welfare and health-care programs go into effect. As fears being promoted by government about the federal deficit and the national debt continue to incite public concerns, there are new provocations for raiding the treasury. The potential for more lost jobs, higher taxes, increased inflation, and an implosion of debt has never been greater. But short of some kind of sudden popular uprising, it is doubtful the American people will be in any position to resist the government's predatory incursions.

The Coming Collapse

The irrefutable conclusion of all these object lessons from history is that personal rights have been co-opted by the so-called experts. Government has, on its own, created today's crisis of debt and the dangerous levels of insolvency that may very well destroy us in the very near future. In the years following the Great Depression, government was spending $4.6 billion of taxpayer funds each year. Today, the United States government spends more than that every single day of the year. And from a total of some 600,000 government employees in the mid-1930s, we now have more than 18.6 million men and women on the payrolls of the government.

Do the vast numbers of government workers make our lives better? Do they give us greater financial, political, social, emotional, or moral security? Do they protect us from crime or offer us practical and helpful services for the salaries we pay them? Do they enhance our freedoms, or do they in reality place this nation at greater and greater risk with every passing day?

By any standard, no government in history has been so profligate as our own. And no people have ever been at greater financial risk. All the lessons of history tell us that the loss of economic discipline destroys nations and people. But how long will it be until the next Easter surprise shakes the foundations of the nation? How long until the next stock-market crash sends Wall Street into panic? But be assured that the next time the market collapses, it will not rebound like the last one. Look at the headlines tonight and ask yourself: How long will it be until something goes desperately wrong with the economy and we lose it all?

Are you prepared for the consequences of a total economic collapse? Are you prepared for the public backlash if Medicare, Aid to Families with Dependent Children, Social Security, or some of the other forms of welfare and social assistance suddenly disappear? That is a genuine possibility. Do you think that the people who have been born and raised on welfare for three or four generations will be able to cope if the system suddenly stops dead in its tracks? Social conditions are already stagnant, and these economic uncertainties may well be the key to the greatest national catastrophe in history. Yes, it *can* happen here.

The fact that our nation is in a financial and political crisis is no secret. There is no one who believes we are doing "just fine" anymore. But there is not much evidence that the people are willing to do anything about these problems, either. More than half of all citizens in this country are taking money from government at this moment. Despite all the evidence that government confiscation of wealth is crippling the nation and that taxes and bureaucracy and profligate spending are ruining the lives of millions of citizens, most people seem to feel that government indeed owes them a living.

Whatever happened to the American spirit? What happened to our sense of individual pride and self-sufficiency? Whatever happened to the spirit of rugged individualism that made this nation the greatest economic success story in the history of the world? We can only wonder. Governor Tommy Thompson of Wisconsin has led lawmakers in his state to try to reform the system and, over a period of time, to phase out welfare entirely. Despite protests from some quarters, these reformers are eager to turn back the clock on government handouts and the tax-and-spend mentality.

There is strong evidence that America's day of reckoning is not far away. Do we care enough to do something about it? Can we respond in time? Do we have the courage to take these matters back into our own hands and make some serious changes at the polls? The only way to turn this situation around is to get involved now and to begin working for positive change. One way you can make a difference is to support only those candidates who demonstrate by their actions and by their record that they are committed to fiscal responsibility.

Stay informed on these issues, watch how your national, state, and local representatives use their votes. Write letters, make phone calls, and stay in touch with these issues. If enough people show that economic discipline is of vital concern, then things will begin to change for the better. In view of our current dilemma, to sit back and watch, or to simply ignore these problems in hopes that someone else will worry about them for you, is the most dangerous course you can follow. But prayer, involvement in citizen action groups, and dynamic engagement with these issues can make a difference. The best defense is a positive offense, and now is the very best time to take a stand.

4

Rising Bureaucracy

THE INDISPENSABLE background to Western democracy is the idea that every individual citizen has, by birthright, the freedom of self-determination. The American founding fathers believed in individual liberty as a right, endowed by the Creator. It was "unalienable." This constitutional view of the independence and autonomy of the individual is essential to our definition of freedom. Each man has the right to succeed or to fail on his own, without the interference or the complicity of government.

But, over time, government has changed this vital covenant. For a variety of reasons, Congress has been persuaded to modify the paradigm of individual liberty in the attempt to rig up a safety net for every citizen and to provide guarantees against the risks involved in every sort of endeavor, from new business to childbirth. Such a prospect was never considered by the American founders. Government was designed as a guardian of law and order; it existed to preserve and protect our essential rights and liberties.

Cradle-to-grave protection was never a democratic notion; rather, it is one of the fundamental principles of socialism—the ideology that has now failed on every continent and in every nation where it has been tried. But for better or for worse, this is the task the American bureaucracy has taken unto itself.

At the March 1994 European "jobs summit," President Bill Clinton said he was perplexed by the critical employment problems in Europe and low wages in America. Neither the president nor his expert policy analysts could make sense of it. But columnist David Lambro says it is perfectly clear: "The evidence is everywhere that both are due to the excessive growth of government, burdensome social welfare costs, and increasingly higher taxes to pay for it all."[1]

The Growth of Government

The biggest growth industry in America today is government. At the federal, state, and local levels, government is growing faster than any industry. Government consumes more revenue than any industry takes in, and for the first time in history there are more workers in the public sector than in all areas of the manufacturing sector combined. In 1994, more than 18.6 million people were employed by government. In 1993, the *Federal Register,* which is the record of activity in the executive branch, grew by more than seventy thousand pages—a record even by standards of the Carter administration.

At the same time, we have read that the Clinton health-care

proposals will mandate a 7.9 percent increase in payroll taxes for all employees. Reports prepared by the Heritage Foundation show that these new costs will shackle private business in this country, and, according to the best estimates, increased costs and higher taxes will lead to the loss of as many as 3 million American jobs.[2]

How will the administration deal with the 3 million unemployed men and women who will suddenly be looking to the government for assistance? The Congressional Budget Office (CBO) projected the Clinton plan would lead to a 27 percent increase in federal taxes—the largest tax increase in history. And the CBO's line-by-line analysis of the actual costs of the plan indicate that its policies would not save the nation $50 billion, as the president once claimed, but would instead cost at least $90 billion additional. That means the president missed his estimate by more than $140 billion. Where will the nation come up with that kind of cash?

Sometimes we forget that government does not have any money of its own. The federal and state bureaucracies do not make money. Government takes the hard-earned wages of citizens and pours them into the public trough.

Furthermore, they never get enough, and year after year the tax hustlers come back for more. Many of the most totalitarian regimes of history actually began as free-market systems that were gradually co-opted by revenue-hungry governments. In such cases, they eventually came to the point, as in the Soviet Union, where the government took everything its citizens could earn and then gave back what the bureaucrats thought the people deserved. Are we headed in that direction? All the signs seem to suggest that we are.

Government is extraordinarily inefficient, and whenever the government gets involved in anything, the situation automatically gets worse. Whenever you find a serious problem in your community, you can be fairly certain that government was involved in creating it. When citizens feel they have a problem only government can solve, they inevitably discover that, the minute government gets involved, their problems become immeasurably worse.

Taxation without Retaliation

The United States Constitution is a fragile instrument; it cannot be changed by whim or even by plebiscite without damaging the vital covenants and principles established by the founders. The Constitution of the United States guarantees each citizen the right to keep and bear arms, and the Declaration of Independence asserts the right of citizens to change the structure of an oppressive government by armed rebellion, which is still a radical idea. But changes in foundational principles by mere custom or by casual modifications of law are not warranted. Thomas Jefferson wrote in the Declaration:

> *Prudence, indeed, will dictate that governments long established should not be changed for light and transient causes; and accordingly all experience hath shown, that mankind are more disposed to suffer, while evils are sufferable, than to right themselves by abolishing the forms to which they are accustomed.*[3]

The patriots held that it was only after long provocation and by force of arms that the constitutional code of citizenship might be altered. Yet, by economics, by law, by diplomacy, and by manipulation of the rights and responsibilities of the individual states established in the Constitution, and especially in matters pertaining to taxation and public welfare, the federal government has already taken upon itself unprecedented and virtually unlimited powers.

Despite the immense provocation, no one rebels! One would think taxpayers would be up in arms. Shouldn't parents be raging against the assault upon their families, their children, their public schools, and the safety of their communities? Shouldn't workers be screaming about the lack of safety in the workplace? Shouldn't employers be outraged about the meddling of federal and state bureaucracies in their business and financial decisions? And what right, after all, does government have to consume more than 40 percent of the entire wealth of the nation while it siphons off $1.5 trillion every year for government spending without making a dent in our national debt of $4.4 trillion?

Thomas Jefferson also said, "I place economy among the first and most important virtues, and public debt as the greatest of dangers," by which he meant that it is the duty of the government not simply to manage its financial affairs professionally, but to live frugally. Government must be economical in its spending habits, and it is no secret that in recent years government has become extravagant beyond all measure.

Jefferson said that financial profligacy, or profusion, can lead only to disaster, and he warned, "We must make our choice between economy and liberty, or profusion and servitude. If we can prevent the government from wasting the labors of the people under the pretense of caring for them, they will be happy." But the alternative is that as government consumes the public treasury it also destroys the people's freedom.

In the mid-1990s, every working man and woman in America is in bondage to the federal government. Even God only asks for 10 percent of our wages. But today every working person in America must work until May 3 for the substance to pay our federal taxes, until May 20 to pay our portion of what Congress spends, and until July 13 to pay off all our federal, state, and local taxes. That means average Americans work more than half a year for the government before they are allowed to keep even the first nickel of their personal wages. That is the longest period of tax bondage—the longest financial obligation to government—in American history. "Tax-freedom day" comes later every year.[4]

In effect, we have become sharecroppers for the master in the White House. We are little more than indentured servants to a ruthless totalitarian regime that holds the power of intimidation, financial retaliation, and even imprisonment over our heads at every turn. The political, economic, and spiritual bondage from which our forefathers fled when they first came to America now enslaves the entire nation. We are bound by an onerous form of "taxation without representation" the founders of this nation would never have endured.

Government Out of Control

Wherever the state has been allowed to become all-powerful, to grow out of control, dwarfing the interests of the community and consuming the productivity of the nation, the consequences have always been disastrous. Ancient Egypt and the Roman Empire provide historical precedents for the out-of-control growth of government.

Egypt was a remarkable kingdom that survived for more than four thousand years under thirty-two separate dynasties before it finally faded into irrelevance under the Roman Empire. In the early days government administration was remarkable. Highly placed eunuchs, priests, and scribes administered the agriculture, industry, arts, and sciences of the day, and in the beginning the system seems to have worked quite well. The scientific and artistic achievements of the kingdoms of the Nile are still stunning to most observers.

But changes were bound to come, and after 1085 B.C., Egypt went through a series of divisions and internecine struggles provoked by religious and nationalistic disputes. Rivalries and even civil wars became dangerously common, so that by the eighth century B.C., Egypt had to be divided into eleven separate states. Instead of the open and peaceful communities of the second and third millennia B.C., the nation was now a bizarre network of walls and canals and man-made barriers set up to segregate ethnic groups and to allow for regional defense.

The regionalization of the Egyptian culture promoted the rise of local cults and an assortment of local and provincial governments. Just as religious and social unity had promoted order, growing disunity led to chaos and decay. As dozens of councils competed with each other, factionalism and infighting increased. Bureaucratic meddling only made things worse, and soon the entire structure began to collapse.

In the end Egypt fell to a succession of alien empires, first to the Cushites of Sudan; then to the Assyrians, who occupied the nation in the mid-seventh century B.C.. The kingdom was then conquered by the Persians, who ruled it off and on until the entire kingdom fell to Alexander the Great, who was recognized as Pharaoh in 333 B.C.. But rather than settling in Memphis, Thebes, or any of the ancient capitals, Alexander established his base of operations at Pharos, just off the Egyptian coast. Here, on a tropical island, there was no taint of the corrupt systems of administration that had divided and destroyed the empire.

Among other contributors to the decline of the Roman Empire was the drop in productivity, made worse by bad national policies. Burdensome regulations and taxes made every form of trade, farming, manufacturing, and even common labor unprofitable. Small farms had already been swallowed up by the large estates under the control of a few powerful families. In time, however, corrupt officials and government functionaries found ways to confiscate the wealth and property of even the greatest estates.

These farms were nationalized very much as those in the Soviet Union during the Bolshevik reforms, and predictably, production and revenues immediately collapsed. Most of the estates eventually went to weed and seed, and they became eyesores for travelers, deserted by all but the homeless peasants. And no amount of persuasion or coercion could persuade tenants to reclaim these lands. Some of the best farmland in all of Italy became freehold property no one cared to claim.

All of this was complicated immeasurably by the meddling of government, and as the bureaucracy consumed the sources of wealth, national prosperity was progressively eroded. The efforts of the emperors and the senate to manage the nationalized industries damaged productivity even further and led to outright abandonment of not only the best farms but businesses, homes, properties, and possessions of every kind.

The emperors, aided by the senate, preyed on the wealth of the prominent families. In the attempt to pay the army and feed the growing hordes of starving peasants, the industrious classes upon whom the empire depended were driven into poverty and/or exile. The only ones able to survive these burdensome conditions were a few of the most powerful aristocrats who protected their dependents, workers, and slaves from political oppression by bribery, brute force, or some sort of personal influence with the throne.

These conditions placed enormous burdens on families. Under so many pressures, the population declined. Childbearing became undesirable. Little by little a general barrenness came about among women of all social classes. As life became untenable, life itself seemed to retreat. Very similar conditions are reported today by mission agencies that work in the drought-stricken nations of Africa. When societies begin to collapse, and when even nature turns its back upon a people, life dies in the womb. Nature rebels.

Losing Control

The Roman Empire was a thousand years old when the emperor Diocletian came to the throne in A.D. 284. Power was now concentrated in the emperor and his personal council. Unfortunately, the Romans never developed a practical form of representative government with the capacity to deal with the complexities of such a vast regime. Everything hinged on the strength and perception of the emperors; and when the leader showed signs of weakness, the empire suffered.

The bureaucracy grew so large that at one point there were more people on the government payroll than there were taxpayers to support them. The whole administrative system became overcentralized, and as Russell Kirk observes, "When the center could hold no longer, the bough began to break."[5]

In time, most of the free population in Rome were unemployed—thus they became what Arnold Toynbee has described as an "internal proletariat." Such people were bitter and jealous revolutionaries who worked from the inside to destroy the empire. Even though there was no work for the lower classes, the rulers believed these people had to be fed and amused to prevent violent outbursts. In large cities in every province, the consuls resorted to the form of bribery known as bread and circuses in order to keep the masses under control. Large quantities of corn, grain, meat, and wines were distributed daily to the poor, who crowded in ever growing numbers in the ghettos of the capital.

These spectacles and entertainments were designed to keep the masses amused and preoccupied. Under Diocletian this policy of placating the turbulent crowds, known formally as "euergetics," went from an act of occasional generosity to an absolute necessity. Public welfare, along with the most extravagant and bloody entertainments, were free to the common people. Even as these events demonstrated the cheapening of human life and the debased morality of the people of all classes, they were nevertheless a desperate attempt to preserve the tenuous order of the state. They were a last-ditch effort at keeping the crowds in check.

Naturally, as the population began to shrink, the tax base declined as well. Surviving members of the wealthy classes were taxed exorbitantly to support the least-productive members of society—meaning not just the masses of unemployed poor but also the emperor and his hangers-on. This led to increasing dissension and frequent violence between all classes and races.

So what was the effect of the attempt to placate the masses? In his treatise on the impact of all these social and economic factors, historian Michael Rostovtzeff observes that "the peasants hated the landowners and the officials, the city proletariat hated the city bourgeoisie, the army was hated by everybody, even by the peasants. The Christians were abhorred and persecuted by the heathens, who regarded them as a gang of criminals bent on undermining the state."[6]

Russell Kirk adds that suspicion and intolerance quickly spread between all classes in the empire. "Between the senatorial and equestrian families on the one side, and the masses of free citizens in the cities on the other, between the freedmen and the native-born Roman citizens; between the citizens, urban or rural, and the millions of slaves; between the urban populations and the peasants—among all these social elements, little sympathy endured."[7] It should come as no great surprise that in such an environment, when the empire finally did fall to the Goths, many Romans actually considered it a blessing.

The All-Powerful State

From these examples, it can be seen that the improvident growth of government and the exploitation of citizens through excessive taxation and overregulation will destroy the initiative of labor and contribute to the decline of industry and productivity. It is very likely that we in America will undergo some intense political and financial testing in this decade. Unless we can get a grip on the bureaucratic nightmare and stop the predations of government—specifically, get government's hands out of our pockets—there is great doubt whether or not America as we know her can survive.

In his lesser-known study *The Old Order and the French Revolution*, Alexis de Tocqueville said that the drift toward centralization by government is the very essence of despotism. The French statesman observed that the rise of the all-powerful state is the root of the waves of egoism, selfishness, and self-seeking that perennially overcome great societies at critical times in history.

As government grows, social authority diminishes. Laws, prohibitions, and increased taxation favor the state but penalize the individual. The purpose of law under such a political regime is not the common good or moral order but the empowerment of the state and the bureaucrats who grow fat and sleek within such a system. Robert Nisbet says, "As the blood rushes to the head of society, it leaves anemic the local and regional extremities."

Individual states, counties, and towns suffer from lack of authority and lack of support. As the federal government grows into the very image of Leviathan—that is, the state as described by Thomas Hobbes in his famous book—the impersonal mass of mankind under an autocratic government is left rootless and alienated in the world. And this entire scenario of collapse and loss of values arises specifically because government has ascended to the place of becoming society's predominant authority—its god, a false god, an idol of worldly power—and therefore stands where only the divine authority should be.

As we have seen throughout these pages, we are facing dark

times in this nation. At times we can see the indisputable image of national catastrophe on the horizon, and the crisis before us is only compounded by the destructive policies of the bureaucracy. Nevertheless, I maintain that there is still hope.

If we are willing to risk the scorn of the media and the bureaucrats, there is reason to believe that good things can still happen. If we can follow the practical plans already being drafted by Christian and conservative groups across this nation—plans designed to bring about positive change, and a renewal of our time-honored traditions—then there is just a chance that we may be able to halt the siege of ideology and corruption in the land.

There is hope that government can be downsized and that the bureaucracy may be brought to task. The battle is not over; but the time is short. Can we afford to wait any longer to get involved?

PART TWO

CULTURAL
DECAY

5

The Decline of Education

FROM the first stirrings of the Latin culture on the banks of the Tiber in 753 B.C. to the sack of Rome in A.D. 410, and then to the assumption of power by the German chief Odoacer in 476, the Roman Empire survived for thirteen dramatic centuries. After the Fall of Rome, the empire continued for another thousand years in its new capital at Constantinople. The Eastern empire, built on the principles of a triumphant Christian faith, survived the Fall of Rome and continued in power and splendor until 1453, when the Byzantine Empire was overrun by the Ottoman Turks.

By that time, a new renaissance of art and culture was bursting forth once again in Rome, and the rediscovery of classical ideas was beginning to stir an awakening of the imagination and a new vitality of thought. The Eastern empire added to the legend. But after the fall of the ancient capital, the character of the empire had changed. It was no secret that the great Roman Empire died a less than noble death.

What did fell the Roman colossus? What brought the majesty of the Caesars to a halt? In his study *The Civilization of Rome*, Donald Dudley says that no single cause, by itself, would have been enough to bring the empire to its knees. Rather, it required a large number of bad habits acquired over a long period of time. What history reveals, Dudley says, is "a number of weaknesses in Roman society; their effects may be variously estimated, but in combination they must have been largely responsible for the collapse."[1]

The Cultural Revolution

Today American society suffers from a growing number of maladies, including many that have lingered for years. Are they comparable to the failings that afflicted Rome? Are they sufficient to bring this nation to its knees? Donald Dudley suggests that the leading factors in Rome's decline were both philosophical and practical in nature. They included, for example, the exploitation of workers and other citizens, and lack of innovation. But he also stresses that one of the key factors in the atrophy and decline of the empire was the loss of curiosity and intellectual integrity in education.

Instead of favoring an education in history and letters, prominent families began directing their sons into the more lucrative and expeditious professions of rhetoric and debate—the training ground for lawyers, politicians, and bureaucrats. The weakening of the quality of leadership and the gradual compromise of the

74

essential principles of government may be traced to the loss of essential knowledge, the loss of a sense of history, and the general deterioration in the overall quality of education.

Honesty and nobility of character disappeared, sexual immorality became rampant, and speaking out against excess or corruption was called treason. To squelch all evidence of resistance to their policies, Roman emperors from Nero on used the army and their personal guard as a sort of thought police to ferret out dissent and punish opponents. While this may be one of the best early examples of political correctness being enforced by government, it was merely one example of the extent to which a government will go to enforce its will upon the people. Thought control, political manipulation, and intellectual exploitation have always been crude and simplistic forms of tyranny. But they are very effective. Witness what is happening in our schools and universities today.

Held in a virtual stranglehold by the liberal teachers unions, many of America's public schools have become ghettos of ignorance and violence. The shocking state of education today is directly attributable to the social agendas being force-fed to teachers and pupils alike in the nation's public schools. Educators today no longer concentrate on the standard curricula of previous generations. Classical learning has been turned on its head in favor of the socially expedient. And instead of educating students in subjects that build moral character and civic virtues, today's textbooks program children with the agenda of the Left.

Predictably, the results are appalling. In one Philadelphia high school, 85 percent of the graduates were reported to be functionally illiterate. The United States has roughly 28 million functional illiterates and approximately 83 million people who are in some way learning impaired. But this legacy of ignorance also has a social component, since 60 percent of all inmates in our prisons are functionally illiterate. In one southern state the percentage of illiterate inmates exceeds 70 percent.

The Dumbing of America

In his book *Why Johnny Can't Tell Right from Wrong,* William Kilpatrick reports that as many as 525,000 attacks, shakedowns, and robberies occur in our public high schools each month. Every day more than 16,000 crimes are committed in or near schools. And despite the increase in metal detectors, as many as 135,000 students carry guns to school each day. One out of every five students carries some type of weapon for personal protection. All these statistics are subject to change, but they indicate the magnitude of the problems.

And the problems do not end at the school door. The suicide rate among young people has gone up 300 percent since the 1960s; drug and alcohol abuse and promiscuity have become commonplace. According to the 1994 edition of the *Index of Leading Cultural Indicators,* in the past decade there has been a 1,740 percent increase in the number of children treated for knife and gunshot wounds at the Children's National Medical Center in the nation's capital. While a growing number of students and teachers are knifed, shot, raped, beaten, and robbed in the schools, the biggest concern of educators is not safety but the implementation of programs such as "values clarification" and "value neutral thinking." The three Rs have been replaced by the three S's—"sensitivity," "self-esteem," and "safe sex."

As a result, more than 2.5 million young people graduate from the public schools of this nation as functional illiterates each year. Many cannot read above a third-grade level; they cannot do simple mathematics; they cannot keep a checkbook; and in some cases they cannot even use a public telephone without assistance. One study reports that as many as 25 million adults read so poorly they cannot understand the warning label on a bottle of poison. And many cannot even fill out an employment application without someone to read it to them.

In 1987, Chester E. Finn, the former assistant secretary of education, found that only 5 percent of seventeen year olds could read well enough to understand technical documents, literary essays, or works of history. Only 6 percent could solve simple math problems with more than one step. Only 7 percent could draw a logical conclusion from a list of scientific facts. In a comparison of the educational attainments of students from the United States and nineteen other industrialized nations, American high school students scored dead last or next to last in every category. Sadly, American students had the highest level of self-esteem and the lowest intellectual attainments of all students tested.[2]

In his best-selling book *The Closing of the American Mind,* Dr. Allan Bloom makes the statement that American high school graduates are among the most sensitive illiterates in the world. In all the standardized achievement tests comparing the educational attainments of U.S. students with young people of the same age from other countries, American students consistently place near the bottom in every category. They are incredibly sensitive. They are environmentally aware. But they are pathetically ignorant.

Where do such problems come from? To what do we owe this sudden plunge into sensitivity and ignorance? Could it be that American students are poorer than the children of other nations? Is it because they are socially deprived? Maybe it is because there is not enough multiculturalism or diversity or sex education in the schools. Or maybe it is because public educators, in order to accomplish their social programs, have turned away from the task of teaching young people the specific information that used to be considered essential knowledge.

The Brainwashing of America

According to the National Education Association (NEA), the cause of ignorance in America today is the "religious right." Everywhere you look, there are signs that the secular establishment has targeted evangelicals and other religious groups for political attack. "Alarms are being raised," writes *Forbes* columnist Thomas Sowell, "that conservative or religious indoctrination will be imposed in the public schools."[3]

But in truth, he says, any real or perceived dangers from the right don't even come close to the dangers represented by the awesome "education" bureaucracy already in place in this country. These "educrats" have been conducting a systematic "brainwashing" of America's children for the past thirty years. He writes:

> *The techniques of brainwashing developed in totalitarian countries are routinely used in psychological conditioning programs imposed on American school children. These include emotional shock and desensitization, psychological isolation from sources of support, stripping away defenses, manipulative cross-examination of the individual's underlying moral values, and inducing acceptance of alternative values by psychological rather than rational means.*

The columnist, an economist and senior fellow at the Hoover Institute at Stanford University, says such practices are employed throughout the educational system today, not only dealing with personal and relational issues but even in such subjects as history and social studies. They are especially prevalent in courses dealing with social issues. These include instruction in sex education, death education, drug prevention, nuclear education, and multiculturalism. Sowell writes:

> *Shock and desensitization procedures range from taking children to morgues and funeral homes to see and touch dead bodies to pairing boys and girls to have conversations with each other about sex, showing ghastly movies of war, or raw movies showing sexual activity or close-ups of childbirth.*
>
> *Verbal examples include classroom discussions of lifeboat dilemmas, where the limited capacity of the boat forces decisions as to who should be left to drown. Sometimes children are asked to decide whom they would sacrifice among members of their own family.*[4]

This highly recognized scholar stresses that these dangerous curricula are part of a nationwide trend implemented by educational psychologists using programmed materials that are distributed to educators, school boards, and curriculum administrators. Included in the packages are detailed guidelines and instructions on how to deal with parents and others who object to the radical techniques. In addition, the NEA has produced an instructional video, booklets, and a militant-action guide for defeating the religious right and like-minded conservatives.

"Mobilizing schoolchildren for the political crusades of the left has also been going on for years," writes Sowell. At one period of time the president's office was routinely flooded with antinuclear letters from schoolchildren, orchestrated and initiated by liberal teachers and their educational curriculum. More recently we have seen multiculturalism being force-fed to children through politically correct textbooks and teaching methods.

How are schools to deal with complaints? Teacher handbooks

offer specific guidelines. When parents complain to the schools, they are to be told, "None of the other parents has objected!" or "You're the only one who has complained." Such tactics are designed to isolate and humiliate those who are rightly shocked by what their children are seeing and doing in school. And when parents come together in groups to resist the indoctrination of their children, the cry of "censorship" goes up loud and clear, and the liberal media are quickly put on the trail. The object is to accuse and vilify Christian and other conservative "troublemakers" in the eyes of the community. But these troublemakers are decent people like you. They are not outlaws; they are your neighbors and friends.

Professor Charles Sykes, author of the best-selling book *A Nation of Victims,* writes in an article in the *National Review* that the NEA liberals have it backward. The battle over school choice, he says, points out just how differently the educrats and the parents feel about the education of their children. He writes:

> *Given the dangers young blacks face in the nation's inner cities—illiteracy, drugs, gang violence—few black parents lose much sleep worrying that their children will be exposed to prayer. The educrats, however, worry about it for them. (Repeat after me: A crucifix submerged in urine is art; a crucifix in a classroom is a threat to our constitutional freedom.)*[5]

Political Correctness

The intellectual coercion we see in schools as well as in other areas of society is yet another manifestation of the spirit of political correctness that pervades our campuses. In only slightly different form, the same kinds of thought control existed in the Soviet Union, Hitler's Third Reich, the French Enlightenment, and the last days of the Roman Empire. The proscription of certain ideas and certain types of speech was a major feature of the Spanish Inquisition and the religious wars of the Middle Ages, each based on the desire to control not only words but thoughts and beliefs. We used to say they can't hang you for what you're thinking. But that is not really true.

Political correctness (PC) is an attempt to eliminate freedom of speech for those who hold traditional values and religious beliefs. It is overt social censorship designed to stifle the truth. But we should also note that the emergence of this hostile ideology is one of the surest warnings that a culture is on the verge of collapse.

Several years ago, Alfons Heck wrote a book entitled *A Child of Hitler: Germany in the Days When God Wore a Swastika.* It is the story of a boy who grew up in the Second World War as a member of the Hitler Youth. He tells of the emotional and psychological programming that took place at that time. And one of the most striking portions of the book is Heck's description of the mind control that induced children to betray their own parents and friends for saying things that were deemed politically incorrect.

Simply saying aloud that Germany should not have invaded Poland, for example, was considered treason. Anyone guilty of saying so was summarily executed by the Reich. And there were countless other examples even worse. Speech was no longer free, and even thoughts were controlled by force. But we know that the same consequences were meted out by the Bolsheviks in Russia, the philosophes in the Enlightenment, and the emperors of the Eternal City during the last miserable years of Rome. In reality, PC is the symptom of a disease as old as time itself.

As always, the battlefield of all these intellectual and moral campaigns is the soul. Arnold Toynbee concluded that one of the effects of collapse in the great empires of antiquity was a "schism in the soul" that causes dissension and recoil, and leads to moral chaos. When the "creative minority" that gives leadership and ideas to the nation begins to lose its influence and becomes an "oppressive minority," the nation invariably enters a time of troubles. The associations of this term with the same term in the book of Revelation is not accidental, and the consequences are much the same.

Nationalized Education

One of the major publications of the NEA's assault on conservative values is called *Combating the New Right*, and it describes the pro-family movement in America as the "barefoot and pregnant coalition." I recently received a copy of a regional NEA periodical called the *Advocate* that gave its readers a five-page cover story warning teachers to "Beware the Invasion of the Radical Right." Another publication, *What's Left after the Right*, written by Portland professor Janet Jones, is a resource tool for educators distributed by the NEA to tens of thousands of schools all over America.

This handbook includes sections such as "The Typical Censorship Scenario," "Profile of a Censor," "How the Religious Right Views the New Age and the Force," and "Friends of Public Education." Throughout this literature, parents who resist on moral grounds are labeled as censors and extremists, while left-wing activists and social reformers are called friends and supporters.

A self-test called "Your Radical Right IQ" is also included. This test is designed to help reinforce the indoctrination and to lock certain names of "friends" and "enemies" in the teachers' minds. It begins by saying, "Administrators in this district know several state and national organizations that will supply resources and supportive assistance to this district in the event of a censorship controversy." Then the teachers are supposed to list and categorize the groups they have been reviewing.

Under "destructive" the teachers are expected to write such names as Focus on the Family, Citizens for Excellence in Education, Eagle Forum, Concerned Women for America, and the Christian Coalition. Under "supportive" they are to list the NEA, the ACLU, and People for the American Way. For an example of their objectivity, consider the remarks of People for the American Way's Michael Hudson at an Institute for Development of Education Activities (IDEA) workshop, in which he told his audience that Focus on the Family and its president, Dr. James Dobson (one of those on the "enemies" list), is a "nationwide force that has a very anti-education agenda" and is "a significant threat to American democracy and to public education."

All across North America, liberal educators and school boards are using such inflammatory literature to support their war against historic American values and authentic content-based education. In many places experimental programs based on the untested theories of so-called experts are being implemented without parental consent or community approval. One such example passes under the innocuous name of "Required Student Learning Outcomes" (SLO). But it is simply another form of value-neutral, outcome-based education, which holds that it doesn't matter whether or not children learn any specific facts, so long as they feel good about themselves and develop "tolerance for diversity." If they can get a basic job, that's enough. This form of behaviorism has crippling consequences and destroys achievement at every level. It does not encourage excellence but mediocrity.

These programs scrap traditional content-based education in favor of the SLO program, which requires that all students demonstrate their acceptance of the politically correct social concepts being pushed by the NEA. If students give the wrong answers, they will not be promoted to the next level. Such PC values would include environmentalism, global citizenship, multiculturalism, and acceptance of homosexuality and abortion rights.

In a report published in *The Christian American,* the president of Citizens for Excellence in Education said that "over 50 percent of the goals do not deal with academics (learning how to think). Most of the value outcomes are politically and socially in opposition to traditional Judeo-Christian values." In a chapter on environmentalism, one textbook currently in use talks about the "carrying capacity" of the earth and tells students that birth control and abortion are essential to the future of the planet.

Over the protests of parents and educators, the government of Pennsylvania has authorized the curriculum for outcome-based education for a three-year trial period. But the lawyer for the House Local Government Committee predicts that all students will learn is that outcome-based education is an experiment that pushes values at the expense of learning. "You don't have to be a fundamentalist to see that it's a concern," says William Sloane. Unfortunately, these dangerous programs have been ignored by too many parents, and they are creeping into schools all over the country at this very moment, virtually without resistance.

The Pragmatic Approach

For more than fifty years, the political Left has denounced religion as the source of all mankind's woes. By casting doubt on traditional values, the education establishment has been setting forth the programs for progressive education first promulgated by John Dewey during the early years of this century. Using many of the controversial theories of Horace Mann, Dewey helped to create the basic plans for compulsory education, which was to be one of the essential tools for the social indoctrination of America's young people.

The proposals of Dewey and Mann were controversial and extremely unpopular with parents, especially as they began to discover what their ideas entailed. Mann had said, "Education, then, beyond all other devices of human origin, is the great equalizer of the conditions of men—the balance-wheel of the social machinery." At the same time, John Dewey maintained that education was its own reward. He said, "Education is a social process," and he insisted that "education is not a preparation for life; education is life itself." In short, he rejected the idea of preparing young men and women for careers in the real world. His aim was to socialize them and transform them into creatures of the state.

It is important to keep in mind that compulsory public education was carefully structured by the leftists as the main way to accomplish their social goals. As Samuel Blumenfeld concluded in his important book *NEA: Trojan Horse in American Education,* "The most potent and significant expression of statism is a state educational system. Without it, statism is impossible. With it, the state can and has become everything."[6] This was Dewey's goal, and at first his systems received strong resistance from all sectors of society.

Writing in the April 1994 issue of *Chronicles* magazine, Samuel Francis says that it was inevitable that leftist intellectuals and the pushers of radical educational programs would come to align themselves with the federal bureaucracy. In empires of the past—including Athens, Rome, Elizabethan England, and seventeenth-century France—the cultural elites attached themselves to the government. They knew that the way to get the favors and the positions they wanted was by cozying up to the king. Today, the NEA and other radical groups go to government because they know there is no sympathy for their causes among parents or the public. Only government is blind enough to the needs of the people and hungry enough for power at any price that it will indulge and give financial support to the forms of education that will destroy children's lives.

Francis says, "Unable to peddle its garbage on the market, incapable of duping or flattering wealthy patrons into supporting it, and despising the prospect of working for a living like everyone else, the cultural elite has no other recourse but to rely on bureaucratic mechanisms to sustain itself, its privileges, its productions, and its power."[7] The early educators in this country stuck to their radical agenda over the decades, and by sheer dogged persistence they were able to outlast most of the mainstream resistance. People who felt threatened by the new ideas, including most Christians, eventually fled from the debate. So today, thanks to the power of the federal government and the taxpayer dollars it provides, a radical education agenda is flooding into America's classrooms and putting another generation of children in peril.

John Dewey's method was to apply the humanistic philosophy of pragmatism to education by teaching that learning comes through doing. This is the perspective that values physical and emotional experience over facts and practical knowledge. It is a type of learning that leads inevitably to denial of the importance of history and tradition. It rejects existing cultural and moral values in favor of "diversity" and "tolerance." It is hard to overemphasize the damage that is being done to traditional values. Dewey's influence on education theory is still being felt not only in the schools but in the universities and in government.

In the final analysis, the theories of modern education can be summed up as a basic denial of the value of Western tradition and a repudiation of the role of religion in the welfare of the community. Educators push not only the denial of the existence of God but militant hostility to any form of Judeo-Christian religion. That is what the whole debate about separation of church and state is all about.

At least among the organizers and union leaders, professional educators say that creationism cannot be taught because it requires belief in God, morality cannot be taught because it requires reverence to the Bible, and traditional history cannot be taught because it speaks of the important place of God and our religious values throughout the entire record of human affairs.

Numbers Don't Lie

In his well-documented analysis of the cultural changes of the last thirty years, David Barton reports that between 1963 and 1990, SAT scores of college-bound students plunged more than 80 points. At the same time, illegitimate births have soared from 15 per 1,000 to 35 per 1,000 for girls aged fifteen to nineteen. Total pregnancies for unwed girls between fifteen and nineteen have soared from 100,000 in 1963 to 650,000 in 1987. Sexually transmitted diseases among teenagers have soared from 350 cases per 100,000 to 1,200 cases; and premarital sex among teenage girls has jumped from 23 percent to 70 percent.[8] At the same time, the divorce rate in this country has shot up from 2.2 per 1,000 in 1962 to 4.7 in 1990. Single-parent households have risen from 4.6 million to 10.9 million. And the incidence of violent crime leapt from 250,000 in 1962 to 1.7 million in 1990. In short the court-mandated removal of prayer, devotionals, and any exposure to religious values from our schools has been the major contributing cause of the moral breakdown in our society.

What's interesting is that the people who are carrying out this dangerous agenda are not sending their children to the public schools. They send them to exclusive private schools where they can be protected and educated as the liberal elite of the next generation. None of those in power, from the White House down, want their children subjected to the tyranny of the public schools. The cultural elite refuse to put their own children into those politically correct ghettos. According to one news report, as many as 40 percent of the teachers in the Chicago public schools send their own children to private schools. No doubt the figures are much the same in many other cities.

Thirty years ago, every schoolchild in America understood the premise of Western civilization. They were well versed in the heritage of our nation, and they understood the background to our struggle for independence and freedom. They understood that honesty, hard work, and personal integrity were essential, along with faith in God and a commitment to our fellowman. And like their parents before them, including many thousands of immigrants, they believed in the value of the American way of life.

Today, however, we can no longer take such attitudes for granted. Students are taught that the Founding Fathers, the great writers and thinkers, and all the values of those "dead white European males" were perverse and imperialistic from the start. Teachers in our schools and universities set about to redefine the world for our young people. They make it their task to set the record straight.

Openness and relativism became the great insights of modern education. As Allan Bloom attests, students were taught to believe that the most dangerous person in America is the man or woman who believes in an absolute standard of truth. Bloom says, "The study of history and of culture teaches that all the world was mad in the past; men always thought they were right, and that led to wars, persecutions, slavery, xenophobia, racism, and chauvinism. The point is not to correct the mistakes and really be right; rather, it is not to think you are right at all."[9] Teachers say that everything is relative; there are no absolutes.

Consequently, millions of students today have no views or values they wish to defend, no belief in cultural or religious values, and no respect for their heritage as Americans.

The English language is being redefined in America's classrooms today. Advocates of politically correct speech have begun to rewrite the entire lexicon of Western thought and to invent a new vocabulary of "victimization" more suited to a cultural tradition of bigotry and exploitation. In his important book on the politicization of the university, *Illiberal Education,* Dinesh D'Sousa says, "Instead of cultivating in young people those qualities of critical thought and civil argument that are the essence of a liberal education, university leaders have created sham communities where serious and honest discussion is frequently drowned out by a combination of sloganeering, accusation, and intimidation."[10]

Cultural Relativity

The game plan of the deconstructionists in the universities has been to eradicate the past and indoctrinate the young men and women of this nation with a new view of society and a radical political ideology. According to these theories, there are no absolutes, no sources of ultimate truth and meaning, and all "values" are of equal importance. So, by this view, the principles of Mao Tse-tung are just as meaningful as those of George Washington. Students today learn about the writings of Maya Angelou, Toni Morrison, and Judy Bloom instead of Mark Twain or William Shakespeare. And they know a great deal more about Madonna, Ice-T, and the 2 Live Crew than Bach, Beethoven, and Brahms.

Thanks to the shoddy education they have received, most students have no means and no desire to challenge such fraudulent ideas. They have no grasp of history or ideas. They have been taught to respect diversity and multiculturalism, and they have been taught that their heritage of freedom gives them plenty of rights but few responsibilities. There are no causes they are willing to fight for, no great and noble truths they would die for. Millions of young Americans have been stripped of their past and, very possibly, their future as well.

As students are infused with these revolutionary ideas, they lose any sense of esteem for American heritage, for the values of Western civilization, and for the virtues and the beliefs that made this nation unique. And because they have no sense of history, they are easy prey for radical beliefs and practically any political theory being pushed by liberal teachers and professors. The prevailing orthodoxies of the "cultural elite" have become the models for behavior and belief, and the emptiness in the souls of young people today is just one indication of the damage that has already been done.

The collapse of educational standards is one more expression of a society turned in upon itself—a nation at risk. Professor Charles Sykes, in his book *A Nation of Victims,* suggests that the meaning of right and wrong is being redefined by the secular society. In order to remove the restraints of Christianity and traditional moral values, educators have turned to the teachings of behaviorism and modern psychology, which hold that behavior is simply the result of conditioning. Bad behavior is not sin but merely nonproductive action. Crime is the result of poor socialization. And to overcome such problems, we don't need churches but more "therapy."

The rise of the "therapeutic culture" in America, says Professor Sykes, amounts to the ascendancy of a substitute faith—its roots are certainly in the false theology of humanism. "Filling the vacuum created by the decline of institutional faith and the collapse of the moral order it has provoked," Sykes observes, "psychoanalysis has assumed many of the functions traditionally performed by religion, and has done so by translating many of the theological and existential issues of human life into therapeutic terms."[11]

The degeneration of philosophy and science into relativism is just one more indication of the moral poverty of American society. It is evidence that we have become corrupt. In one of his most perceptive statements, Russell Kirk says, "Without Authority vested somewhere, without regular moral principles that may be consulted confidently, Justice cannot long endure anywhere. Yet modern liberalism and democracy are contemptuous of the whole concept of moral authority; if not checked in their assaults upon habitual reverence and prescriptive morality, the liberals and democrats will destroy Justice not only for their enemies, but for themselves."[12] In their fierce determination to deny their own guilt and to deny any possibility that a divine judge may be a witness against them, the modern scholar denies all moral authority.

President Theodore Roosevelt once said, "Americanism means the virtues of courage, honor, justice, truth, sincerity, and hardihood—the virtues that made America. The things that will destroy America are prosperity-at-any-price, peace-at-any-price, safety-first instead of duty-first, the love of soft living, and the get-rich-quick theory of life." At that time, at least, people still understood the value of their cultural heritage.

Relative Disaster

These were the values of a disciplined, dedicated, and caring people. While Americans of that day were reasonably tolerant of individual differences, they were not blind to careless, stupid, and irresponsible behavior. Justice meant swift and certain judgment, not moral blindness. But sadly, we have come a long way since the muscular Americanism and fortitude of Teddy Roosevelt and the Rough Riders.

But make no mistake: When relativity becomes the prevailing orthodoxy of a culture, the character of the people will wither and die. Both the individual and the nation as a whole will be reduced to selfishness and expediency. Pragmatism will become the new law of life, and moral discretion will have no power to restrain evil. Albert Einstein, the father of the science of relativity, was shocked by the tendency of intellectuals and social pundits to confuse his mathematical models with moral behavior. He saw this as a deadly mistake, and he said so.

He understood many things about the nature of matter, space, and time, but the great scientist said repeatedly that ethical behavior depends on the existence of an inner moral strength that is fixed and permanent. Good and evil are never relative; right and wrong are never arbitrary. "The real problem," he said, "is in the hearts and minds of men. It is not a problem of physics but of ethics. It is easier to denature plutonium than to denature the evil spirit of man." The prophet Jeremiah said, "The heart is deceitful above all things, and desperately wicked; Who can know it?" The father of relativity knew that to be true.

Many people will recall the controversial remarks a few years ago by Ted Turner, the founder and chairman of CNN and the Turner Broadcasting Network in Atlanta, when he offered to pay a million dollars to anyone who could come up with a realistic moral code to replace the unrealistic and worn-out Ten Commandments. That is a lot of money, but apparently nobody was able to come up with a satisfactory replacement. Today's liberals are selling their goods from an empty wagon, yet, with no values of their own, they are determined to eradicate those that have contributed to the progress and moral vitality of Western civilization for the past two thousand years.

But that is a large part of our problem today. For six thousand years we have had a practical, reliable, proven, and authorized set of rules from the hand of God himself. But man, in his pride and arrogance, refuses to acknowledge or live by them. But without the support of biblical values and the principles of Scripture, we have no other moral foundation.

Young people today are convinced that Einstein proved that everything is relative. But Einstein never said anything about moral or cultural values in his studies of physics. He said that time and space are relative, under certain circumstances, at the outer limits of physical theory. But he spent the last years of his life trying to tell people that his ideas applied only to science and not to ethics or morals. He was horrified by the atomic bomb, and he would certainly be opposed to what the liberals have done with his ideas today.

The Neoclassical Spirit

There is no denying that the influence of such revolutionary thinkers as Einstein, Freud, Marx, Nietzsche, and Darwin upon modern educational and political theorists has been profound. But even deeper in the substratum of the intellectual ideology of today's liberals are the ideas of the scientists and philosophers of the Enlightenment. Rousseau, Descartes, and Voltaire may be the legitimate fathers of the revolutionary spirit that first appeared in the French Revolution, then in the Russian Revolution, and most recently in the violent outbursts of the sixties.

Behind these philosophers was a group of English writers of the previous century, including John Locke, Thomas Hobbes, and David Hume. These men, in turn, owed a debt to the early scientists, such as Isaac Newton, Galileo, and Copernicus, who first demonstrated that nature operates by logical and predictable principles and that everything physical can be described and defined in intimate detail, not through theology or philosophy, but by physics and mathematics.

This chain of intellectual inquiry, which developed during the neoclassical age, led certain men to the world of ideas and letters. The birth of new learning encouraged them to question everything—life and death, man and nature, God and science. But instead of the secure and finite world described by conventional theology, where men had lived by the mercy of a patient heavenly Father, these new thinkers began to see themselves as creatures of Nature.

They were inhabitants of a vast and orderly universe whose boundaries were infinite and whose processes were not mysterious or religious but mathematical and precise. When they came to believe that all of life is a process of cause and effect, it would be only a short jump to the notion that no other force or agent was required. At best, God had been misrepresented; at worst, perhaps he might not exist at all.

In general, the seventeenth-century philosophers did not leap to that conclusion, but it is impossible for us today to understand how earthshaking such concepts must have seemed to the men and women of that time. Though they had made incredible advances, the science of that age was still partial and incomplete; and of course, theology and philosophy had practically no means of responding to the challenges that these facts posed for them.

It would take years—more than a century, in fact—for the complex emotional and spiritual issues they raised to be resolved by the church. The implications of these changes were shattering to the traditions and beliefs of the old way of life. Revelation suddenly had less appeal, and empiricism (meaning hard-nosed, practical research, which Locke had described as "cold philosophy") was becoming the only reliable source of truth.

In France, René Descartes proposed a new philosophy based

on the principles of Galileo and Copernicus, and he developed a series of tests of knowledge based on what he called "skeptical hypotheses." He used this analytical method to challenge his own sense of perception and experience, and he came to one irreducible truth: the phenomenon of thought. This led him to the statement *Cogito ergo sum,* or "I think, therefore I am." For two centuries this simple axiom offered confirmation for the elegance of rational thought. Today, however, it may be seen as an indication of the change of focus from the external to the internal.

But consider the changes that were taking place in the mind during this remarkable age. If everything visible and invisible could be explained by natural philosophy and the new science as the consequence of causes set into motion by Nature itself, men reasoned, then what did this say about supernatural explanation and about the nonscientific events of the Bible? John Locke, among others, attempted to unite the findings of the new science with the Christian tradition, but his methodology inevitably led to a profound religious skepticism.

The Cult of Reason
Locke began to look to the classical models of Greece and Rome for a basis for a logical synthesis of science and faith. Reason alone was to be his guide, but he had not discarded faith entirely. There were some, such as Hume, who were already prepared to challenge the truth of the Bible, but the atheist perspective was not yet a fully conceived hypothesis. This would not be the age to assault openly the tenets of Christianity or to deny Scripture. That would be reserved for the men of the following century.

The immediate consequence of these new ideas was much more mundane, for the discoveries of science seemed to say that everything real could be described by empirical evidence, by mathematical principles, or by some kind of physical equation.

Carried to its logical conclusion, the new thinking would totally discredit the higher functions of insight, intuition, and inspiration. This would, however, become a major obstacle for art and poetry, and it would ultimately give reason priority over imagination in all things.

But there was a side effect that even the reformers had not anticipated. The attempt to escape from the dangers of fanaticism and unreason through pure science would eventually become a new kind of fanaticism and a new threat to society—the Cult of Reason—which would dominate the Enlightenment and well beyond.

Among John Locke's many important works were *A Letter concerning Toleration,* which expressed the idea that no one can dictate the form or content of another man's religion; *The Reasonableness of Christianity,* dealing with his own beliefs; and *Some Thoughts concerning Education.* These essays would have great influence on popular thought in France and America during the eighteenth century. Locke's famous treatise, the *Essay concerning Human Understanding,* published in 1690, contains the famous statement, "Let us suppose the mind to be, as we say, white paper, void of all characters, without any ideas; how comes this to be furnished? . . . Whence has it all the materials of reason and knowledge? To this I answer, in a word, from experience."

Locke's notion suggests that the mind at birth is a blank slate, a *tabula rasa,* upon which the experiences of a lifetime are to be written. The character of the experiences will determine the character of the person. His argument suggested that environment is more important than heredity in the development of thinking and ideas. He also claimed that the only reality is that which can be perceived by the senses, and anything that cannot be detected by sight, taste, touch, smell, or hearing is of no concern to science.

This flowering of the neoclassical spirit among the scientists, poets, and philosophers of the seventeenth and eighteenth centuries represented a deliberate attempt to follow the models of the great classical thinkers—to imitate the styles and methods of the Greeks and Romans. However, in the process of theorizing the ideals of reason, education, and enlightenment, their positions became assertive and doctrinaire.

What Rousseau demonstrated in his writings was an immature emotionalism that discarded traditional standards and values in favor of liberation and self-determination. His writings appealed to the spirit of rebellion, putting natural freedom ahead of austere virtue. The "high old Roman virtue," which had been transmitted from the fall of the empire to the Renaissance and the Reformation, implied self-sacrifice, endurance, and submission to a higher good. For Rousseau this was a perverse and unnatural demand. The dominant passion of the human spirit, he believed, was self-interest, and he taught that only repression could cause men to give up this natural impulse.

But even Rousseau realized that pure, unmitigated self-interest would be hostile to the common good, so in concurrence with English writers such as Jeremy Bentham and John Stuart Mill (who popularized the notion of "the greatest happiness for the greatest number"), he proposed that *enlightened* self-interest is the quality to be sought after. "And this," says Allan Bloom, "is the best key to the meaning of enlightenment."[13]

The Source of Truth

At the heart of this age-old warfare is a basic disagreement over the source of truth. That fact has been evident throughout this discussion, and it is nowhere more visible than in the precepts and dogmatic positions of the educational establishment. Those who subscribe to the liberal agenda will see the idea of moral or spiritual restraint as a needless hindrance to their political interests. But the lesson of history is that no society can exist without it.

Without a foundational code of morality, law has no meaning. And without spiritual convictions, the code of responsible citizenship has no force. So, to what do we attribute the crisis of education and cultural authority in America today? Is the battle over diversity, multiculturalism, and political correctness just one more manifestation of the centuries-old dispute over the source of truth?

Francis Keppel once said, "Education is too important to be left solely to the educators." That is a wise maxim. What happens in the classroom will shape the character and values of the next generation, and we can be certain that our nation's hopes for the future grow dimmer and dimmer as the quality of education deteriorates another notch with each generation. As long as educators with a liberal social agenda set the standard, you can be certain that we are losing the culture war.

My own position is that the classrooms of America have become the focal point of the warfare between the sacred and the profane, and the struggle for the hearts and minds of the next generation must be seen as a guerrilla war between two rival forms of authority. The most dangerous aspect of the battle is not that the quality of education is weak: Millions of people who have gone on to great careers and advanced degrees came from poor educational backgrounds. The danger is that young people are being morally strip-searched and intellectually abused by this system.

The most lasting danger is that young people are being indoctrinated with alien ideologies that are destructive to America's traditional values and our heritage of faith. It is not just that our children's knowledge of science or history or art is inferior, but that their souls are being laid bare, and they are being steeped in destructive humanistic concepts that leave them in moral and spiritual chaos.

Under these conditions, even their bodies grow weak. Their minds are sterilized. They are ground down to a level of less than mediocre performance, and their right to excel, to rise to their own level, and to hold time-tested beliefs is being blocked. I cannot say that all of this is happening in every school all at once. Surely there are still many schools that stand by the truth and by our heritage of virtue and morality. But the trend is overwhelmingly in the opposite direction.

From the record of history we can see that the caliber of education in one generation will determine the prospects for the next. It has been said that the values taught in the public schools today will become the laws legislated by Congress tomorrow. That is why it is vitally important that men and women of conviction must first acknowledge the scope and the complexity of the challenges before us and then react with haste.

And there is no more vital arena for engagement than the education of our children. Unless you have no interest in the laws that will be legislated in this nation in the coming decades, then you and I are obligated to take up moral and spiritual arms to resist the fraud that passes for education in the universities and schools of this nation. History confirms that we cannot afford to fail in the task. To ignore the decay, and to neglect what former education secretary William Bennett has called the spiritual *acedia,* or sloth, of public education today, *will* lead to the death of this nation.

6

Weakening of Cultural Foundations

IN HIS comparative study of several great civilizations of history, Samuel Eisenstadt raised questions about the character and durability of culture. "The fact that similar causes for the respective declines of different empires have been found by various historians gives rise to an important question," he said. "Are there similarities in the basic features of the social structure of these empires?" Looking at the work of a half dozen historians and the themes each has proposed for cultural decline, Eisenstadt wanted to know if the apparent similarities in great societies were merely apparent or if they were historical and legitimate.

He eventually decided the similarities were actual and concluded that "despite the great difference in cultural back-ground—most of these empires have shown similar characteristics, and that these characteristics provide the key to an understanding of the processes of their decline."[1]

Unfortunately, it doesn't take a historian or social scientist to tell us that great societies can go into decline. The headlines do that forcefully enough. Social disintegration, rising crime, economic disorder, political disunity, educational failure, cultural degradation, and the deterioration of moral standards are undeniable factors of our daily life. The basic unit of civilization, the family, is clearly in chaos in this country, while the institutions of marriage and childbirth are under assault.

From environmentalists we get the idea that human life ranks somewhere between insects and plankton. And every attempt to restore a consensus with regard to the importance of probity and balance in our lives leads to armed resistance from civil libertarians, cultural revisionists, and advocates of politically correct social theories. Issues such as virtue and moral restraint—which were vital topics of discourse in Greek and Roman times—are dismissed as inappropriate and prejudicial subjects today. Instead, we are inundated with social and political schemes that are alien to our heritage of virtue and self-reliance.

Challenging Authority

The political ideology known as liberalism is, by definition, a philosophy dedicated to overthrowing the status quo. The liberal worldview that first came into being during the Enlightenment placed man rather than God at the center of the universe. As we saw in the preceding chapter, the architects of rationalism in eighteenth-century England and France held that man, by reason alone, could penetrate the secrets of nature and build a better world—a utopian paradise. In time, they felt, all problems could be solved through social planning and rational action.

Naturally, these liberal thinkers were hostile to aristocrats, the church, the military, and most other forms of authority. They believed in "natural rights," and they came to believe in "change for the sake of change." They were constantly looking for new answers to the old questions. But the problem for us today is that liberalism is incapable of giving us any lasting answers. Since this view is hostile by definition to the traditional foundations of culture, once any idea becomes accepted and when it assumes the status of an established value, it comes to be seen as an orthodoxy that must be debunked and overthrown.

This kind of liberalism leads to constant change and revolution. And even as they wage war on what they perceive as the sources of pain, its adherents continue their relentless pursuit of change. And we ask ourselves: How can such convictions lead to anything but chaos and disorder?

James Burnham's definition of liberalism, in his book *The Suicide of the West*, explains why political correctness has become such a dominant feature of modern liberalism. PC thinking grows out of the need to sympathize with the underprivileged and the hurting. It demands that the dominant culture, regardless how virtuous or how long established, must change to accommodate the emotional sensibilities of even the smallest and least-represented minorities. Cultural relativism and historical revisionism, by the same token, spring from the liberal's desire to deny inconvenient facts and to change appearances by redefinition of everything, from history to language.

"I rather think," Burnham writes, "that the attitude toward tradition furnishes the most accurate single shibboleth for distinguishing liberals from conservatives; and still more broadly, the Left from the Right, since with respect to *change* the revolutionary and the reactionary are merely pushing the perspectives of liberals and conservatives toward their limits" (emphasis added).[2]

Hubert Humphrey, who was vice president under Lyndon B. Johnson and a noted liberal leader in the 1960s, said in a *New York Times Magazine* article, "It is this emphasis on changes of chosen ends and means which most sharply distinguishes the liberals from a conservative in a democratic community. The dictionary defines a liberal as 'favorable to change and reform tending in the direction of democracy.'" And Humphrey adds, "Liberals recognize change as the inescapable law of society, and action in response to change as the first duty of politics."[3]

In the conclusion to his impressive study, Burnham writes that liberalism, by dint of its commitment to change at all costs, leads inevitably to national suicide and the destruction of civilization. He says, "Liberalism permits Western civilization to be reconciled to dissolution . . . for if Western civilization is wholly vanquished or altogether collapses, we or our children will be able to see that ending, by the light of liberalism, not as a final defeat, but as the transition to a new and higher order in which Mankind as a whole joins in a universal civilization that has risen above the parochial distinctions, divisions, and discriminations of the past."[4]

With Change Comes Loss

This is a compelling but frightening portrait from one who speaks with undeniable authority. In the 1930s, Burnham had been one of the lights of the communist movement in America. He wrote extensively and participated in political activities. However, like other young intellectuals such as Sidney Hook and Max Eastman, Burnham soon recognized the dangerous brutality and intolerance at the heart of socialist ideology and made a complete turnabout, becoming a leading voice among American intellectuals committed to traditional values and conservative politics.

In this century, intellectuals, scholars, and others among the so-called social elites have expressed an almost nihilistic fascination with change. And they have done so with such passionate intensity that many ordinary people have been persuaded that any change is for the best and that anything new must be an improvement over the unhappiness and apparent chaos of our lives. But as James Burnham has illustrated, it is precisely this sort of complacency that allows the dangerous social doctrines of fundamentalist liberals to perform their task of deconstruction.

In his analysis of democratic institutions and the risks to civil society posed by the various repressive regimes of this century, Jean-François Revel offers this perceptive observation:

> *There have been natural cataclysms in history, epidemics, droughts, earthquakes, and cyclones, and they have killed millions, destroyed cities and crops, annihilated artistic and intellectual treasures, devastated the infrastructures of nations. Yet these plagues are nothing compared to those that have been caused by human action. The most destructive catastrophes are man-made, and above all statesman-made. They come from his appetite for conquest and domination, from the dead-end political systems he thinks up, his uncountable religious or ideological fanaticisms, and, especially, his obsessive needs to reform societies instead of letting them change at their own pace.*[5]

Obviously, sensible, constructive change is essential to every organization, and a wise government will strive to be flexible and responsive to the timely issues and trends that demand change. But change must never be an end in itself.

Statesmen, public officials, and bureaucrats who create change for their own purposes are dealing with dangerous forces that do not often respond to casual manipulation. Whether it is peace in the Middle East, nuclear disarmament, demilitarization, reinventing the health-care industry, or nationalization of industry, government must be responsive to the will of the people and not go crusading for causes because, as Revel states so precisely, man-made plagues are by far the worst disasters mankind must face.

The deterioration of public education is largely responsible for our children becoming adults with virtually no knowledge of their own history as a nation. Pride in their nation or state is often condemned as dangerous nationalism. And the separation of church and state has stripped at least an entire generation of their heritage of faith and values. So when Americans vote for change merely for the sake of change, they are contributing to the perpetuation of the liberal agenda that leads to the systematic weakening of our cultural foundations.

Dangerous Loss of Faith

All of this illustrates how vital a proper knowledge of history and literature—in short, culture—is in a free society. Robbed of our past, we will accept any future. But history and literature offer ample warnings about the risks of mindless change. In their encyclopedic reference work *The Columbia History of the World*, authors John A. Garraty and Peter Gay remark on the irony that the seed of national decay is often discovered in this idea of change for the sake of change. With change, they say, comes loss. And the greater the change, the greater the loss.

As time passes and as traditions and beliefs weaken, the foundational principles that were once considered essential to the nation and its great society come to be seen as old-fashioned and undesirable, and youth in particular conclude that *"whatever is, is bad."* The advance guard of reformers and activists demands change from the ground up. But what they fail to recognize is that loss of the foundational principles and core values that made the culture great will lead inevitably to the weakening and ultimate collapse of the entire nation. Again, no nation that loses its raison d'être can long survive.

In the conclusion to their twelve-hundred-page tome, Garraty, Gay, and a panel of scholars at Columbia University conclude that perhaps the most significant change in our own time has been the gradual weakening of morality and religion. "Morality, like religion," they say, "has the double aspect of satisfying an emotional need and serving a social purpose. Without morality—some inner restraint—society must assign two policemen to watch every citizen day and night. And without a religion which sustains conduct or at least organizes the facts of life and the cosmos, men seek in vain for the meaning of their existence."[6] One need only recall what we have recently learned about the brutality of the socialist police state in Poland, Germany, and Communist Europe to recognize the truth of these words.

We react to the chaos in American cities and towns and call for more police, more money for crime prevention, more prisons, and more and bigger government, but then we disregard the most critical need of all, which is the historical imperative that all elements of society hold a high view of their citizenship: that is, that all of us demonstrate by our attitudes and behavior that we have a respect for and commitment to ethical responsibility, that we support the moral and ethical values upon which a civilized society depends. But can any society survive when stripped of its sources of meaning and moral restraint? The evidence of history says no. Force always follows in the wake of lost faith.

A Generation of Change
In their book *Destructive Generation,* two former editors of the

radical magazine *Ramparts* write, "The New Left did not want to patiently infiltrate institutions in the American mainstream with whose purposes they were openly at war and whose ends they intended to subvert; they wanted to create their own institutions and make 'a revolution in the streets.'"[7]

The antiwar marches, the sit-ins and teach-ins and love-ins had their desired effect, and Americans came only too quickly into the streets. But the revolution did not remake America after the communist model as the radicals had hoped. What it did do was to change the values of the American mainstream and to give unprecedented credibility to all the beliefs and immoral behaviors of the "liberated" culture of the Left.

Suddenly, the nation that possessed the greatest birthright of freedom in human history was accused of brutality and intolerance. Black was white, and wrong was right. Everything was turned around backward. What turned off the New Left and their well-meaning fellow travelers were the officials, administrators, and authorities who resisted them.

Those who held power were called "straights," and anything that seemed to represent custom or tradition was called "repression." Unfortunately, the confrontation was so strident and so pervasive that all too often law-enforcement officers responded to the demonstrations and other emotional situations with excessive violence, and this only made matters worse. It seemed to confirm what the hippies were saying all along.

The transformation of the culture was so broad and so complete that it eventually infiltrated into every level of society. Schools, government, and political organizations began to adopt leftist policies and to accede to all the demands of the radicals. And the more the straights and conservatives resisted, the more vigorous the attacks became. In their book, Peter Collier and David Horowitz explain:

The Sixties might have been a time of tantalizing glimpses of the New Jerusalem. But it was also a time when the "System"—that collection of values that provides guidelines for society as well as individuals—was assaulted and mauled. As one center of authority after another was discredited under the New Left offensive, we radicals claimed that we murdered to create. But while we wanted a revolution, we didn't have a plan. The decade ended with a big bang that made society into a collection of splinter groups, special interest organizations, and newly minted "minorities," whose only common belief was that America was guilty and untrustworthy. This is perhaps the enduring legacy of the Sixties.[8]

Demoralization of America

The most destructive social forces in the culture today are those that have been transmitted to the middle class and become ingrained sociological patterns in American society. Not the least of these has been the influence of rock and roll, which has demonstrated from its beginnings a desire to break down the high moral standards of the culture and to level society. By the last decade of this century, the popular music of this nation has become alien and frightening. Much of today's rap music incites "cop killers," and death metal promotes violence, sexual and chemical abuse, satanism, hedonism, and utter self-destruction.

Young adults and even small children who become fixated on MTV and VH-1 are indoctrinated with dangerous ideas about sex, violence, and flagrant disrespect for every form of authority. Teenagers and young adults, like orphans of the storm, carry these destructive emotions inside them without any hope of redemption through therapy or religion or positive criticism from their peers, parents, teachers, or any other segment of the culture.

What America is wrestling with today is a critical loss of faith that threatens to destroy the nation from within. We are so near to becoming a totally demoralized society that we have to wonder how much longer we can endure. There are already terrible similarities in this nation to the last days of Rome, only our situation is worse. Even in the horrendous climax and submersion of Roman culture, the citizens never dissipated themselves to the level that American civilization has reached in the 1990s.

Consider just the obvious examples of collapse in the daily newspapers. Consider the example of riots in south-central Los Angeles or the evidence of destruction that is so visible in the media today. Consider the slaughter of 1.6 million unborn infants every year since 1973 and the fact that 31 percent of Americans support the use of abortion "in any circumstance" to terminate pregnancy.

But don't stop there. Consider some of the other records our civilization is leaving behind. These changes to the values and practices of Americans can only increase the levels of chaos in American society, thus placing all our moral and cultural foundations at risk. By every measure, the United States is the most violent nation in the world. Violent crime in the four years from 1987 to 1991 increased by 22.7 percent, with 24,700 murders, 106,500 cases of forcible rape, 687,730 cases of robbery, and 1,092,740 cases of aggravated assault reported nationwide. In 1991, there were 3,157,200 reported burglaries, 8,142,230 reported cases of theft or larceny, and 1,661,740 stolen vehicles.

FBI and Bureau of Justice Statistics records also show that the value of goods reported stolen exceeded $15 billion in 1991 alone. In 1990, 19,722 people aged one to thirty-four died as a direct result of firearms, and 25 percent of all deaths of young people between fifteen and thirty-four were caused by gunshot. Among black males, 60 percent of all violent deaths were from firearms; and among whites, 23 percent of violent deaths were due to guns. In just one decade violent crime has risen more than 15 percent in this country.

These are shocking figures, and they are doubly shocking when compared to the relatively low crime rates in Western Europe, Japan, and other major areas of the world. We have recently read of the government's plan to implement a national police force and to double the number of uniformed officers in an attempt to stop the siege of violence in the land. But will this solve the problem? If policemen on America's streets are already hamstrung by strict regulations, citizen action groups, and anti-law-enforcement movements, what effect will a larger force of powerless officers have? It will certainly drive up taxes and the financial and administrative burdens on city and state governments.

Losing Faith in the System

This is one of the most important lessons we can learn from the collapse of Rome. When the people lost faith in the system or simply deserted it, the empire stalled. Later this would become the key factor in the terrors of the Enlightenment, in the swift rise and fall of the military empires that dominated world events of the first half of the twentieth century, and in the decline and fall of the British Empire as well. The people lost faith in the system.

Recently, English scholar F. W. Brownlow observed that the beginning of the end for the British Empire was the Boer War (1899–1902). In the face of endless frustrations and defeats, the English seemed to lose heart, and the empire became little more than a ghost. He says, "The conviction grew that in gaining an empire England had lost too much of its traditional character, and this feeling, joined to foreign competition and disapproval and to difficulties and discontents at home, provided moral cover for a process of disengagement from imperialism that two great wars could delay but not reverse."[9] Similarly, religious wars brought changes to England and France in the seventeenth century, Vietnam wounded something in the American spirit in the sixties and seventies, and Afghanistan broke the Soviet resolve in 1989.

Changes in the historic cultural and ethical foundations provoked a crisis of law and order in each of these nations, and the leaders were either unwilling or unable to respond. As Russell Kirk has observed, the same resistance to statutory law occurred in some European countries over the centuries. Certainly Spain, France, Germany, and Austria-Hungary are examples. And in each case, the consequences were disastrous. But the dangers facing the United States today deserve a closer look.

Degradation of law and order is a critical aspect of the undermining of American society today. Just consider how far we have fallen in such a short time. When Alexis de Tocqueville came to America in 1820, he was anxious to discover the factors that had made the United States such a remarkable nation. Having just come through a revolution of its own, France had thrown off the yoke of monarchy and established a republican form of government. The results of the revolutions in France and America were vastly different, but Tocqueville understood the terms and the distinctions very well.

As he traveled throughout the United States, he spoke with men and women at every level of society, and he was stunned by the openness and the unity of spirit of the American people. His remarkable book *Democracy in America* reports his findings and offers a dramatic contrast to the portrait of American society we have in these pages. Peace and prosperity were everywhere in the land, law and order triumphed, and the people were clearly happy and law-abiding. They were a people "united" in spirit and action.

Habits of the Heart

Tocqueville described America as the greatest experiment in democracy the world has ever known. Mores, which Tocqueville calls "habits of the heart," are the foundation of manners and morals required for life in civilized society, and he said the source of America's greatness was its *mores*—its values established on Christian principles. "What is meant by 'republic' in the United States," he made clear, "is the slow and quiet action of society upon itself. It is an orderly state really founded on the enlightened will of the people."

And he adds, "In the United States republicans value mores, respect beliefs, and recognize rights. They hold the view that a nation must be moral, religious, and moderate all the more because it is free." He said, "I do not know whether all Americans have a sincere faith in their religion, for who can know the human heart?—but I am certain that they hold it to be indispensable for the maintenance of republican institutions. This opinion is not peculiar to a class of citizens or to a party, but it belongs to the whole rank of society."[10]

What most astonished him was that, unlike France, where religion was a source of division and strife, religion in America was the cement that held society together. The Enlightenment in France had taught the people to distrust the church; in America religion was the essential source of values and beliefs. Tocqueville said that America is "the place where the Christian religion has kept the greatest power over men's souls; and nothing better demonstrates how useful and natural it is to man, since the country where it now has the widest sway is both the most enlightened and the freest."

But not all the nineteenth-century statesman's observations were so upbeat. He also considered the potential threats and dangers to a free democratic republic. After all, wasn't history full of stories about great empires that had fallen due to an excess of luxury and abundance? Could a nation be threatened by too much of a good thing? He writes:

But sometimes there comes a time in the life of nations when old customs are changed, mores destroyed, beliefs shaken, and the prestige of memories has vanished, but when nonetheless enlightenment has remained incomplete and political rights are ill-assured or restricted. Then men see their country only by a weak and doubtful light; their patriotism is not centered on the soil, which in their eyes is just inanimate earth, nor on the customs of their ancestors, which they have been taught to regard as a yoke, nor on religion, which they doubt, nor on the laws, which they do not make, nor on the lawgiver, recognizing neither its own nor any borrowed features, and they retreat into a narrow and unenlightened egoism. Such men escape from prejudices without recognizing the rule of reason; they have neither the instinctive patriotism of a monarchy nor the reflective patriotism of a republic, but have come to a halt between the two amid confusion and anxiety.[11]

Then, in a perceptive analysis of the dangers of democracy, Tocqueville goes on to say, "I noticed during my stay in the United States that a democratic state of society similar to that found there could lay itself peculiarly open to the establishment of a despotism." He says, "I was thus led to think that the nations of Christendom might perhaps in the end fall victims to the same sort of oppression as formerly lay heavy on several of the peoples of antiquity."

New World Disorder

Here again the ancient models of collapse are invoked. Could the phantoms that devastated Greece, Rome, Carthage, and the empires of France and Spain come back once again to haunt the American nation? Tocqueville recognized the distinct differences between the ancient empires and the American democracy. He could not believe this nation would fall victim to some type of totalitarianism, since that would be so contrary to common experience. He believed that any such tyranny would surely provoke armed rebellion. So he said that the undermining and destruction of a great democratic nation would have to be slower, subtler, and more insidious:

> But if a despotism should be established among the democratic nations of our day, it would probably have a different character. It would be more widespread and milder; it would degrade men rather than torment them.
>
> Doubtless, in such an age of education and equality as our own, rulers could more easily bring all public powers into their own hands alone, and they could impinge deeper and more habitually into the sphere of private interests than was ever possible in antiquity.[12]

So that we do not miss his point, we should note that Tocqueville says that the despotism of a democratic nation would not be like that of the ancient monarchies or even the imperial regimes of the eighteenth century. Instead of terror and torment, the nation would be transformed by a gradual *degradation* of the people—a demoralization and decivilization—an entropy of the spirit.

The slow decline of culture, slow deterioration of morals, slow degradation of the national polity, and a steady and almost imperceptible increase in the size and authority of government would lead inevitably to the loss of individual freedoms and the ruin of the state. Thus the despots would gain totalitarian control over our lives.

As morals are eroded and as crime and disorder increase in a democratic society, the people cry out for more government assistance and more centralized authority. The rise of federalism is a direct result of the insecurity felt by the nation and the feeling that only the central government can give people the protections they must have. Tocqueville notes that in Europe, social disorder invariably led nations to relinquish freedom for the sake of safety.

Let us consider this prospect for a moment. If a small core of leaders were intent on seizing control of a large, powerful nation, could the appearance of some kind of national crisis be induced? Something like health care, the economy, or law and order for example? And could the media be led (perhaps misled) to publicize this presumed state of emergency to bring about citizen unrest, and could the appearance of crisis, widespread unhappiness, and looming chaos be manipulated to ensure that the central government gains constantly greater authority until the people finally and willingly relinquish their rights and freedoms to a despotic regime?

Whether or not such a hypothetical crisis could be orchestrated in our own time, we know that the propagandists and philosophers of the French Enlightenment manipulated public emotions in much this way during the eighteenth century. In order to transmit their revolutionary ideas to the people, the philosophes and their advocates used every device within their means.

Rationalism, the new science, and the spirit of philosophy that came out of the Renaissance and the neoclassical age awakened new sensibilities in the men and women of letters in both England and France. But these ideas immediately took a revolutionary turn. The connection between the ideas born in the Enlightenment and the social issues of the sixties in this country is not at all accidental. Both revolutions were an attempt to overturn common custom and to install a new revolutionary ethic. Both were attempts to remove moral restraints. And both became open warfare with authority and public virtue.

The British writer Tony Judt recently observed that for some strange reason America always seems to be the final resting place for the outworn ideas of French intellectuals. Long after vogue ideas popularized by the luminaries of the Paris bookshops have lost their allure at home, they come to America and play to standing-room-only crowds in our universities, think tanks, and liberal foundations.

Existentialism and deconstruction still survive among liberals here, decades after they have faded in Europe; and communism, one of the most discredited philosophies in the history of ideas, has plenty of apologists today in the United States government, the Congress, the judiciary, the university lecture halls, and the media.[13]

The Breeding Ground

The forces that introduced the ideas that first excited the revolutionary spirit in France were the books, pamphlets, and tracts published by the new intellectuals. As revolutionists and revisionists emerged from the crowds, newer and even shriller voices began to be heard. The emphasis shifted from the calm and judicious mind of a writer such as the Baron de Montesquieu, a rural judge for ten years of his career but a supporter of individual rights, to men such as Denis Diderot, author and editor of *L'Encyclopedie* (perhaps the first politically correct journal), to Voltaire, Jean d'Alembert, Caron de Beaumarchais,

Comte de Mirabeau, and others. And then the message was picked up by the crowds.

Special newspapers such as Marat's *L'Ami des Peuple* (The Friend of the People) were created, and inflammatory plays were written for the popular theaters of the day. Plus, new ideas and ideologies that debunked all the old values were being tested for effect by the young masters in the universities, the seminaries, and the secondary schools.

Among all these fertile minds there was an unspoken unity, a cohesion of thought and aspiration, and a bond of sentiment that had grown out of ideas awakened in the transition from medieval to modern society. They shared so many sparks of common insight, and these were fanned into flame by the winds of free thought and liberal controversy blowing across the English Channel with the ideas of Newton, Locke, Hobbes, Hume, and Mill.

They shared a common political discontent, a hostility toward both church and state, and a hunger for the new and the modern. The possibility of a new order and a release from the old values stoked powerful emotions and offered a tantalizing vision to their eyes. The dialectical interplay of all these forces gave great momentum to their movement.

The literary salons of Paris were a natural environment for breeding sedition; there were also political societies, such as the Society of the Friends of the Constitution, known as the Jacobins; the deputies of the Legislative Assembly, known as Girondins; and others. Many of these intellectual and political dens preached tolerance, at least in name; they promoted deism over traditional Christian theology; and they raised an alarm about such issues as slavery.

The *Société des Amis des Noirs* (Society of Friends of Blacks) championed abolition in Europe, America, and the French colonies. All these groups were cheered by the revolutionary success of the American patriots in 1776, and they began to dream of imitating the Yankee Revolution in their own country. The *Club Américain* was fomenting rebellion even before the books and tracts of the republican leaders Robespierre and Marat ever made it to the shops and sidewalk stalls of Paris.

Before long, revolutionary booklets in small format, which were portable and easily hidden in a man's coat, were being talked about all over the city, and they were also being distributed to the provinces wherever sympathetic rebels might be found. The literature of the revolution was striking and often funny, caricaturing the aristocracy and arousing the readers to action. But there is no doubt that it had the desired effect.

A Lasting Impression
To this day, Rousseau and the bourgeois emperor of the republic, Napoléon Bonaparte, are still considered heroes to many people in France. I found this fact startling when I lived in France during the late seventies, but I soon came to realize why. Even though Napoléon is generally considered a brigand and a tyrant everywhere else in the world, he represents a brief hour of glory in the history of the French Republic.

And even though both these men contributed to a time of tragedy and disgrace, Rousseau and Napoléon and all the impetuous revolutionaries of that time were the very epitome of the French motto, then and now, *liberté, egalité, fraternité*—liberty, equality, and brotherhood.

But thanks to Rousseau, France is still steeped in the bitter anticlericalism and agnosticism of the Enlightenment. It is constantly rocked by debate and street fights over liberal and socialist ideologies. The loss of their ancient heritage has brought little but suffering and despair. Lord Acton, who was certainly no friend of Rousseau and no admirer of the French Revolution, once remarked, "Rousseau produced more effect with his pen than Aristotle, or Cicero, or St. Augustine, or St. Thomas Aquinas, or any other man who ever lived." How sad to think that he may be right.

The ideas that were aroused in the explosive environment of the Enlightenment were bound to have a broader impact on society. They were a source of provocation in the American and French Revolutions, as well as in the sixties. But how could the people of France, who said they were weary of religious warfare and intolerance, allow themselves to be drawn into another war, and especially into a type of conflict that was almost entirely ideological and revolutionary in intent?

Former Harvard professor Henri Peyre says that the reason France was drawn into an idealistic war was that "eighteenth-century philosophy taught the Frenchman to find his condition wretched, or in any case, unjust and illogical and made him disinclined to the patient resignation to his troubles that had long characterized his ancestors."[14] France had never wanted a revolution. They didn't want a new regime. They were seduced by the idea of "enlightenment." Thus, an environment of revisionism, political intolerance, and liberation from the traditional sources of authority was created.

If there is any lingering remorse for the manifest failings of the Enlightenment, it is the awareness that the ideas unleashed by the radical reformers and idealists of the day have led untold millions, from that time to this, to cast away their confidence and give up on the great reward that might have been theirs through faith. The people who had nurtured the faith of Jesus Christ after the Fall of Rome, who established the church as a guardian of morality and public life, and who fought (like Joan of Arc) for the glory of God, gave up everything they treasured for a humanist dream. They sacrificed their hope of heaven for a man-made utopia.

"The Christian faith alone," writes Christopher Dawson, "offers man a perfection which is not relative and transitory, but absolute and eternal. The Christian faith alone has measured how deep is the need of humanity and how great is the possibility of restoration. If it seems to neglect the material world, that is not because it treats the material world as unimportant, but because the restoration of the spirit must precede and condition the restoration of the body."

The revolutionists had said that religion was an empty promise, that its idea of heaven was a fantasy, that its doctrine of the soul was a myth that could not be proved by science, and that the mind of man could bring forth its own heaven on earth. But Dawson says the antagonists confused the vast differences between the City of God and the City of Man. "The divine life that is in the Church is not limited in its effects to the human soul, it overflows onto the body, and hence onto the whole material universe."[15]

Jesus said, "The Kingdom of God has arrived among you" (Matt. 12:28, TLB). The kingdom of heaven is not some future estate: It is not simply pie in the sky, as skeptics claim. Jesus said that it is here, and it is here now. And those who know this to be true have to wonder why anyone would settle for an illusion of victory in the temporal world when the offer of life in the everlasting kingdom of God is such a magnificent promise.

A Contrast of Opposites

There is no way to cover all the implications and extenuations of the Enlightenment and its impact upon twentieth-century mores and values in less than book length, and there are several important studies cited in these pages that do that very well. But I hope that the review in this chapter and the next one, on the loss of tradition, will at least shed some new light on the connections between the social and political crises of our own time and the ideologies that first appeared during those dramatic early years of the modern age.

What we should see in such a survey is not just the little details and all the disturbing pathologies that emerged in the character of French and British culture during the period, but the way all cultures may be destroyed from within. Greece and Rome gave way to greed, corruption, and moral degeneracy much as the nations of the seventeenth, eighteenth, and nineteenth centuries gave way to the impulses of humanism.

Please hear again these words that ring out from history: A nation that loses its raison d'être cannot long survive. A nation does not have to be overrun by a foreign enemy to be utterly destroyed. Sometimes the most dreadful aliens are those who dine at your own table. And a nation does not collapse only when it has been vanquished by barbarian hordes. Rome wasted away long before the barbarians ever arrived. The great pity for the Goths who claimed Caesar's throne was that it was simply an empty chair. The glory had long since departed.

How will our own great nation survive all the changes and cultural tranformations that have come about in just the past three decades? Many people in this society have been flirting with revolutionary ideas and political notions that assault the very foundations of the American way of life. Is there hope that these people might learn something from the lessons of the Enlightenment that may help us to avoid its excesses? Will they see that in all the great empires that have fallen there are warnings that cannot be ignored?

Somehow we must find ways to preserve the freedoms we have purchased at so great a price without succumbing to the false theology of humanism, the hazardous ideologies of modern socialism, and the liberals' lust for change, which pose such threats to our cultural heritage. The challenge is not an easy one, but the monster of deconstruction will not go away unless we confront it.

In the next chapter we will continue our survey of some of the threats and challenges that first began taking shape during the Enlightenment. To see how the ideas of humanism and social liberalism born in England and France eventually impacted our own culture, it will be important to see how the weakening of cultural foundations led to a general loss of respect for tradition. From that point we will be in a better position to examine the significance of the rise of materialism and immorality.

7

Loss of Respect for Tradition

THE PERIOD of time that marked the transformation of
society from the final hours of Rome to the birth of the modern
age may be characterized as a revolution of the mind. All across
Europe, Asia Minor, and North Africa, the Roman Peace had
transformed the world of tribal factions into a unified whole.
Barbarians, Scythians, Macedonians, Jews, Egyptians, and Afri-
cans all lived side by side and worked under the same banner.
And wherever Roman law prevailed, the world came to understand the meaning of unity. Even the remotest cultures gained a
vision of the prospects for civilization.

Over the span of a thousand years, through the Renaissance,

the Reformation, the Holy Roman Empire, and the Age of Faith, which emerged during the Middle Ages, a singular view of man, informed by Greek thought, strengthened by Roman virtue, and uplifted by Christian values, persisted in the hearts of men. A foundation had been laid, upon which the concepts of the modern world could at last be built. But as we have just seen in the previous chapter, something dramatic changed at the cross-roads of the Enlightenment—something from which society has never quite recovered.

The Change of Heart

In the discussion of cultural foundations in the preceding pages, we saw that the Renaissance in Italy and France awakened many new ideas about nature, society, and the dignity of man. Science, art, and philosophy assumed a new importance in public and private life. With the rediscovery of classical learning, there came a new stimulus to analytical thinking. There was a new focus on the prospects for human achievement, along with a much wider spectrum of imagination and invention.

The Enlightenment, which came later, was a rejection of traditional values and an attempt to dislodge the restraints imposed by traditional theology. But despite the intellectual euphoria it aroused, these new ideas did not add to the happiness or peace of the people. In particular, the revolutionary ideas of Rousseau, Voltaire, and Diderot did not enhance their sense of security or their faith and contentment. Even though the French Revolution may have freed the common people from bondage to the king and the corrupt aristocracy, it also stripped them of their ancient heritage, their reliance upon a code of moral values, and many of their finest virtues. But most of all, it robbed them of their secure traditions and beliefs.

To see the impact of all these changes, it is important to take our look at the Enlightenment a step further. We will touch briefly upon certain similarities in the ancient Mediterranean cultures, but it is in the events of eighteenth-century France and the flowering of the Enlightenment that we see the similarities to our own society. And nowhere are the comparisons more striking than in the general loss of respect for tradition brought about by the "new thinking" of the age.

As so often happens, one of the principal causes of the disturbances of the late eighteenth century was the lack of money. French contributions to the religious wars of the sixteenth and seventeenth centuries in England and France, and the American Revolution, drained the royal treasury and put the kingdom in peril. The government was unable to raise revenues because the aristocrats who controlled the large estates were exempt from taxation. The nobles who created the tax laws had made themselves exempt, and when the king called for a voluntary contribution to restore the bourse, the aristocrats refused to cooperate. They were not about to support any type of tax that might jeopardize their own property or wealth.

Put into a state of emergency by the lack of funds, Louis XVI summoned the States General in 1789. This political body, similar to the British Parliament, had not met since 1614, and when they assembled, the aristocrats tried to take over the meeting. This provoked a bitter controversy and noisy disruptions. A famous painting from this period illustrates the verbal brawl that ensued.

In addition to the ongoing financial crisis in the government, the harvest that year turned out to be disastrous. Wheat was scarce, the price of bread skyrocketed, and in all the cities and towns of France the people were already up in arms. Because of problems with the Assembly of Notables and his fear of public unrest due to the food shortages, Louis called the soldiers into

Paris to help keep the peace. But rather than calm the situation, this act alarmed the people. So on July 14, 1789, they stormed the old prison, the Bastille, demanding weapons for their personal protection. By most accounts this was the true beginning of the French Revolution.

End of the Monarchy

In the ensuing months, a bill of rights, called the Declaration of the Rights of Man and Citizen, was drafted by the assembly guaranteeing equality and freedom of thought, speech, and religion. The document proclaimed that the authority in France would no longer be the king but "the will of the people." This concession to the rebellious crowds preserved the peace for a time, but it was to be short-lived. In fact, by acceding to the people in this way, the government actually relinquished its power and signed its own death warrant.

Between 1789 and 1792, a war was waged on rank and privilege. The nobles and aristocrats were stripped of their titles, and their positions were given to faithful supporters of the Revolution. Tax privileges were revoked, and the landed gentry were denied participation in government, the judiciary, or the military. There no longer was any recognition of the great estates, of royal or religious orders, or of the guilds. Nor was there any advantage by virtue of inherited wealth or position.

A document called the Civil Constitution of the Clergy nationalized all church lands and possessions in 1791 and called for popular election of priests and bishops. Clergy were to be considered civil servants paid by the state. They were forced, on penalty of forfeiture of all their rights, to swear allegiance, not to God, but to the new Civil Constitution. These actions, however, divided even the liberals among themselves, especially after the pope publicly condemned the Revolution.

In 1791, unruly crowds were once again at large in the capital. The old guard and those who were terrified by the implications of the assault on the church and the nobility turned out to protest. Facing them were the liberals, along with the peasants in their thrall, who also took to the streets demanding more rights and privileges. The confrontation of all these forces set off a chain of events that would ultimately bring an end to the monarchy forever.

The king was encouraged by his advisers to call for a counter-revolution, and he immediately began making proclamations that were meant to overrule the actions of the republican consuls. But when it became clear that the revolutionaries and the crowds of commoners were infuriated by his actions and that now there was imminent danger of physical harm, Louis and his queen, Marie Antoinette, fled to Varennes, near the German border. But they were quickly captured and brought back to Paris for trial.

Threats of war with Austria and Prussia, combined with the urgency of the uprising now taking place in the streets of Paris, persuaded the rebels to bring their charges against the king. With the authority of their newly formed republic, Louis was found guilty of conspiracy. He was executed by guillotine in January 1793, and Marie Antoinette met the same fate in October of that year. From that point the Revolution entered a radical and bloodthirsty phase.

The Reign of Terror

Maximilien Robespierre, chosen to head the Committee of Public Safety, promptly suspended the constitution and assumed dictatorial powers. In the reign of terror that followed, thousands of men and women of all classes lost their lives. The assurances of victories by the French armies helped to restore calm, but a fatal stroke had been taken against the national character.

When Robespierre was himself executed for treason, it was clear that there was a volatile momentum to this revolution that was beyond anyone's control. Perhaps those who lived through the revolutions in Eastern Europe and the Soviet Union in 1989 and 1990 would understand this feeling, as would those who are enduring the current crisis in South Africa.

From 1795 to 1799, the leaders of the republic set up a government under a modified cabinet known as the Directoire. A brash young officer who had won several important battles entered Paris with his army and overthrew the Directoire. Thus, Napoléon Bonaparte created his own military dictatorship called the Consulate and named his companions and personal aides to be the bureaucrats who would administer the republic.

Napoléon brought much-needed stability to the nation, but for the next fifteen years there was no peace. His forces occupied parts of Spain and Portugal, challenged Austria and the German states, engaged the English, Prussians, and Swedes, and even occupied Moscow briefly before being driven back with heavy losses in the winter of 1812. Napoléon's army was defeated again in 1813, and when he returned to Paris in 1814, he found the capital occupied by his enemies.

Exiled to Elba after that defeat, Napoléon returned a year later, regrouped his army, and led them to Belgium to challenge the allies at Waterloo in 1815. It was there, in June of that year, that Napoléon's forces were finally crushed by the British and Prussian armies, costing more than thirty-one thousand French lives and nearly twenty thousand of the other side. After this final humiliation, Napoléon abdicated the throne and was exiled permanently to the island of Saint Helena in the South Atlantic, where he remained until his death in 1821.

During the thirty years from the execution of Louis XVI to the death of Napoléon, the *ancien régime* (the old order of France) was effectively destroyed. Land was confiscated from the nobility and the Catholic Church; families of privilege or noble heritage were either killed, ruined, or driven from the country; and the sources of wealth dried up in short order. This so-called abolition of feudalism promoted egalitarianism, but it also damaged the economic welfare of the nation virtually beyond repair.

Before long, France was a land almost entirely in the hands of illiterate peasants without the skills or resources to develop agriculture or industry. Foreign traders and bankers settled in France and seized control of valuable estates and lands, establishing financial domination over the French. Administrators who had gained a small measure of authority during the Directoire were mostly low-level bureaucrats or small farmers without the skills or resources to encourage any sort of renewal. Likewise, a few speculators had made fortunes during the war, but the economy was in shambles, and it remained so for decades.

Symbolism over Substance

Assessing the achievement of the Revolution, historian Geoffrey Bruun writes, "The *philosophes,* like many eloquent writers before and since, failed to foresee the impact their phrases might have on the immature and the inexperienced. The oversimplified, seductive doctrine that all the evils and abuses of society could be remedied by drafting a code of laws based upon 'the nature of things' captivated an entire generation."[1] When the intoxication of their victory began to wear off, however, the people found a nation in deep despair.

Perhaps the most illustrative example of the utopianism of revolutionary thinking is found in the opening lines of the French Constitution of 1793, which says: "The French people, convinced that neglect or defiance of the Natural Rights of man are the sole causes of human misery, have resolved to set forth . . . these sacred and inalienable rights in a solemn declaration." The debt to the writings of Thomas Jefferson is apparent. But unlike the American documents, there is no evidence here of faith in the Creator whom the patriots of 1776 acknowledged as the Source of the Rights of Man.

In the final analysis, the achievements of the French Revolution were more symbolic than successful. For decades after the Revolution, democracy failed. Weak leadership, poor administration, and general apathy among the voters contributed to a growing sense of chaos. Throughout the nineteenth century and much of the twentieth, the nation has swung violently from one reform initiative to another—from liberal to conservative and back again in a single decade, sometimes in a single year.

Once the pride of the Roman Empire and once the dazzling kingdom of the Sun King, Louis XIV, who made the name of France renowned in every corner of the world, France became a destitute nation, struggling for a new identity. Today France is still paying the price of the tyranny that came in the names of such heroes as Rousseau, Voltaire, Diderot, d'Alembert, Montesquieu, Beaumarchais, and their English precursors.

Clearly any evidence of reason in the disasters of the late eighteenth and early nineteenth centuries was nullified by the violent emotions and idealistic sentiments of the reformers. "As for the Age of Reason," writes David Ogg, "the period might equally well be called the Age of Sentiment, for the first of these was gradually displaced by the second, and the Romantic Revival was the result."[2] Order was lost in a burst of passion and discontent, and the hope of peace utterly disappeared.

The theologian Karl Barth has said that the eighteenth century was the birthplace of the "Absolute Man": Liberal ideas helped to create a new man, a *natural* man who could look into his own humanity and, with a sense of smug self-satisfaction, report that he alone is master of his fate and captain of his soul. Yet the fate of man in our century has perpetuated, not the image of the captain and master, but the alienated individual, lost in his own isolation and self-induced madness. The image of modern man popularized by literature and the arts is not that of a hero but of a lonely and broken figure, lost in time and space. He is a creature without roots, corrupted by hedonism and self-indulgence and freed from all attachments to the past. Rather than the absolute man, he might better be labeled an absolute disaster.

We are often quite out of touch with the age in which we live, and we are unable to make sense of our daily lives. The mounting body of statistical evidence regarding divorce, debt, family dysfunction, violence, neighborhood crime, and other forms of disturbance makes the point only too well.

Deconstruction of Reality

The discomfort we feel with present conditions is disturbing, even if it is remarkably pervasive. Our feelings of insecurity clearly have a great deal to do with the problems of modern society and with the state of decay in the culture at large. For the past half century, academicians and philosophers have been telling us that life is essentially meaningless and without purpose. Science is the only reliable standard, we understand, but science is cold and heartless. Science does not feel. In addition, the secularization of popular culture has left a majority of Americans without the traditional sources of faith, hope, and virtue upon which their fathers and mothers once depended.

In many ways, religion and expressions of faith have been banished from the public square, and in the absence of commonly held absolutes and moral standards—those values that have traditionally been derived from faith in God—everything has become relative. Ethical standards are reported to be, at best, arbitrary. The modern idiom claims that every proposed standard of values is authoritarian and potentially fascist. Values, such as right and wrong, are condemned as forms of absolutism, and suddenly the twilight zone of unreason and irreality returns. But when all our structures of experience are broken down, where will we turn for comfort? If right and wrong truly have no meaning, we must ask, how should we then live?

From the standpoint of cognitive philosophy, the theory that provides the most convenient explanation for this unsettling description of society is called deconstruction. As an aspect of the specialized area of philosophy called phenomenology, deconstruction first appeared in the United States in the 1970s, initially as a reaction against the linguistic theories of formalism, structuralism, and semiotics. Each of these deals with the content and context of language—the way words convey meaning.

Its most ardent proponent was the French phenomenologist Jacques Derrida, who wrote numerous essays and a book, *Of Grammatology.* Deridda's theory holds that the meaning of language is subtle and elusive. Words in all their forms betray a host of linguistic and philosophical presuppositions; therefore, verbal communication is meaningless until language itself can be reduced, deconstructed, and sifted for prejudice and bias. And who better to perform this task, the philosophers would ask, than the experts themselves?

Theories come and go, and on the surface this one appears no more harmful than the hundreds of others that have disappeared over time, except for the incredible vogue the deconstructionist ideology has had in the universities. Deconstruction and its companion in the plastic arts, post-structuralism, deny that there are any reliable criteria for establishing worth and value in communications—either in arts and letters or in our daily experience.

Meaning is always vague, and value judgments such as "good" or "bad" or even "in questionable taste" are irrelevant and dangerous.

Obviously, such theories have provided the mantle of legitimacy for much of the modern art and literature of our day. Minimalist and nonrealist works could only pass for art in an environment stripped of standards. In fact, I would even say that the plague of ugliness and ignorance that assaults our eyes and ears in virtually every medium today became inevitable once the established principles of form and judgment were removed.

If ugliness or perversity cannot be identified and rejected, as they have always been, then the whole idea of critical evaluation is meaningless. Without some reliable source of values, as Dostoyevsky and Sartre concurred, "everything is permitted."

Indeed, critic and scholar René Wellek has said that the barrage of critical theories and radical ideologies being bandied about today as a result of the deconstructionist and Marxian critique of texts has turned this entire field of study into a modern Tower of Babel. Never has there been such ferment in the arts. Every poseur with a theory can gain a ready audience, leaping from crackpot to celebrity virtually overnight.

I think immediately of the great number of so-called New Age philosophers who dominate the speaking circuit and the lecture halls of our great universities. Not satisfied with mere art and literature, today's linguistic critic becomes tomorrow's social philosopher, pronouncing upon all the institutions of society and civilization.

New Ideas for Old

135

So what does deterioration in the field of textual criticism have to do with the loss of tradition and the decline of culture? Just that. Civilization appears to be in decline, society is facing the most pernicious crisis of cultural authority in modern history, and the intellectual leaders and opinion makers who are best situated to help us make sense of the apparent chaos and trauma of modern life—to try to put our lives back into some sort of perspective—insist that communication is biased, nonrational, and meaningless. Everything else is relative, they say, and there are no longer any acceptable standards for perceiving value or truth. In short, nothing matters.

Unfortunately, the human spirit cannot exist in a vacuum. We strive for order and reason just as instinctively as we crave air, water, and sunlight. So the war on reason and common values being waged within the intellectual community does a great deal more than simply amuse the scholars: It actually undermines all the traditional standards of civilization and culture. Because ideologies influence what we believe about truth and the meaning of life, rising chaos and confusion in these areas threatens to drive our entire civilization backward toward a state of nihilistic self-destruction and lawlessness; in other words, to turn society over to the barbarians.

Such a prospect is not only frightening, it is also contrary to the hopes and dreams of the nation. In the midst of World War II, several months before Pearl Harbor, and while Great Britain was fighting the Axis powers virtually all alone, *Time* magazine publisher Henry Luce called upon Americans "to seek and to bring forth a vision of America as a world power. . . ." He declared this the "American Century" and described a vision of America as the leader of the free world. That editorial cheered many Americans for decades and coined the term *American Century,* which historians and economists have since applied to the second half of the century.

By 1989, however, a Wisconsin university professor, Thomas J. McCormick, concluded that America's era of influence and political hegemony was already finished. He admitted that the United

States had achieved great material prosperity, but he blasted the government for its perverse fixation on military spending and overseas investments, which had brought the United States economy to the verge of bankruptcy. His book, *America's Half-Century,* claimed that the United States was not only unable to win the cold war, but we could no longer even continue to think of ourselves as a global superpower.[3] Had McCormick waited just six months to publish his book, perhaps he would have witnessed via satellite the collapse of the Communist governments of Poland, Hungary, Czechoslovakia, East Germany, Latvia, Lithuania, Albania, Bulgaria, and Romania. He might have seen the execution of Nicolae Ceauscescu and the toppling of one of the most repressive regimes of modern times. He would probably have seen the ousting of Mikhail Gorbachev and the bloodless coup that ended the seventy-year history of Soviet communism.

Even cynical network correspondents were intrepid enough to proclaim to the entire world that America had, in fact, won the cold war. In a short time, even the skeptics were able to see the Berlin Wall hacked to rubble and the nations of Europe turning to George Bush and the American people for ideas and instructions on democracy, commerce, and religion. But McCormick's book was early, and his political theories were off the mark.

At the end of another important book, *The Closing of the American Mind,* the distinguished professor and social theorist Allan Bloom offered a different perspective. He said, "This is the American moment in world history, the one for which we shall forever be judged. Just as in politics the responsibility for the fate of freedom in the world has devolved upon our regime, so the fate of the philosophy in the world has devolved upon our universities, and the two are related as they have never been before."[4] The book was published in 1987, but even then Bloom saw that doubt, negativity, and relativism were eroding the institutions of society and that the rise of anti-American sentiment ever since the 1960s had greatly devalued the culture.

Even though he was optimistic that the American character was still strong and resourceful and that it could weather terrible disasters—as it had done at least twice in the twentieth century alone—Bloom went on to say, "The gravity of our given task is great, and it is very much in doubt how the future will judge our stewardship."[5] Bloom did not claim an American century or settle for half a century. Rather, he said this was a moment that would determine the context of every succeeding moment of the American way of life. In truth, it always comes down to the individual and to a particular moment. That moment is the instant in which you decide how you will respond to a critical challenge. Will you side with the forces of deconstruction or of production? And will you agree to the calumnies heaped upon the nation in the name of political correctness—along with its accusations of imperialism, racism, sexism, and ethnocentrism—or will you reject them?

Bloom's position was that the tendency of academics to toss out the two thousand years of learning codified in the great works of Western civilization was intellectual suicide. It was tantamount to inviting a new dark age. If the American empire is to survive, he believed, it would be because the American people chose to recognize and honor their heritage and traditions in every area of life. He hoped they would turn away from the things that would tend to degrade, dishonor, demoralize, and deconstruct their heritage and values, and choose in their own moment of history to renew their commitment to basic truths.

The Religion of Humanity

Existentialism, nihilism, anarchism, socialism, deconstruction, and perhaps even the mindless consumerism of our day are the frail flowers that have blossomed from the withered roots of humanism. During the Enlightenment, a large segment of society cut themselves loose from the tether between man and God. The consolation of faith in God and the benefits of divine intervention in the daily affairs of men were repudiated.

Robert Anchor, in his study of the Enlightenment tradition, suggests that one of the problems of the Enlightenment is that the "religion of humanity" brought forth a culture that was self-seeking, antisocial, and detached from the traditional sources of meaning. The creators of the Enlightenment fashioned a society without standards of justice, without standards of merit and authority, and without a higher moral purpose or even a willingness to admit that there may ever have been a moral purpose. Their allegiance was to the merely utilitarian, the materialistic, and the immediately gratifying. And they left to posterity a new view of humanity based on flimsy evidence, superficial illusions, unnatural passions, and an immense ideological gullibility.

The philosophers cast off the noble and heroic in favor of the common and prosaic. They drove away people of culture and virtue even from their own class who might have helped restore reason and order. The cry for liberty, equality, and brotherhood only served to imprison the children and grandchildren of the Revolution in a dismal bond of fatalism and failure.

But lest we forget, we are their heirs. Physically and metaphysically, we are their progeny. The modern liberal democratic society in Europe and America must now come to grips with the legacy left to us by those enlightened progenitors. And we must decide what we will make of our inheritance.

Perhaps no culture has so imitated another and with such disastrous effect as the culture of the 1960s in America imitated the French Enlightenment. If the philosophes and "new men" invented by the Enlightenment were self-seeking, antisocial, and detached from the sources of meaning, the children of the sixties were all of these and more. Their war on prejudice and establishment values was targeted at the very fabric of American society. Their aim was to assault traditional values at the heart and soul of the culture.

The radicals made it no secret that their aim was the overthrow of this nation, and their appearance, behavior, language, and odors were merely the first efforts at intimidation. They had a deep loathing for middle-class values, for the suburban snobbery of their own affluent upbringing, and for the conventional ethics that still survived in weakened form in America's churches, country clubs, and boardrooms.

The Best and Brightest?
The French philosophes had a double standard of justice—their own and everybody else's. The hippies, the Weathermen, the Black Panthers, and the Communist-backed Students for a Democratic Society had an even more startling vision of justice. "Free the prisoners," they chanted. "Free *all* prisoners!" These young leftists were not motivated by any hope of improving the system, but of destroying it entirely. They were committed to total anarchy, to abolishing all existing standards of merit and authority and judgment.

Their spirituality was mystical and primitive. They turned to Native American cults and the worship of Mother Earth, combined with an obsession with drugs, free love, liberal multicouple living arrangements, and the total destruction of every custom or habit that smacked of "middle-class morality." They fully expected to overthrow Christian virtue and bring forth a new and exotic paganism in America. This is precisely what was implied by the flirtation with Hinduism, Buddhism, and Zen by rock groups of the sixties, such as the Beatles and the Rolling Stones.

To the utilitarianism and materialism that first appeared in the seventeenth century, the hippies added another one: a stark, pagan, and ritualistic "commune-ism" in its most naive and primitive form. Robert Royal of the Ethics and Public Policy Center in Washington, D.C., once remarked that the social phenomenon that blasted America in the sixties was "something like a Copernican revolution." Even if the movement was lacking in science, it did indeed change the way we view the world.

John Powys, in his book *The Meaning of Culture,* said that culture is the essential quality and character of a nation, and the principle that defines it. It is, he said, "the bedrock, the final wall, against which one leans one's back in a God-forsaken chaos." Given such a view, what assessment would someone from another country have made of the state of American culture in the sixties based on the accounts they saw in the media? And what would they have decided about the integrity and virtue of American society based on the individuals they met in our centers of higher learning? And if universities attract the best and brightest, and if they are the training ground of the "new intellectuals," what did the culture of the sixties contribute to the quality of intellectual life on American university campuses?

Jean-François Revel, who did observe these things from Paris, has often said that "criticism is the engine of democracy." He accepts the value of intelligent debate in resolving controversies. But he also believes that the rebels of 1968 were after much more than criticism. They were after *change* in a big way, and they were armed "with an ideology of destruction and hate aimed at the very existence of democratic civilization." He writes:

> To say a system that had done more than any other to spread well-being and social justice deserved to die, as did the young rebels of the sixties, was to reveal a profound and thorough gap

between reality and the concepts used to apprehend reality. To recall how stupendously large this gulf was, bear in mind that the revolt against democratic capitalism was led by young people in the best universities, who had access to all the information they could ask for. Yet they chose as their political role models men like Fidel Castro, Mao Zedong, and Che Guevara, whose achievements were not in the area of good government but mass terrorism, not social justice but economic incompetence, not the expansion of liberty but criminality. And this sort of insanity, which was at times carried all the way to acts of terrorism (on the theory that to fight injustice you have to kill bankers and politicians), found some support, at least some "understanding" even among the liberals![6]

Those who say today that the hippies were "noble but naive" are missing the point. In an address to the Heritage Foundation in 1991, Heather Richardson said, "What we suffer from, in great measure, are the by-products and excesses of generally well-intentioned but misguided policies put into place to satisfy some half-right ideas."[7] Her remark was made in reference to public policy in the nation's capital during the 1990s. But I would suggest that it applies just as well to the sixties and even to the twentieth century from start to finish.

No matter how noble the aims of the radicals, we are still their victims, just as society still suffers from the misguided principles of idealistic college deans, civil libertarians, and others who have applauded the assault on tradition. When we see neighborhoods torched, innocent people dragged from their cars and beaten, and the integrity of the law corrupted to placate some liberal notion of "individual rights" or "social equity," we can be sure that society is out of touch with reality and taking its motivation from the tortured logic of the Enlightenment.

The disintegration of the nation begins with internal struggles between various groups. Secular against religious, tradition-minded against innovators, and progressives against reactionaries. Such conflicts are recorded among the Sumerians, Babylonians, Egyptians, Greeks, and Romans. Intense political and social polarization leads first to verbal confrontation and then to open warfare. As we have seen, the French Enlightenment operated on the same sort of dynamic, as did both the English and the American Civil Wars.

Disagreements over fundamental cultural values quickly degenerate into armed conflict. Arnold Toynbee points out in *A Study of History* that our modern time of troubles began with the religious wars of the sixteenth and seventeenth centuries in Germany, France, and Great Britain. He points out that full-fledged collapse generally takes centuries to complete, as it did in Greece and Rome. But by the mid–twentieth century, thanks to the disaster of two world wars, Toynbee believed that Western civilization had already entered the final stages of breakdown.

The Search for Transcendence

What we have seen in these pages has been the pathology of an idea that, no matter how far you trace it, has roots that go even deeper. In the 1960s it appears as a "proletariat" of pampered rich kids, which we now identify as the "hippie movement." In the nineteenth century it was the succession of liberal reformers—Fabians, socialists, romantics, and materialists—seeking freedom from political, social, sexual, and artistic restraints through their search for the "sublime." In the eighteenth century, it was the French philosophes in their quest for "enlightenment." In the seventeenth century it was rationalism and the "scientific method" that allowed men to peer into the quantum of the universe.

Earlier, in the Renaissance, it was the birth of the new human-

143

ism, which claimed to discover within man a spark of genius and divinity. And in the empires of the Mediterranean world—including Egypt, Greece, and Rome—it was a quest for order and balance that reflected the harmony of man and nature. But the roots go ever deeper.

Clearly there is a philosophical turn of mind at work in each of these movements. There is a sense of grappling with the fundamental issues of reality, but the search is deeper still. It is a quest for ultimate reality, and I would suggest that it all comes back to one basic theme. Man has been engaged in an adventure as old as history in search of the missing piece of himself. We seek a sense of connectedness that has been missing in the ordinary ebb and flow of our lives, and we cannot be satisfied until some reconciliation is made between that which we now possess and that which we can scarcely live without.

Christopher Dawson has said, "In the present order of the world, the relation of spirit and matter, as well as the relation of the natural and the supernatural, has become dislocated." I believe that is the heart of the matter. But I would add that what is often missing for so many of those who look solely to the culture or to philosophy and ideas for meaning is the harmony between the reality we know and the greater truth we seek.

The search for the divine presence is natural and inevitable, but if we seek for it through enlightenment or other social movements, we are bound to be disappointed. Saint Augustine said, "God is more truly imagined than expressed, and He exists more truly than He is imagined." We imagine God because we need him. But the reality of God is greater than our imagination and more certain than our need.

The apostle Paul wrote that he lived in the hope that "the creation itself also will be delivered from the bondage of corruption into the glorious liberty of the children of God."[8] He longed for release from the agonies of his physical life and deeply desired a restoration with the life he knew God had already provided in Christ. He said, "For we know that the whole creation groans and labors with birth pangs together until now." If the universe itself groans in anticipation of that fulfillment, how much more are we bound to live in distress amid our materialistic and unfulfilling surroundings.

"Not only that," says Paul, "but we also who have the firstfruits of the Spirit, even we ourselves groan within ourselves, eagerly waiting for the adoption, the redemption of our body."[9] What Paul was saying, beyond the simple statement of his personal hope, was his belief that the merely temporal and the merely physical are not the natural domain of the soul. We are liberated from the encroachments of the world, the flesh, and the devil only as we come into willing subjection to the divine reality. For two thousand years Christians have believed that we find the fulfillment that is missing in the merely physical through religious faith. That is, our reality is completed in Christ.

But that reality is precisely what was lost at the crossroads of the Enlightenment. In tossing out seventeen hundred years of tradition in the search for the new reality and the new humanism, men lost their connection to the divine and to the harmony that they could find only through unity with the divine will of God. Following in their footsteps, modern society has subscribed to a theology of change, and thus we have subverted traditional values without which our culture cannot survive. In the name of liberation and diversity, we have lost the possibility of connection, which alone gives life to the soul.

145

The Common Bond

In *Habits of the Heart,* Robert Bellah says that cultures are dramatic conversations about things that matter to their participants. It may be a casual discussion or even a debate, but culture demands an active dialogue with constant and constructive interaction. In the fabric of our daily lives, the many-colored strands of traditions, values, opinions, achievements, and ambitions are all woven together to make up the characteristic design of our culture. While each thread may represent a different set of values and experiences—values that may sometimes be at odds with the strands that surround it—it is the integrity of the design and the unity of purpose that make American culture unique and desirable. And most important, it is the strength of the material that gives it its beauty and value.

In recent years so much attention has been given to our individuality and freedom of expression that we have put the entire fabric of culture at risk. We have been tolerant of values that are inimical to the health of the family and the long-term interests of the American people. We have allowed, even encouraged, an escalation of lawlessness and open defiance that is dangerous and self-destructive. Perhaps we should remember that from a theological perspective, lawlessness is the very essence of sin.

Violence, hatred, and rage flame out of control in our cities and towns today. And under such benign-sounding names as "choice," "free speech," and "liberation," we permit hotheads and radicals to make a mockery of sacred landmarks and institutions as old as the nation itself. The atmosphere of permissiveness, in turn, threatens our survival as a nation.

Robert Bellah points out that, contrary to popular opinion, this nation is not simply a collection of individuals with nothing in common. We have a great deal in common, including language, ideas, values, beliefs, and aspirations. What gives life meaning is not our individuality and independence but the fact that we are part of the greater tapestry of culture. We are strands woven together with great passion and skill into a mosaic of colors and textures that, by virtue of their sheer complexity, reveal the most remarkable patterns. Those patterns are discerned through our common culture.

The fabric of American culture has survived for more than three hundred years, and until very recently it has been a tapestry that dazzles the eye. Are we really willing to throw all of that away for the sake of change? Are we willing to cast away our great tapestry for a heap of string? Culture and tradition are interwoven at every stage of our national life, and to assault one is to do damage to the other.

Just as the loss of tradition was destructive to the French Republic and as the loss of foundational principles and values contributed to the collapse of the ancient empires, the tendency to underestimate the importance of traditional values in this country (and especially at this time) threatens this nation with unprecedented disaster. If we continue to allow political polarization and social fragmentation to rip out the threads of society, be assured that we will see the fabric of America's future disintegrate before our eyes.

What people want most in life is a sense of purpose and a feeling that things really matter. We want to know that it is all worthwhile and that, in the end, everything does work out for the best. The American educator Robert M. Hutchins once said that effective communication in our age depends on a lot more than telephones, computers, and shortwave radios. What makes communication possible, he said, is "common understanding, a common tradition, common ideas, and common ideals."

It is not our uniqueness or our different racial, social, and cultural qualities that make communication possible in American society, but the willingness to concentrate on the ways in which we are alike. What we should learn from the lessons of the past is that our chances for survival as a culture are best when we work together in harmony and in the unity of shared hopes and dreams.

As a nation we need to concentrate on the beliefs and values we have in common and hold firmly to those things that bring us together. And as individuals, we need to find comfort and security in that dynamic connection with the eternal that unites us to the ultimate Source of meaning and truth.

8

Increase in Materialism

ACCORDING to *USA Today* reporter Anita Manning, kids are under a constant barrage of negative images, racial hatred in popular music, sexual violence in videos, sexual irresponsibility on television sitcoms, and many other destructive behaviors that are troubling to parents. And not least, kids are being sucked into lifestyles of greed and materialism by the commercialism and hype they consume. Marian Wright Edelman, president of the Children's Defense Fund, told the reporter that parents need help. "We're selling consumption and materialism as a measure of our success," she says. Ms. Wright Edelman says parents should use any code of ethics they can muster to counter the negative messages from the popular culture. They need to give their children positive examples in the home. But how are parents to instill values in their children? What are the sources of ideas and beliefs that can bring back the security of the home? Edelman says, "They also need help from other institutions, good institutions such as the schools and churches and synagogues."

Indeed, it is about time that parents and others stopped accepting the materialistic standards of the marketplace and got back to traditional values. It is time to take back the culture from those who have substituted materialism for morality. The entire package of modern broadcasting on both television and radio is designed to exploit kids with messages that saturate them with materialistic desires. We are turning kids into consumers, all right. And their insatiable desire for possessions and adult experiences has robbed a great many of them of their childhood and the deeper values and attachments that make life worth living.[1]

The Medium Is the Message

When Marshall McLuhan said that "the medium is the message" in the late 1960s, he suggested that newspapers, magazines, and the broadcast media are not merely carriers of certain types of information. They are themselves the message. The message is not always the medium, but every message is influenced by the way it is presented in the total context of its presentation. The glitzier and slicker the medium, the more seductive the message. What people consume is not just specific information but the total package—the message and the medium. No wonder kids are so easily captured.

Even if McLuhan's ideas are somewhat abstract, we can see today just how much the American culture has consumed the message of the mass media. Young people as well as adults are saturated with the hype, the commercialism, the facile morals and manners of the Hollywood crowd.

A survey conducted by University of California professors Richard Easterlin and Eileen Crimmins found that teenagers of the early 1990s were more interested in making money than their counterparts in the early eighties. The study measured attitude changes over a twenty-year period, from 1966 to 1988, and included input from two separate surveys: a University of Michigan survey of seventeen thousand high school seniors and a survey of two hundred thousand college freshmen at UCLA.

What Easterlin and Crimmins discovered is that 60 percent of the young people considered "a chance to earn a good deal of money" to be their top priority. That is a 15 percent increase in just ten years. On the other hand, when asked to rate their interest in "an opportunity to be directly helpful to others," only 45 percent responded positively—which was a 5 percent drop from the earlier survey.

The researchers found that a much higher percentage of young people say that making a lot of money is "very important." However, the number who say that work should be a very important part of their life has dropped from 75 percent ten years ago to 35 percent today. The interpretation seems obvious. The kids expect to have a lot of money, but they don't want to work hard to get it.

A larger percentage of young people think that it is very important to try to give their own children a better opportunity than they had; however, they believe the way to do that is by giving them money and things. They do not associate time spent with children as a very important factor. A decade earlier, 44 percent said mothers should spend more time with their children. Today, only 25 percent of those surveyed believe that to be very important.

The Consumer Lifestyle

In this country both federal and state governments have established product standards. They regulate the kind of product information that may be published by manufacturers and advertisers, encourage consumer education, assist consumers in action claims of various kinds, including antitrust suits, and attempt to make sure that consumers have a voice in Washington.

Government policies give specific guidelines regulating product safety and design features, ensuring a certain level of quality and usefulness. But where are the standards that protect consumers from values fraud? Where are the policies that help us to avoid the cheapening of life caused by the hype, commercialism, and creeping materialism in contemporary society?

In a recent feature for *Worth* magazine, Michael Lewis, a senior editor at the *New Republic,* showed just how materialistic Americans have become. There have been two great changes over the past forty years in the way Americans shop, he said. One is a gradual shift toward "a pattern of consumption that has little to do with the simple satisfaction of needs." And the second, he says, is the rise of the shopping mall as "a place to satisfy this peculiar lack of needs."

At the end of World War II there were just eight shopping centers in America. Between 1970 and 1990, however, another twenty-five thousand shopping centers and malls suddenly sprang up from coast to coast. To examine the strange customs that prevail in America's malls, Lewis visited three—three vast shrines to the materialism of our age.

Horton Plaza, in San Diego, is an expansive mall that Lewis describes as "a delightfully improbable combination of Moorish palace, art deco studio, French brothel, and Florentine villa." With more than one million square feet of shopping space, it is one of America's largest. Larger still is Cherry Creek Mall in

Denver, 1.4 million square feet of retail space under one roof, with 130 separate shops and department stores. Among its pricey tenants are Lord & Taylor, Saks Fifth Avenue, Neiman-Marcus, Foley's, and a string of upscale chains that, Lewis notes, "suggests anxiety in the soul of the developer."

But the Mall of America in Minneapolis/St. Paul is far and away the largest mall in America. When the Mall of America opened in 1992, says Lewis, "it was spoken of in the same breath as electricity, the cotton gin, and the first landing on the moon." The description of this modern bazaar is more like a statistical abstract. It has 4.2 million square feet of space, 358 stores, 46 temporary cart stalls, 12,000 permanent employees, 12,750 parking spaces, and 20 acres of roof. It houses nine nightclubs, eight art galleries, a historical-research center, and an amusement park in the middle, where even the Junior League has come to meet. The mall also publishes its own newspaper—not about the economy or the strife in South Africa but about unusual incidents in the mall.[2]

The Crisis of Values

When David Riesman, Nathan Glazer, and Reuel Denney published *The Lonely Crowd* in 1950, they explored the changes that were taking place in society during those postwar years. The discussion showed that the strength of the American character had already declined in many ways, and fewer and fewer people were emotionally secure. They described three character types: the tradition-directed, the inner-directed, and the other-directed.

The principal discovery of that Yale University study was that the major population shifts and technological developments of the period had reduced the significance of tradition as a guide to behavior and self-esteem. Lacking strong roots, more and more people were simply mimicking the culture around them. And lacking either strong faith, a strong sense of self-worth, or strong moral values, many people accepted the tawdry values of Hollywood and television actors as a way of blending in with the standards of the mass culture around them. They believed they were simply adapting to the new "modern" standard of living.

Michael Lerner, best known as the architect of Hillary Clinton's "politics of meaning," is an activist liberal with little sympathy for traditional values, and he clearly believes ours to be a culture of exploitation. Nevertheless, Lerner agrees with many conservatives that one of the most disturbing problems in America today is "the crisis of selfishness."

In a February 1994 editorial in the journal *Tikkun,* Lerner writes, "Reacting against the selfishness and materialism that are sanctified by the competitive market—and that undermine our ability to sustain loving relationships—people hunger for communities of meaning that provide ethical and spiritual purpose. They are offered instead a myriad of nationalistic, religious or racial pseudocommunities that never challenge the 'look out for No. 1' mentality of the market. So people soon find that their daily lives at work or in family life are just as empty as ever."

The problem is that many people have become convinced that happiness can be purchased. As Lerner says, at bottom this is a sign of spiritual weakness. As society's inner resources grow weak, our dependence on things increases, and our highly commercialized culture is only too happy to encourage these bad habits. But it was not always this way. For most of our history, Americans placed greater stock in a man's character than in his possessions. The American Dream held that, by hard work and self-discipline, we could achieve success. And success was not measured in material possessions alone.

Benjamin Franklin said, "The great part of the miseries of

mankind are brought upon them by false estimates they have made of the value of things." The common wisdom of the day taught that greed, luxury, and self-indulgence were the passions of a weak character. And the frugal nature of the pioneers taught that the treasures to be valued most were the virtues of honesty, good character, and moral strength. The poet Allen Tate affirmed this view when he said, "Religion is the sole technique for the validating of values."

But at some point these traditional virtues were lost. At some point the legacy of faith, values, and selfless endurance apparently disappeared. Charles Colson writes, "Societies are tragically vulnerable when the men and women who compose them lack character. A nation or a culture cannot endure for long unless it is undergirded by common values such as valor, public-spiritedness, respect for others and for the law; it cannot stand unless it is populated by people who will act on motives superior to their own immediate interest."[3]

A sophisticated society such as ours is made up of a whole wide range of unspoken commitments. We agree to respect one another's privacy, property, and personal dignity. We agree to abide by a common code of ethics or legal and moral restraints, to commit ourselves to our own loved ones and family, and to be responsible members of our community—to pay taxes, to lend our voices in public issues, and to contribute to the common defense.

When the culture is vital and thriving, we value our role as responsible citizens. We agree to support those causes that are good and worthy and to eschew those that are bad and destructive. We agree to behave honorably and to resist those things that would tend to harm or injure our neighbors. Underlying these commitments is what used to be called a "common code of decency," which is a set of values born of shared values, strong character traits, and a strong moral sense. And, yes, in such a society we do accept the idea that we are our brother's keeper. Our neighbors depend on us just as we depend on them.

Misplaced Priorities

As natural as these ideas once were in American society, a growing number of people no longer accept that traditional view of virtue, character, and faith. Perhaps the group that most objects to objective standards is that large group of men and women known as baby boomers, who have had an overwhelming influence on the beliefs and behaviors of this nation over the past three decades. Between 1946 and 1964, more than 75 million boomers were born in this country. Prior to World War II, the highest average birthrate was about twenty births per thousand women, but during those boom years, the birthrate topped twenty-four per thousand. Today, the boomers are the largest segment of the population.[4]

But as the boomers have begun to enter middle age, there is a very different mood in the country. The children of the boomers, known as baby busters, are entering the picture, and the expectations for these young people are much less optimistic than we might wish. The boomers had a profound effect on American culture. They were there for the birth of rock and roll, the radical revolution of the sixties, the hippie generation, and the Vietnam era. They were the first wave of the Me Generation and the Yuppies, and their children display the social and emotional results of the boomer legacy—the offspring of parents who were too consumed with their own success to spend time with their children.

Of course, the boomers are still a major player in American culture. They are the generation for which the term *consumerism* was coined. Shaped in many ways by television and the commercialism of the media, the boomer generation has been the era of materialism and greed—they seem to have a passion for "stuff." While many are now opting for simpler lifestyles and less conspicuous consumption, their values have nevertheless changed the canvas of American life. Their values still influence popular tastes.

Many analysts agree that there are profound changes taking place in this country today, and the implications for the well-being of the family are disturbing. In its annual report entitled *Free to Be Family,* the Washington-based Family Research Council (FRC) says that the prospects for children have never been bleaker. In an editorial comment, the editors state, "The family in America today is undeniably weaker than at any point in our nation's history." Substantiating such a perspective is the fact that one child in three is born out of wedlock today. Half of all American children will spend at least part of their childhood in a single-parent household. And at least 20 percent of all children, or one in five, will grow up on welfare.[5]

As the background to the dramatic changes brought about by rising divorce and the skyrocketing rate of out-of-wedlock births, the single greatest problem facing the nation today is the breakup of the family and the isolation of an entire generation of American children. The FRC report indicates that parents today spend 40 percent less time with their children than parents did just a generation ago. From about thirty hours per week in the mid-1960s, the amount of parent-child interaction dropped to just seventeen hours per week in the mid-1980s. Americans spend less time with their children than any other people on earth.

Obviously children in single-parent homes are deprived of parental attention by the demands of work and school. A University of Virginia survey shows that employed mothers of preschool children spend less than half as much time with their children as nonemployed mothers. But even in two-wage-earner

157

families, the innocence and freedom of children has been compromised. Kids are scheduled, picked up, and delivered, and they are deprived of the simple pleasures their parents and grandparents enjoyed as children. There is no time for long walks, kicking cans, or watching the clouds. Children are forced to follow schedules for the convenience of their parents. And they soon become victims of the consumer mentality.

Assessing the Damage

What are the implications of such conditions? The FRC study also says that crime begins when childhood ends too soon. Depriving children of their childhood and healthy growing-up experiences not only robs them of a very important part of the learning process but it apparently causes many to turn to gangs, promiscuity, and other destructive behaviors as a way to get even with society. Children who do not receive proper love and guidance are targets of opportunity for those who prey on children.

Amitai Etzioni, who has written on the need to restore the values of home and community in this country, has said that if Americans ran their businesses the way they run their homes, the entire nation would grind to a halt. What if parenting were an industry? he asks. Could it survive under today's brutal conditions?

As farming declined, most fathers left to work away from home generations ago. Over the past 20 years, millions of American mothers have sharply curtailed their work in the 'parenting industry' by moving to their work outside the home. By 1991 two-thirds (66.7 percent) of all mothers with children under 18 were in the labor force, and more than half (55.4 percent) of women with children under the age of 3 were. At the same time,

> *a much smaller number of child-care personnel moved into the*
> *parenting industry.*[6]

The comparison is striking. What would happen if more than half
the available jobs in industry were lost and the workers were
replaced with fewer, less-qualified people who were told to continue the same level of production and with the same quality that
the full force had previously delivered? Etzioni says anyone who
tried such a thing would be considered crazy. But this is precisely
what has happened to parenting in America. Instead of raising
them in loving homes and friendly neighborhoods, parents deposit
their children in "kennels for kids," and the results have been
devastating, not only for the children but for our entire society.

Etzioni continues, "Children require attention and a commitment of time, energy, and above all self. . . . The notion of
'quality time' is a lame excuse for parental absence; it presupposes
that bonding and education can take place in brief time bursts,
on the run. Quality time occurs within quantity time. As you
spend time with children—fishing, gardening, camping, or 'just'
eating a meal—there are unpredictable moments when an opening occurs, and education takes hold." Quoting Barbara Dafoe
Whitehead, "Maybe there is indeed such a thing as a one-minute
manager, but there is no such thing as a one-minute parent."[7]

Throughout history, people have believed that things are
gradually getting better and that, thanks to the marvels of "progress," human welfare is constantly improving. They have anticipated that situations for the individual and the family would
eventually reach some stage of perfection. The idea of making the
world a better place was a very realistic hope—at least that was
the assumption for many generations.

Unfortunately, the reality has been far different. During this
century, things began to change. Whether we blame the mass

media for the loss of traditional values or the church for the diminishing importance of religion in American homes, things have simply gotten worse in America's homes, and the prospects for the future are growing dimmer by the day.

Looking at History

Are there precedents in history for these conditions? Are there lessons we can learn? The Roman poet Livy wrote that over time greed and self-indulgence led the Romans into dangerous excess. All of this was set off by absorption with the vice of luxury. "For it is true," says Livy, "that when men had fewer possessions, they were also modest in their desires. Lately riches have brought avarice and abundant pleasures, and the desire to carry luxury and lust to the point of ruin and universal perdition."[8]

In his descriptions of the decadence of the Roman Republic, during the wars with Greece, the great historian Polybius wrote that this preoccupation with luxury led to absolute self-indulgence, which led in turn to the most sordid carnal indulgences. "For some young men indulged in affairs with boys, others in affairs with courtesans, and many of them in music and drinking parties and all the expenses associated with such activities.

"So great was this eruption of self-indulgence among the young men," Polybius adds, "that many paid a talent [roughly a thousand dollars] for a boy bought for sexual pleasure and many paid three hundred drachmas for a jar of caviar. Marcus Cato was outraged by this and, in a speech to the people, complained that one might be quite convinced of the decline of the republic, when pretty boys cost more than fields and jars of caviar cost more than plowmen."[9] Clearly the morals of the empire had grown corrupt, and economic values had become degraded as well. But how do such conditions relate to the problems in our own society?

The roots of modern materialism, despite the protests of

scholars, grow very much within the same soil as philosophical and dialectical materialism from which socialism and communism have sprung. Materialism denies any reality beyond the realm of immediate experience. What you see, they maintain, is what you get. Karl Marx and Friedrich Engels believed that people are motivated by material needs. Therefore, living conditions, physical circumstances, possessions, and the general economic welfare are all that really matter in life. There is nothing beyond the here and now.

The Greek philosopher Democritus had said that everything in the universe can be broken down to one basic element: the atom. Beyond that, he said, there is no greater reality. No spirit, no soul, no life after death. These ideas were awakened again during the Enlightenment. In the nineteenth century they were taken to their logical conclusion, and G. W. Hegel added the dialectical component to the ancient theories of the Greeks. The defenders of these ideas were deadly serious about them. As we know now, tens of millions of people who disputed the cold rationality of the materialist doctrines in Eastern Europe, Soviet Russia, China, and many other places were simply murdered by their leaders.

The bourgeoisie of the Enlightenment is the proletariat of the communist ideology. And the self-indulgent, greed-driven, materialistic society of the 1990s is the natural offspring of the socialistic dialectic. It was only natural, in such a climate, that religious faith and values would begin to fade away in modern society. And it was also inevitable that morality, tradition, and our cultural foundations would slowly begin to collapse.

Reflecting on Virtue

In his book *The Moral Sense,* James Q. Wilson says that in today's intellectual climate people are no longer receptive to reflection on issues of morality and virtue. Those who do still feel strongly about traditional values tend to feel like refugees in an occupied nation. Whenever we speak of virtue, Wilson says, we feel as if we are supposed to do it in private. Otherwise, we may either be charged with violating the separation of church and state or, even worse, of being "unsophisticated" and old-fashioned. As Frank Rhodes found out at Cornell, the very idea of public morality is offensive to the intellectuals.

But Wilson finds these conditions very disturbing. "If we are to live as fugitives in so alien a world," he says, "it is necessary to find a way of speaking that will not offend anyone. We need a code word for virtue or morality. That word is 'values.'"[10] It should not be surprising that the idea of "values" is under attack today. But the question is whether or not society can survive in a morals vacuum. Can we live without a tradition of shared values and beliefs? And can we continue forever in a moral chaos where only materialistic values prevail?

This same pattern may be seen in detail not only in the empires of our own time but in the collapse of the ancient civilizations of Egypt, Babylon, Syria, and Carthage. The city of Carthage, which holds special interest for me, was a spectacular example of the rise and fall of a great power. At its height, the city of Carthage had an internal area of seven square miles, and homes in the center of the city were as much as six stories high. The houses had internal courtyards with fountains and greenery, and even indoor plumbing.

There were wells throughout the city, and the citizens were able to collect and use rainwater. Agriculture and animal husbandry were highly advanced there, and the battlements around the city were able to hold off even the strongest of enemies for months and years without threat to the inhabitants.

Unlike their cousins in the great cities of Sidon and Tyre, the

Carthaginians were largely nonpolitical in the beginning, and their military power was dedicated first to defense, second to maintaining freedom of the seas, and only third to conquest. The naval and military strength of Carthage was dedicated to commercial exploits, and while its forces were large and fearsome, they did not so much march to take slaves or to make conquests as to penetrate new territory and secure new markets for their goods.

First and foremost, the Carthaginian empire was built on commerce. They loved wealth and luxury, and they lived to buy and sell goods. Their Punic fleets settled and built the city of Málaga in southern Spain as a Carthaginian port. They also established a base at Cádiz, and artifacts found recently in Great Britain suggest that they may have had some traffic there as well. The ancient historian Herodotus reports that the Carthaginian empire once included more than twenty thousand square miles of the Tunisian plains, plus most of the littoral of North Africa— all of the territory now occupied by Morocco, Algeria, and Tunisia.

Salvian, the fifth-century bishop of Marseilles, called Carthage the queen and mother of all the cities of Africa, "the eternal rival of Rome, first in arms, then in courage, and finally in splendor and dignity!" He boasted that Carthage was the most formidable adversary of Rome, and within its city walls was everything needed for a truly great nation. Academies of liberal arts, schools of science and philosophy, gymnasia (secondary schools) of language and manners, plus great temples, arenas, and government houses—all were within the walls.

Among the most influential people in Carthaginian society were their learned scholars, military leaders, diplomats, judges and lawyers, consuls, and governors. And while other great cities of the time lacked adequate police protection, Carthage was, at least until late Roman times, a model of authority and popular restraint.

Seeds of Corruption

But just as Salvian heaps praises on the city in the most extravagant language, his condemnation of its vices is no less remarkable. He reports that the citadel of Carthage was a city "seething with every kind of wickedness, thronging with people, thronging still more with iniquities, full of riches, but fuller of sins, where men surpass one another in the vileness of their evil passions, strong among themselves for supremacy in greed and impurity, others enfeebled with wine or distended with gluttony, others crowned with flowers or reeking with perfumes, all weakened by degrading forms of luxury, nearly all sunken in deadly errors, not all dizzy with wine, it is true, but everyone drunken in sin."[11]

He specifically mentions the proscription of orphans, the oppression of widows, and the torture and mutilation of prisoners for sport at the hands of barbarian gladiators. Proscription was the issuance of a kind of death warrant against a person or a group, and in Roman times it was used to bring about execution without involving the state. It may be that, in their desire for order and simplicity, the Punic leaders believed that the proscription of unwanted orphans and widows would reduce the amount of poverty and suffering in the city.

Certainly it would have helped to prevent the rise of an underclass of rebels and brigands. Yet there is a great deal of evidence today suggesting that the Punic culture became increasingly acquisitive and bloodthirsty over time. In an atmosphere of decadence, life in Carthage lost much of its character and significance. Their lives of materialism and corruption finally consumed them.

As the Carthaginian empire expanded, the emphasis of their

religion also began to change. The merchants of Carthage achieved great wealth, and their exploits and adventures upon the seas were unrivaled by any other race of men. But these people were apparently persuaded that they were at the mercy of the gods, and only dark and sinister deeds could preserve them. So over a period of time they ceased worship of Baal Hammon, the hereditary god of their ancestors mentioned repeatedly in the Old Testament, to the worship of the earth goddess Tanit. Sacrifices to the goddess of fertility were supposed to ensure productivity, long life, and even greater profits.

At one time scholars denied that the Carthaginians practiced such rituals, but it is clear that infants were sacrificed to Tanit. Ornately carved funeral monuments, some of which depict actual scenes of infant sacrifice, were set up in the cemeteries and sacred precincts of the city to acknowledge the blood offerings made to the goddess in exchange for blessings on the Punic fleet. Several of these monuments have been preserved intact and can be seen today in Tunisia's renowned Bardo Museum.

When I visited the funeral gardens and cemeteries at the Realm of Tanit, I saw the tiny stone coffins of infants who were murdered and burned as sacrifices to the pagan goddess. The sight of thousands of these coffins lined up, row upon row upon row, was chilling. Twenty years after that first visit, I still remember the sense of sorrow I felt then. I recall wondering what horrors the mothers and fathers of all those innocent victims must have endured at the hand of their demon gods.

But this was the ironic fate of Carthage. This is how a city of improvident wealth and monstrous rituals became one of the most unusual milestones in the march of Western culture. The cult of greed had grown so intense that murdering their own children apparently meant nothing. But we must ask ourselves, how is the murder of 30 million innocent children in America over the last twenty years any different? Isn't the rite of abortion our culture's sacrifice to the gods of materialism and greed?

Unwanted pregnancies they're called today. Children who do not deserve to live. Evidence of our sin and our culture's insistence on "rights" and "choices" over God's gift of new life. Call it a cult of selfishness, of greed, or of materialism. But call it what it is. The Phoenicians murdered many thousands of children. And, yes, they burned their young. But in the entire history of Carthage or of Rome, they never killed 30 million in the name of "a woman's right to control her own body."

The cult of Tanit was a terrible, bloodthirsty affair, but they never hid their deeds behind a cloak of hypocrisy. They called it what it was. It was murder, and it was a sacrifice to the gods of materialism and greed. So is abortion today.

Religion and Reality

For Christians the question is not whether Jesus Christ is the "Savior incarnate in a man" but when he will come again to rule and to reign. No one knows the day or the hour. And no one knows how great the disorder must be before the Messiah returns. Who knows what losses we must first sustain? And who knows what might provoke the great final outpouring of divine wrath that will bring about the judgment of mankind? We certainly cannot live as if there were no other options and nothing to do until that moment arrives. But the price of victory will be to endure that great moment of truth and to survive the test by fire.

A few months ago I read an article by Dr. Robert Wuthnow, a scientist and researcher at Princeton University, about his study of the relationship between faith and materialism in American society. In 1992, Wuthnow and his colleagues conducted a survey of two thousand men and women in the work force in this country on the relationship of faith and values in their daily lives and activities. The results were disturbing.

> *Religious traditions provided earlier generations of Americans a moral language that helped curb the pursuit of money. Faced, as we now seem to be, with a sense that materialism has gotten out of hand and that we are unable to resist its power, some of us might hope that religious faith would still be a source of wisdom and guidance in these matters. Yet the results from our study are at best mixed.*[12]

More than 89 percent of those surveyed told Wuthnow that "our society is much too materialistic," and 74 percent said materialism is a serious social problem. Another 71 percent said society would be better off if less emphasis was placed on money, and 90 percent said that "children today want too many material things." Nevertheless, 64 percent said, "I think a lot about money and finances," and 84 percent said, "I wish I had more money than I do."

What the study revealed is that even people who have religious values are emotionally divided over the problem of materialism. More than 78 percent believed that a beautiful home and a new car were either "very important" or "fairly important"; 71 percent agreed that "having money means having more freedom"; and 76 percent agreed that "having money gives me a good feeling about myself." After analyzing these and other data, the researchers concluded that "faith makes little difference to the ways in which people actually conduct their financial affairs."

Spiritual Emptiness
In *The American Hour,* Os Guinness writes, "Americans with a purely secular view of life have too much to live with and too little to live for. Everything is permitted and nothing is impor-

tant." Thanks to the secularization of our age and the degree to which Christians hide their faith (in order to avoid embarrassment), the marks of character have grown soft, often invisible. Many people today have traded their faith in the eternal verities for the cheap substitute of material possessions, and predictably the soul of the nation has grown weak.

Secular answers to society's problems are hollow and unfulfilling, and, Guinness warns, "once growth and prosperity cease to be their reason for existence, they are bound to ask questions about the purpose and meaning of their lives: Whence? Whither? Why? And to such questions secularism has no answers that have yet proved widely satisfying in practice."[13]

In short, materialism has failed us. The false faiths of our age have failed us. Freudianism, Marxism, deconstruction, and social permissiveness have all failed to render the great social order or peace of mind their adherents promised. None of these seductions have enhanced the meaning of life or made up for the poverty in our souls. "Even secular humanism turns out to be, not the bogey its enemies feared, but an oxymoron its supporters regret—for secularism does not produce humanism; humanism requires, not secularism, but supernaturalism."[14]

The human spirit requires more than mere physical food for its deepest hungers. It needs spiritual meat. And the soul of the nation cannot survive when greed, lust, selfishness, and ambition are our only criteria of value. Whether in Europe, in Soviet Russia, or in modern America, materialism is a disease that destroys character. The only cure for our spiritual emptiness is a return to the moral values that made this nation great. And such values only come through faith in God. Guinness says:

> *The lesson is clear. When morality is strong, laws need not be. So if the scope of freedom is to widen, that of law should not. There*

is therefore great folly in the current notion that, because morality is a private affair, anything is right in public "so long as it does not break the law." Under the guise of this maxim, liberals seasoned in crusades against environmental irresponsibility have presided carelessly over a massive moral erosion of their own. Moral principles have been hacked down, special proprieties bulldozed to the ground. All that is not legally prohibited is socially allowed. Someday these radical rule-breakers will wake up to a world without rules. Then they will lament either the moral dust bowl they have created or the dense underbrush of laws they have had to grow hastily in its place.[15]

Please hear what is being said here. The notion that we can have virtue or strong character without a framework of moral values is false. When morality is jettisoned for the sake of material possessions or personal pleasures, the loss to the individual and the nation is inestimable. Character must be built on a foundation of moral values, and without religion there can be no genuine morality.

In the following section we will explore some of the moral and ethical dilemmas that confront this nation as we stand at the gateway to a new century and new millennium. We will examine briefly the threats to order and decency, and some of the promises offered by the various visions of truth competing for our devotion.

We need to know what we can discover from the record of society's failures that may point us toward a better way. We need to know which resources will be most helpful in averting national disaster. But we especially need to know how faith can, in fact, make a difference in our lives. These issues will be addressed in the final section.

PART THREE

MORAL DECAY

9

The Rise in Immorality

AN ATTITUDE of exploitation and dishonesty seems to touch every area of life today, and no sector of the population is more affected by it than the young. A 1993 report by the Josephson Institute of Ethics in California found that 33 percent of high school students and 16 percent of college students, in a sample of 8,965 surveyed, admitted they had stolen from a store in the past year; a third of high schoolers and college students said they would lie on a resume or job application to get a job; 16 percent of the younger group and 18 percent of the older students said they had lied on an application at least once.

One in eight college-age young people admitted inflating

expense claims, lying to an insurance company, lying on financial aid forms, and borrowing money with no intent of ever paying it back—all in the previous twelve months. More than 21 percent said they would falsify a report if it would help them keep their job; 39 percent said they had lied to their employer; and 35 percent had lied to a customer in the past year.

Do such statistics reflect some local phenomenon? Is this merely a temporary trend or some kind of isolated aberration? Apparently not. The researchers who conducted the survey say these respondents are not "moral mutants." Instead, they are typical of a growing segment of the American population today. At the conclusion of their study, they decided that the negative dispositions of these young people "often developed in an atmosphere where cheaters regularly prosper and honesty is not always the best policy." In other words, these traits simply represent coping mechanisms for a corrupt society. "Their misbehavior," the analysts report, "is more often the product of survival strategies and coping mechanisms than moral deficiency."

But can this be true? Young people today can cheat and lie and steal, and that is not a moral deficiency? First the sociologists tell us "There is a hole in the moral ozone layer," but then they quickly tell us that dishonesty is simply "coping." Condemnation for immoral behavior is rare these days. There seem to be very few things for which a person can be punished anymore.

On April 28, 1994, the secretary of the navy announced plans to punish a large group of Naval Academy midshipmen who were involved in the worst cheating scandal in the school's 149-year history. The cheating incident occurred in December 1992 when students in a tough electrical-engineering course got advance copies of the exam over the academy's electronic-mail system. Of the 134 midshipmen who had at least some advance knowledge of the test, 24 were expelled, 47 received lesser punishments, 25 were disciplined separately, and 38 were exonerated.[1]

What is particularly telling about this incident, however, is not that students would try to cheat on an exam. Cheating has become an accepted practice in many schools today. What is noteworthy is that several students reacted with surprise and anger when told that they would be punished. How could they be blamed for cheating when most of them didn't see anything wrong in what they did? "It used to be that people just came here and all these things were assumed," said one young man. "The idea of integrity wasn't that hard to grasp. . . . But the whole world has turned upside down. Our class—we grew up at a time when nobody in our entire lives, in any institution, was ever there to tell us what's right or wrong."

The sad part is that the analysis of the midshipman was partly correct. The honor code at Annapolis does specifically warn against cheating or cribbing on exams, and every class is reminded of the 1976 cheating incident in which a group of honor students was expelled. But throughout the culture, and especially in the schools and colleges, disobedience, dishonesty, and cheating have been tolerated. Indecency is more and more common, and it seems there is hardly any sort of standard left for judging right and wrong.

Moral Deregulation

Senator Daniel Patrick Moynihan outraged his fellow liberals when he broke another bit of bad news in the *American Scholar,* saying, "The amount of deviant behavior in American society has increased beyond the levels the community can 'afford to recognize' and that, accordingly, we have been redefining deviancy so as to except much conduct previously stigmatized, and also quietly raising the 'normal' level in categories where behavior is now abnormal by any earlier standard."[2]

Along with all the other changes that came out of the 1960s, there has been a vast moral deregulation in American society, which has led to higher crime rates, the destruction of the traditional family, and an explosion of psychoses and mental disorders. But according to the liberal perspective, the way to deal with these problems is not to punish, reform, or give moral guidance for these maladies, but to define them away—to define deviancy down.

Just a few weeks after Moynihan's article appeared, it was followed by an article by *Washington Post* columnist Charles Krauthammer in the *New Republic* called "Defining Deviancy Up." While Moynihan has focused on the efforts of intellectuals, social pundits, and the mass media to redefine promiscuity, homosexuality, and other behaviors once commonly labeled as sins, Krauthammer took another tack, showing how the same group of activists are trying to prove that traditional American lifestyles and Judeo-Christian values are corrupt, exploitative, and abusive, and that all aspects of the culture are deviant.

"The net effect," writes Krauthammer, "is to show that deviancy is not in the heart of criminals and crazies but thrives in the heart of the great middle class. The real deviants of society stand unmasked. Who are they? Not Bonnie and Clyde but Ozzie and Harriet." The guilty parties, the social critics claim, are you and I, the average American. The writer goes on to say, "The moral deconstruction of middle-class normalcy is a vast project. Fortunately, thousands of volunteers are working the case. By defining deviancy up they have scored some notable successes. Three, in particular. And in precisely the areas Moynihan identified: family life, crime, and thought disorders."[3]

What both these writers—one liberal and one conservative— have described is the rampant deconstruction of moral values by sociologists and intellectuals over the last half century. In the name of liberation we have denied young people and their parents the wise counsel that has been expected in civilized nations since the dawn of time. As a consequence, we are witnessing what can only be described as the suicide of society.

Sociologist James Q. Wilson says that sometime in the 1960s society talked itself out of having a moral sense. In the process, he says, "we may have harmed vulnerable children who ought to have received surer guidance from family and neighborhoods." He adds pointedly, "We may have promoted self-indulgence when we thought we were only endorsing freedom."[4] But we should not be surprised when children who have been denied moral guidance act out behaviors that are dishonest and destructive. If morality is merely relative, it cannot easily be enforced. And if we excuse the most outrageous violations of decency, we should not be surprised when our nation is turned into urban jungles by the immature and irresponsible behavior of its sons and daughters.

Political Indecency

In a discussion of moral values in the inner city, *Newsweek* columnist Joe Klein said,

> *It is impossible, of course, to pinpoint the precise moment when moral relativism became acceptable public policy—but in the sixties, the structures of moral authority were systematically removed from the poorest neighborhoods. A series of legal judgments made it harder for teachers to discipline their students and for housing projects to screen their tenants; the cop on the beat was seen as an occupying force and removed. The moral consequences of programs like welfare were never considered. Instead of nurturing virtue, popular culture celebrated intemperance— and intemperance, as Adam Smith pointed out 200 years ago, may addle the rich, but it devastates the poor.*[5]

177

The dangers and the enormous costs brought about by the moral conflict throughout society are crippling the nation. And just as the floods, fires, hurricanes, tornadoes, and storms of the past three years have changed the physical landscape, the storm of immorality sweeping the land at this hour is changing the moral topography of our country. Never in history has there been such an assault on faith and values. Never have we been at such risk.

The loss of religious values and the enormous growth of the secular state have brought about changes that no nation has ever been able to survive. Throughout the history of this nation, moral education has been an essential aspect of public education. Textbooks such as *McGuffey's Reader,* used by generations of young Americans, offered stories that encourage good moral judgment and good citizenship. Teachers believed it was their duty to tell students about such things as integrity, honor, and duty. And they drew upon the best source material in the world: the Holy Bible.

The whole history of Western civilization derives from these traditions, and without an understanding of Christian moral values and the role of the Bible in public life, no one can begin to understand the true character of the American experience. As Carl Henry writes, "The ideals that lifted the West above ancient paganism had their deepest source and support in the self-revealed God who was and is for Christians the *summum bonum* or supreme good."[6]

As we discussed in chapter 5, every schoolchild in America once understood the moral heritage of this country—but that is no longer the case. The result has been that traditional values and any moral instruction that suggests our Christian heritage have been banished. But in the absence of the commonly held absolutes and standards—the mortar and cement that literally hold society together—discussions of right and wrong are no longer allowed because they involve value judgments. Thus, the props have been taken out from under the edifice of culture. Everything is relative; nothing is absolute. No wonder moral responsibility is disappearing.

Immoral Indoctrination

The plan of liberal educators has been to eradicate the past and indoctrinate young people with their own socialist political agenda. The humanist perspective says there are no absolutes, no sources of ultimate truth and meaning, and no predominant value system. Due in part to the poor quality of the education they receive and the lack of moral guidance in the home, many students have no way of doubting or challenging the lies they are being told.

In many schools students are being programmed with ideas about the sacredness of the environment and the moral significance of tolerance and diversity. Under the rubric of multiculturalism, they are told that American history is a record of abuse and exploitation. Our Founding Fathers were slavers who killed the Indians and practiced imperialism.

They are also taught radical individualism with little or no discussion of the responsibilities that must always accompany rights. At least two generations of young people have been brainwashed by the secular culture. "Your parents are from the old days," some have been told. "They don't know what's going on anymore. You can't trust your parents, so trust us, your teachers. We have the latest information. We offer you the keys to the future."

So students are infused with revolutionary ideas. They quickly lose respect for their heritage of freedom. They believe that Western civilization is a bad idea that does not deserve to be preserved. And because their knowledge of history has been corrupted, many of them become easy targets for the political ideologies of liberal teachers and university professors. The cultural "elites" have become their models for behavior.

The souls of our children are being emptied by design. Religion and exploitation are linked in hundreds of ways: The Pilgrims did not celebrate Thanksgiving to honor their God, but to thank the Indians for their help in the new land. Sharing the gospel with the Indians was actually an attempt to corrupt the purity of the Indian culture, to steal their heritage—certainly not an indication of the desire to share the love of Jesus Christ with them.

Battles are taking place at this hour in our schools, workplaces, and homes over the sources of moral authority in this nation, and the Christian ethic is taking a beating. And the doctrine that is being preached today from the political soapboxes and church pulpits of this nation is not the Good News proclaimed by the saints and apostles but a dangerous socialist compromise that can only lead to the death of this nation.

If you doubt that statement, just pause to consider the values that are being elevated by government, the courts, and the intellectual establishment in this nation today. If you have any doubt that there is a concerted effort to purge the landscape of traditional values and to instill a new politically correct agenda based on diversity, then take a look at the beliefs and the implied political agenda of one recent appointee to the United States Supreme Court.

In its review of the public record on Supreme Court Justice Ruth Bader Ginsburg's position on social issues, Focus on the Family offered this list of her published opinions:

1. The traditional family concept of the husband as a bread-winner and wife as a homemaker must be eliminated.

2. The federal government must provide comprehensive child care.

3. The Homestead Law must give twice as much benefit to couples who live apart from each other as to a husband and wife who live together.

4. In the military, women must be drafted when men are drafted, and women must be assigned to combat duty.

5. Affirmative action must be applied to equalize the number of men and women in the armed forces.

6. The age of consent for sexual acts must be lowered to 12 years of age.

7. Prostitution must be legalized. She wrote: "Prostitution as a consensual act between adults Is arguably within the zone of privacy protected by recent constitutional decisions."

8. All-boy and all-girl organizations must be sexually integrated, as must all fraternities and sororities. The Boy Scouts and the Girl Scouts must change their names and their purposes to become sex-integrated.[7]

This woman, who was praised as a moderate by the press and the administration as well as by some conservatives, quite clearly has goals that are counter to the interests of this nation. If some or all of these ideas are put into place, the already weakened foundations of the family will be damaged beyond repair. Such policies have the potential to create division, hostility, and deep distrust between men and women. They may endanger the whole basis of Western civilization.

Unhealthy Values

In a March 1994 interview in *Advocate,* a publication for homosexuals, United States Surgeon General Dr. Joycelyn Elders said that the antihomosexual sentiment in this nation is due to an irrational fear of sex. She endorsed the agenda of gay-rights activists and criticized the Boy Scouts of America for being "homophobic." Christians are to blame for the problems in this nation, she said, because they are suspicious of sexuality. "I think the religious right at times thinks that the only reason for sex is procreation," she said. "Well, I feel that God meant sex for more than procreation."

As chief of the world's largest health system, Dr. Elders wants sex education to begin in kindergarten. Ideally, she would like to give condoms to all schoolchildren over the age of five. And high schoolers need to be taught how to have safe sex. "We taught [kids] what to do in the front seat," she told a national media group. "Now it's time to teach them what to do in the backseat." As for those who disagree with the spread of "abortion rights," Elders said Christians need to "get over their love affair with the fetus."

If you wonder how the surgeon general's ideas have fared in the past, it would help to examine her record in Arkansas, where she was commissioner of health under Governor Bill Clinton. Under Dr. Elders's policies, the state went from the fourth to the second highest teen pregnancy rate in the nation. Syphilis infections went up 130 percent, and the rate of HIV infection among teens went up 150 percent.

Recently Elders said she is concerned about the alarming rise of sexually transmitted diseases in the nation, but she does not want to outlaw prostitution to try to stop it. In fact, she wants to give all prostitutes the Norplant contraceptive treatment, allowing them to continue to sell their sex without risk of an unwanted pregnancy.

It is clear from statements like these, and many other policies coming out of Washington, that the leaders of this nation do not have the answers to America's problems. We should see that these and other schemes from the radical Left are destroying our moral integrity and substituting a whole range of unhealthy values. A recent study by the Alan Guttmacher Institute called "Testing Positive" showed that at least 25 percent of Americans are currently infected with one or more of the twenty sexually transmitted diseases at large in the land today.

The Center for Disease Control reports that in 1992 there were 120,000 cases of syphilis, 1.1 million cases of gonorrhea, and 4 million cases of genital herpes in this country. They say that 54 percent of high school students are already sexually active. A study by the Responsible Social Values Program (an education system for teaching abstinence to kids) indicates that the federal government spends $160 million each year teaching kids how to have safe sex, but by federal policy, it totally ignores abstinence as the only reliable safeguard against pregnancy and disease.

The Moral Vacuum

The moral vacuum in this country has not come about by accident; rather, it has been created by design by the Left. Despite the fact that Christian values were designed into the entire political structure of this nation by the founders, today's political elites have decided that God and the Bible have no place in American public life. But not all Americans are happy with such changes. Not many of us believe we are better off than we were thirty years ago. Robert J. Samuelson said in a January 1994 *Newsweek* column that Americans are sick and tired of government's smoke screen that the economy is the cause of our problems. What troubles Americans most, he says, is the permissiveness and immorality that are shredding the nation's social fabric.

In a survey of its readers published in June 1994, *Newsweek* found that 75 percent of the respondents believe that America is in moral and spiritual decline. Crime, drugs, family breakup, and low ethical standards were considered to be the leading indicators of moral turmoil. In addition, 72 percent said they believe the questions about President Clinton's character have limited his ability to govern effectively or to exert moral leadership. But is anyone in authority paying attention to these attitudes of the public?

Relative values, moral ambivalence, and cultural relativism are the paramount dangers to the American family today. We are on a slippery slope of moral relativism, and a growing number of children and young adults are sliding down to their own destruction. How can anyone scanning the headlines deny these facts? *Moral relativism* is just another term for immorality. Immorality leads to lawlessness, and lawlessness always leads to anarchy. Arnold Toynbee showed that once anarchy sets in, it cannot be reversed. Have we perhaps reached that point already?

Erwin Lutzer has said, "Those who wish to create a secular state where religion has no influence will of necessity bring about meaninglessness, lawlessness, and despair. Such conditions often spawn a totalitarian state, instituted to restore order by brute force. When a nation loses its moral roots, a dictator often arises who takes away personal freedoms to restore order."[8] That is certainly the risk we face today as we see godless ideologies being enacted by government. But the dangers are greater yet, for when any nation violates the moral boundaries established by God, they place civilization itself at risk.

Inside the Revolution

Where do such bizarre and destructive ideas come from? One major source was Herbert Marcuse, the philosophical guru of the Left who wrote long and detailed treatises spelling out the radical agenda and tactics for undermining and overthrowing the United States and its capitalist system. Years before Vice President

Al Gore became the point man for ecology, Marcuse had described the need for a radical environmental movement, a women's liberation movement, and an all-out assault on traditional moral values. As a doctrinaire Marxist, his goal was nothing less than the total defeat of capitalism.

"If the New Left emphasizes the struggle for the restoration of nature, if it demands a new sexual morality, the liberation of women, then it fights against material conditions imposed by the capitalist system and reproducing this system."[9] He found an army of willing soldiers in the universities during the sixties and seventies, many of whom are now at the forefront of the deconstruction movement as tenured faculty.

Art, style, and fashion were other important tools of the revolution. Marcuse urged the hippies and other radicals to attack the English language from every possible direction. Profanity and obscenity would be important tools. The use of sexually explicit curse words has a double impact, he said. "It turns easily against sexuality itself. The verbalization of the genital and anal sphere, which has become a ritual in left-radical speech . . . is a *debasement* of sexuality." It demeans the existing culture and degrades common experience.

By the same measure, he said that slang, argot, and black dialect (which he called the language of oppression) were important ways to undermine the traditional culture. Language had to be assaulted and made hostile to the mainstream culture. And music could have similar powers in destabilizing the status quo. He said, "I have already referred to black music; there is also a black literature, especially poetry, which may well be called revolutionary; it lends voice to a total rebellion which finds expression in the aesthetic form."[10]

"Art can indeed become a weapon in the class struggle," he said, "by promoting changes in the prevailing consciousness."

Painting, sculpture, theater, and music had to be stripped of "conventional values" if the revolution was to succeed. "While, in the arts, in literature and music, in communication, in the mores and fashions, changes have occurred which suggest a new experience, a radical transformation of values, the social structure and its political expressions seem to remain basically unchanged, or at least lagging behind the cultural revolution." But by the time he died in 1979, all these things were under assault.

In the decline of Greece, the music of the young people became wild and coarse. Popular entertainments—including the theater, music, and public spectacles—were brutal and vulgar. All pretense at art had long since been abandoned. Promiscuity, homosexuality, drunkenness, and other kinds of self-indulgence dominated the daily life of the citizens. And the loss of moral and social restraints led to riotous excesses and decadence.

Comparisons with our own society are obvious. The arts in this country have sunk to deplorable levels. Violence, vulgarity, and obscenity are the rule in popular entertainment. Bloody movies are acted out in real life by psychopaths. And, needless to say, abortion, euthanasia, and the desertion of both children and spouses is now common. We should recognize that it is only in the degree of their dissipation that we are any different from Greece or Rome. The excesses of our day are just as dangerous and potentially as extreme if they are not checked.

Politics of Corruption

It is only too clear that we are witnessing a new barbarian invasion. As in Egypt, Carthage, and Enlightenment France, our barbarians are mostly homegrown. As in the late period of the Roman Empire, adultery and promiscuity are common. Young men and women of the elite classes in Rome refused to marry or to be tied down by the demands of hearth and home. Childbirth was avoided by every means, and young men who should have aspired to public office or other important positions turned instead to drunkenness, gluttony, gambling, blood sports, and unbridled sensuality.

Edward Gibbon observed that the leaders of the empire gave in to the vices of strangers, morals collapsed, laws became oppressive, and the abuse of power made the nation vulnerable to the barbarian hordes. But how are we any different today? Isn't contemporary culture in much the same state of dissipation and moral weakness?

In her study of the "politics of immorality" in ancient Rome, British historian Catherine Edwards says that contraception, abortion, and exposure were common ways to prevent childbirth in Rome. Husbands refused to recognize any child they did not believe to be their own. "Until accepted by its father, a Roman baby did not, legally speaking, exist."[11] Today, abortionists and their supporters have declared that the fetus of a human being is not a human being until it is born. We can only wonder if the same is true for dolphins, whales, or black rhinos. Is it all right to abort these creatures or to smash the eggs of spotted owls?

In the fatal last hours of Rome, local leaders, businessmen, and successful farmers were exploited and abused by the state. Their wealth and privileges were confiscated for the benefit of the emperor and as a way of paying the exorbitant debts of the state. The senators and elite classes were not held to the same laws or standards as the common people. They made themselves exempt from most laws and taxes, and even as the empire was dying from hunger, abuse, gang violence, and debauchery, the elites indulged in shocking excess.

Such destructive behavior led to the utter destruction of many great families, either through debt, dissipation, or flight. Though it was considered treason punishable by death, entire families fled from the authority and domination of Rome, taking up residence in the far west or in other remote provinces so that they might avoid penalties imposed on them by the emperor and the bureaucracy. For many, and perhaps all, life had become intolerable.

In this environment, bloody civil wars broke out throughout the empire. Only radical reforms could have prevented total disintegration. The collapse of society began each time with a period of obvious moral decay that degenerated into anarchy and rebellion. Strong leaders, such as Augustus and Diocletian, would rise up at critical periods and smash the rebellious crowds with brutal efficiency, and on three occasions they were able to save the empire. But each occasion brought about a perceptible increase in despotism. By the early fourth century, freedom no longer existed anywhere in the empire.

Throughout the four and a half centuries of the Roman Empire, bloody spectacles were a common entertainment provided for the people in the great cities. These included circuses, gladiatorial events, the persecution of Christians, and other amusements, all of which attest to the fact that human life had lost its value and meaning.

Slaves were openly flogged by their masters for the slightest indiscretions, and no citizen would have thought to challenge a master's right to murder his slaves—for real or imagined offenses. One story from this period describes the rage of a ruthless master, who hired thugs to take whips and flog a disobedient slave all through the public streets and finally to kill him as an example to the crowds. When life was cheap, it was a small step from killing an unwanted child to the cold-blooded murder of another person.

Class Warfare

In the dark days of Rome's collapse, the military could no longer maintain order anywhere in the empire. Immorality among the upper classes was equaled only by the loss of restraint among the lower classes, who were little better than wild beasts by this time. The general degradation in manners, commerce, and public behavior was so pervasive that no political system could even hope to delay the coming eruption.

In earlier days the classes had been rigidly separated. Patricians were not allowed to fraternize with, let alone marry, the plebeians. By the same token, slaves and other non-Romans were always kept within strict limits, and their freedom of access was forcibly controlled. However, the lusts and corrupt appetites of influential citizens brought about changes in all these things, and by the fourth century there was a total relaxation of moral and social restraints.

Barbarians were brought to Rome first as slaves, then as gladiators, then as soldiers, and eventually as stewards and administrators of great estates. The sons of barbarians gained virtually unlimited rights and privileges. In a bizarre and eye-opening little book called *The Secret History*, which was not discovered until after his death, the historian Procopius provides shocking details of the lives and love affairs of Emperor Justinian, his wife Theodora, the great General Belisarius, and his conniving wife, Antonina.

The narrative shows how dissipation had become a national pastime. Empress Theodora was easily the most outrageous immoralist of all. The former courtesan was a vulgar libertine and a notorious adulteress who was known to be involved sexually with her manservant. This was not a casual relationship, but just one of her many affairs. But when she was taunted by members of her own class for her adultery, Theodora had the lover flogged publicly and sent away—to disappear into anonymity, says Procopius, and possibly even to his death.[12]

Catherine Edwards provides additional details of life and

manners under Justinian, revealing especially the increasing debasement of honor and virtue, and the pernicious decline of character. Entertainment grew bawdier and more bizarre. Orgies, love feasts, and erotic spectacles of many kinds became common, and every kind of vulgar display was allowed. Homosexuality and bestiality were practiced openly, even among the nobility.

In addition, musicians and native dancers were imported from Africa, Asia, and exotic lands beyond the borders of the empire to entertain and indulge the passions of the emperors and their friends. Laborers, prostitutes, circus performers, and slaves began to mingle in society as never before, and members of the elite classes boasted of their sexual exploits with slaves and peasants.

While Rome Burned

There is in history perhaps no better example of the degree to which a nation can suffer at the hands of its immoral leaders than that of Rome under Nero, who ruled in the late first century. During that dark time, there were many periods of corruption and scandal, and the ruling classes were soaked in sin and immoral extravagance. After he had plotted and conspired to kill most of his adversaries, Nero decided that he wanted to be remembered as a great artist, musician, and poet. He even shocked the people of Rome by racing his own chariot in the arena. He commanded that members of the patrician classes attend his musical evenings at which he would play various instruments and sing the songs he had composed.

The emperor had no talent in any of these things, however, and his skills were so deplorable that he finally had to resort to hiring audiences of five thousand or more to attend his concerts and cheer for him. Young men of the equestrian class, as well as crowds from the lower classes, were trained and rehearsed in applauding the emperor. Later, when Nero toured Greece, he demanded that he be allowed to participate in the Olympic games; but, of course, all first prizes had to be awarded to him.

Nero's fascination with such trivial matters incurred expense, humiliation, and a loss of focus for the empire. But the historian Suetonius writes that the most damaging aspect of the emperor's reign was his passion for building magnificent palaces and monuments. "In nothing was he so prodigal as in his buildings," says Suetonius. The estate he built for himself, which he called the Golden House, was so enormous that it contained pastures, woods, vineyards, corn fields, and an enormous lake. He had flocks of animals and even wild beasts roaming at large within the walls.

After the great fire in Rome, which most blamed on the emperor himself, Nero launched a terrifying persecution of the Christians, claiming they had set the fire that burned half the city. Then, as the ultimate demonstration of corruption, he had many of the believers dipped in pitch each night, crucified on high crosses within the palace compound, and set ablaze to provide illumination for his nightly games and entertainments.

By the time Christianity was legitimized in the West, the pagan world was spiritually impoverished, lacking any common beliefs or values that could help bring about moral or political renewal. Many people in all classes believed that the empire was doomed—for them it had already become, as they called it, "a dead world." The empire was suffering from intellectual fatigue, and the spiritual wasteland within the souls of the people reflected the barrenness of their hopes and aspirations.

The farms no longer produced adequate provisions; crafts and small industries floundered; and the engineering and architectural skills that had been the renown of the empire were lost over a period of time. The great buildings fell into disuse; the best estates were taken over by homeless people; and swimming pools and fountains were used as bathrooms and cesspools. Finally, society devolved into two classes—the rich who could not work and the poor who would not work.

Thirteen centuries after Romulus murdered his brother and proclaimed himself king of Rome, the chain of events he set in motion came to an end. His settlement in the Apennine hills had begun as a refuge for renegade slaves escaping from their harsh masters; but thirteen centuries later, the masters in Rome had become slaves, and slaves were their masters.

Lessons for Our Time

Even though Nero and the emperors and patricians of Rome may be extravagant examples of corruption, the type of dissipation they represent is different from the moral failings of our own time only in degree. Because Nero had silenced all his detractors and because he held the power of life and death over the people of his time, his avarice and corruption grew naturally beyond all bounds. But his particular sins are still with us today. Great men and women in places of great esteem are subject to precisely the same temptations. Recent events prove that fact. The lesson we can learn from Nero is that if we are to avoid the fate of the ancient empires, it is essential to recognize that society cannot simply wink at moral weakness and hope to survive. Small sins grow into big ones. And the sins that infect the leaders of a nation will soon enough infiltrate every level of society.

John Silber, president of Boston College, has suggested that the younger generation in this country desperately needs to rediscover the historic foundations of morality that made the United States the greatest empire of modern time. They need to see that moral responsibility is still a respected trait, not only in their homes and families, but in their schools, in the world around them, and in public office. There needs to be a renewed interest in the beliefs and values that make life in a modern, technologically advanced nation possible. If our moral values are not renewed, he says, then all that awaits this nation is the inevitable disintegration that has toppled empires since the beginnings of history.

"Many moral laws," writes Silber, "no less than laws of physics, are enforced by nature. With regard to lives of specific individuals and with regard to specific nations at specific times, their ends can be foretold at least in the manner of the Hebrew prophets. Occasionally lions do roar and even the deaf can hear." Corruption and immorality are never invisible. But what we must see is that these attitudes and behaviors are warnings of impending disaster.

"One could foretell that the virulence of the Third Reich would lead to war," says Silber, "as one can foretell the poverty, misery, and despair awaiting a pregnant, unmarried, drug-dependent teenager and the wretched life awaiting her unborn child. In limited situations in which issues are sufficiently specific we can know that many of our moral injunctions were discovered and preserved for the single purpose of reducing human misery and increasing the opportunities for our own well-being."[13]

This is, I believe, one of the most important lessons we can learn from the record of moral decay in the great empires. The moral and ethical traditions that derive from Christianity are not arbitrary. They are not the product of cultural or personal bias, but of the law of a loving and personal God who cares for us so much that he has told us, through the prophets and through the Holy Bible, how to live in security and good health. That way is the way of decency and moral behavior. It is the way that teaches love for God and man.

The problem in our time is that the simple truth of God's law has been corrupted by those who deny his existence and his

absolute truth. During the French Enlightenment, the encyclo-
pedist Denis Diderot said, "The first duty is to say no!" The
philosophy of the revolutionary is always one of denial. That is
why Marcuse and his lot are against culture, against the freedom
of self-determination, and against traditional morality and responsible behavior. All such attitudes are born of an ideology that
seeks to make a god of mankind and a myth of God.

That is the way of the world, and it is also the way of the
intellectual. One of the most perceptive analyses of the sources
of corruption in modern society comes from the British historian
Paul Johnson, who offers this assessment and prescription:

> *One of the principal lessons of our tragic century, which has seen
> so many millions of innocent lives sacrificed in schemes to
> improve the lot of humanity, is—beware intellectuals. Not
> merely should they be kept well away from the levers of power,
> they should also be objects of particular suspicion when they seek
> to offer collective advice. Beware committees, conferences, and
> leagues of intellectuals. Distrust public statements issued from
> their serried ranks. Discount their verdicts on political leaders
> and important events. For intellectuals, far from being highly
> individualistic and non-conformist people, follow certain regu-
> lar patterns of behaviour.*

In his brilliant review of the damage brought upon society by
ideologues such as Rousseau, Karl Marx, Bertolt Brecht, Jean-
Paul Sartre, and others, Johnson makes it clear that ideologies
without moral context are the source of despair in modern times.
Contrary to their own claims, intellectuals and idealists are the
worst sort of doctrinaire conformists. They insult and assault
tradition because they are rebels against society. They do it
because it amuses them. And, in particular, they attack morality

and Christianity, as Julian Huxley once said, because the very idea of the existence of a just God who condemns sin interferes with their sexual desires.

"Taken as a group," writes Johnson, "they are often ultra-conformist within the circles formed by those whose approval they seek and value. That is what makes them, *en masse*, so dangerous, for it enables them to create climates of opinion and prevailing orthodoxies, which themselves often generate irrational and destructive courses of action. Above all, we must at all times remember what intellectuals habitually forget: that people matter more than concepts and must come first. The worst of all despotisms is the heartless tyranny of ideas."[14]

Moral Anarchy

But sadly, while a segment of the population recognizes that continued toleration of deviance and immorality can only lead this nation to ruin, the liberal intellectuals and idealists who set the pace of the culture are leading us toward those very vices. Without the traditional restraints of plane or parachute, as one writer has expressed it, they act as if we could defy the laws of moral gravity.

"No one seems to remember," writes Jacques Ellul, "that there has never been a society without a moral code, and the chief thing lacking in our Western world is precisely an ethical code and a system of accepted values." This French philosopher and social critic says, "As soon as there is even a tiny blossoming of values, the intellectuals rise up to reject it and jeer at it. In doing so, they give no proof that they are free and intelligent, but demonstrate only that they are impotent and have surrendered to the madness in which negation becomes an end in itself."[15]

I would add that not all radical intellectualism is especially pro-Marxist or pro any particular point of view. Rather, its defining characteristic is that it is "anti-everything," and especially anti–status quo—as in the Enlightenment. Intellectuals, as the term is used here, are essentially ideological and moral anarchists who attack every orthodoxy. In their own vernacular, they are anal obsessive brats, kicking, screaming, and throwing temper tantrums against the hard-won wisdom of the world. And when they express such petulance, they do not represent courage or objectivity but the forces of darkness in the world. They speak the language of the destroyer, who sneers, "Surely not!"

As negative as such a portrait may appear, I must hasten to say that there are many people in every sector of our nation—even in government, even in the universities, even in the union-controlled public schools—who do not fit the stereotype and who stand for moral probity. There are even some Christian intellectuals. And there are many places—that may or may not subscribe to Judeo-Christian values—where good things are happening and where there is still hope. The fact that the flood of immorality is cresting and that at its current pace it may soon wash all of us away—the good, the bad, and the indifferent—does not necessarily mean that there are no allies in the crowd.

Furthermore, I very much believe that we can redeem the time. But the flood of events is coursing against us. The tide of history is not simply rising, it is at its highest point and cascading upon this nation in enormous swells and breakers. It will do no good for anyone to swim out there alone. To stand against the tide, to overcome, to change the trend, to avert disaster, we will need a movement. A movement of men, women, and children with strong convictions will help; but a movement of God would be even better.

As I think of our great need in this late hour, I am reminded of the Scripture that says, "For the eyes of the Lord search back and forth across the whole earth, looking for people whose hearts are perfect toward him, so that he can show his great power in helping them."[16] In that promise there is hope. For in Christ, our hearts are perfected and made holy, set apart for God. God can still use dedicated warriors. He used the martyrs of Rome even in their tragedy, showing through their courage and conviction the dynamic power of faith. The blood of the martyrs was the seedbed of faith, and it is doubtful the Christian church could have survived the Fall of Rome if it were not for the sacrifices made by the early saints—without the example of commitment they showed the world.

But God may have another plan for us, something quite different. And only in his power can we hold onto any hope of overcoming the sources of corruption in our midst.

There may be another Great Awakening. There may be some other great event or some terrible tragedy that will bring the nation to the point of *metanoia*—a change of heart. But be assured that until Christ himself comes again to rule and to reign, there will be resistance—from principalities, powers, and the rulers of the darkness of this age. And that will be the subject of our next chapter.

10
Decay of Religious Belief

IT WAS billed as the greatest gathering of religious and spiritual leaders in history, and men and women came from all over the world to take part. While the organizers of the World Parliament of Religions had only expected about sixteen hundred registered guests, more than six thousand actually showed up, representing several mainline Protestant denominations, along with Catholics, Jews, Baha'is, Muslims, Hindus, Buddhists, Sikhs, Zoroastrians, Jains, and Wiccan witches, plus other religions.

The event was surrounded by controversy from the beginning, not only because of the absence of evangelicals, but because of the loud confrontations that erupted on several occasions. At one point

Chicago police had to be called in to quell disturbances between Muslim factions. Louis Farrakkan, leader of the militant African-American Nation of Islam, addressed the assembly, as did the Dalai Lama (the exiled leader of Tibet and a prominent Buddhist spokesman) and Cardinal Joseph Bernardin, the archbishop of Chicago. Charles Colson came on the evening of September 2, 1993, to receive the Templeton Award for progress in religion, which included a million-dollar prize. This also stirred controversy.

For days the secular media applauded the Chicago meeting and called it a first step toward tolerance and cooperation in religion. However, when one group of ecumenicists attempted to proclaim, "We are all one. We worship the same God," Buddhists protested loudly. "We reject that statement," they said. "We have no concept of God in our religion." Despite this disagreement, a special convocation met at Chicago's Grant Park for the reading of a Declaration of Global Ethics that proclaimed the solidarity of those in attendance to the human values shared by all the world's great religions.

A New Syncretism

Solidarity, globalism, and unity were also themes expressed just two months later when more than two thousand women delegates from half a dozen mainline denominations met in Minneapolis for a conference called "RE-Imagining," aimed at formulating a broader role for women in the Christian church. According to published reports, conferees prayed to the goddess Sophia, the ancient goddess of wisdom, proclaiming Sophia is the tree of life to those who lay hold of her.

The women celebrated Communion as an invitation to the banquet table of creation. Their sessions included chants that employed explicit sexual imagery honoring Sophia and acknowledged that they were "women in [her] image."[1]

Among cosponsors of the event were the World Council of Churches (WCC), the Women's Division of the United Methodist Church, Church Women United, International Fellowship of the Least Coin, and various denominations whose funds were especially designated for the creation of a theology of women. On learning of the group's activities, however, several churches were upset. Some 185 Presbyterian congregations vowed to withhold support from the Presbyterian Church U.S.A. (PCUSA) until some kind of disclaimer or condemnation of the conference was published.

Unmoved by the threats, the PCUSA headquarters in Louisville, Kentucky, refused to make even a token response. The denomination stands to lose approximately $2 million in support, as well as members. Already the mainstream body has lost nearly 4 million members over the past twelve years, due primarily to its controversial positions on ecumenical and liberal theological issues. Even so, Presbyterian leaders won't budge from their position.

But problems of concern are surfacing in other places as well. An article by Joseph A. Harriss of the Paris bureau of *Reader's Digest* reports that evidence discovered in KGB files in Moscow after the collapse of the Soviet Union indicates that the WCC has been infiltrated with Communist operatives for more than thirty years. KGB communiqués dating back to the 1960s describe the systematic infiltration of all levels of the WCC and the reshaping of its policies away from traditional Christian theology toward political causes designed to undercut Western democracy.

But despite the exposure of these activities, along with detailed information giving code names and identities of many operatives still working in the organization, the WCC defends its policies and continues to support organizations such as the African National Congress, which has funneled money to the South

African Communist Party, and the Patriotic Front in Zimbabwe, which has murdered at least two hundred whites and seventeen hundred blacks, as well as nine missionary families. It also supports a program called the Special Fund to Combat Racism, whose recipients are kept strictly secret.

What kind of theology comes out of such an organization? As just one example, the first official event·at the meeting of the WCC General Assembly in Canberra, Australia, was a pagan purification ritual in which delegates walked through the smoke of burning leaves while insect noises were played on loudspeakers. Aborigines in loincloths danced in circles around the group, while the Reverend Chung Hyun Kyung called on the spirits of the dead. In his remarks, the South Korean minister called for attendees to read the Bible from the perspective of "birds, water, air, trees," and to think "like a mountain." Afterward, one disappointed delegate protested, "Pagan culture has infiltrated the WCC." An Anglican minister of Indian origin said, "I left that behind to become a Christian."[2]

The Holistic Approach

While Protestant churches, councils, and conferences are warring over the fundamental principles of Christian doctrine, and while the pope continues to battle liberals in the Catholic Church over a wide range of issues, New Age beliefs are making a comeback in mainstream America. Perceiving the lack of direction in the church, thousands of men and women of all social backgrounds are reportedly turning to "the wisdom of the East" for spiritual nourishment.

In mid-1994, three new books on the teachings of the Chinese philosopher Lao Tzu, who lived twenty-five centuries ago (when Athens and Carthage were at their height), were topping the best-seller lists in many bookstores around the country. In addition, classes in martial arts, conditioning exercises, and meditation techniques based on ancient metaphysical teachings are becoming popular in clubs and spas from coast to coast.

An assistant professor of Chinese at Washington University in St. Louis told *USA Today,* "It's all part of the new age movement. It was introduced in the '50s and '60s with the hippies and the beat movement and now it's becoming 'yuppified.'"[3] Teachings on tai chi chuan and Taoism offer a holistic approach to everything from health and psychology to business ethics and political activism. Why this sudden upsurge in interest? According to the writer, the spiritual and physical balance taught by such disciplines appeals to those of the aging baby boom generation, who are still looking for some kind of meaning in their lives.

"A lot of people today are more spiritual," says a tai chi instructor in Arizona. "It's the era. We're changing. We've been materialistic, and now we're trying to compromise, to become more spiritual, too."[4]

For the Jesus Seminar that meets twice annually, the task is a critical examination of the reality of Jesus of Nazareth through textual criticism of the Gospels. Little by little and piece by piece, this group of liberal theologians is pruning the Gospels and reporting that Jesus never said most of the things recorded in the New Testament. The scholars have appointed themselves the task of showing that Christ never did the miraculous feats recorded in the Scriptures, never made any claims of divinity, never intended to found a religion, and died essentially a failure, leaving behind a confused, hypocritical, and error-filled church.

Though they do not say it in so many words, these "scholars" take the position that the disciples and apostles who wrote the books of the New Testament were dissemblers and deceivers who fabricated and extrapolated to create a religion of their own invention. They fleshed out the stories of Jesus and embellished historical accounts to suit their own fantasies. The gospel first delivered to the saints was, in reality, merely a conspiracy by fallible men.

To set the record straight, the members of the Jesus Seminar recently published their own much-revised edition of the Gospels, to which they have added the Gospel of Thomas. This apocryphal work, little known and uniformly discredited by most traditional scholars, is clearly incompatible in tone and content to the books in the New Testament canon.

The critics fail to explain how a fraud undertaken by a couple of dozen Palestinian rustics could have transformed the world and risen to the very center of ethical, moral, and philosophical debate over the past two thousand years. Nor do they explain how it is that Jesus Christ still works in the lives of men and women today. The tragedy for many believers is that, by their skepticism and their claims to scholarship and authority, this group has made a mockery of Christ and his words.

Most who know Jesus as Savior and Messiah will disregard the words of the Jesus Seminar. But thousands, perhaps even millions, may be denied the promise of salvation through Jesus Christ because of the words of these scholars.

A Theology of Oppression

The loss of faith and religious values in a nation is itself a form of idolatry. When we take down the image of God, we lift up the idol of man. From the reality of revealed truth, societies and their leaders sometimes attempt to substitute temporal values based on political expediency and personal ambitions. Suddenly, man takes the place of God, and traditional beliefs are adapted to make room for a new theology. This was the exact process that took place in Egypt at the end of the first millennium B.C., in

Greece in the fourth century B.C., in Rome in the second century A.D., in the Renaissance with the birth of new humanism, and in the French Enlightenment.

The sudden renewal of New Age cults in our own time, along with radical syncretism and the attempts to rewrite the Bible, is a portent of America's loss of faith. In spite of the protests of today's antagonistic secular society, men and women cannot live by bread alone. We are spiritual beings, and there is hunger in the human soul that demands something beyond the here and now—a reality beyond the merely physical life of the body.

Even during the height of Communist atheism, the bureaucratic leaders of the Soviet Union understood something about these longings of the soul. They were determined to control every aspect of human thought and action. They regulated the affairs of people in all classes and professions. They controlled industry and agriculture, and even established the prices of goods. But that was not enough for them.

Along with all the other discoveries of the past three years, we now know more about the "cult of praise" that surrounded the diabolical leader Joseph Stalin. Stalin's orders were given the importance of papal edicts. Even his offhand remarks were taken as law and enforced by the secret police. In the days of Marx and Lenin, the Soviet regime had a certain ecclesiastical character. Portraits and busts of these leaders were everywhere, and outright veneration of both men as saints was encouraged. As in ancient Rome, the ruler was a god, and the Soviet people were his worshipful subjects.

It is apparent now that the Soviet Union was atheistic in name only. The Christian church in Russia dates back to the ninth century, and a sense of religious devotion was long established in the people. How would the Marxists deal with this fact? When the German philosopher Ludwig Feuerbach published his treatise *The Essence of Christianity,* claiming that God was merely a human invention, Marx took it as validation of his own views. Feuerbach's assertion that the Christian God was merely an expression of the inherent good and evil in human nature fit in perfectly with Bolshevik principles.

Feuerbach said that man created God in his own image and that the idea of a great and powerful being who controls human destiny is absurd. Belief in God, he said, has created grief and suffering for centuries by separating mankind from his own innate spirituality and divinity. The idea of a Supreme Being with greater authority than ourselves reduces mankind to intellectual poverty, placing us in the grasp of a powerful church and governments that exploit humanity in the name of religion.

Marx said that man is a "species being," by which he meant that man's purpose is to "advance his kind." Traditional religion and economic policies bring out the worst aspects of human behavior, he said. Private wealth allows men to become greedy and self-serving. So property must be returned to the state so that human behavior can return to its natural purpose of serving our fellowman.

In a work written shortly before publication of the *Communist Manifesto,* Marx called for the elimination of private property, the creation of a new proletariat of workers led by a cadre of handpicked leaders, and the abolition of religion. The Marxists were critical of religion in general, but they especially detested Christianity. Christianity taught people to esteem personal freedom, moral responsibility, and a higher allegiance that would have threatened the "dictatorship of the proletariat" prescribed by Marx and Engels.

Therefore, the purges of religion were carried out in the name of the people. Millions of Christians were massacred by the Red Army. Much the same thing happened under Adolf Hitler in the

Nazi purges of the 1930s and 1940s. The SS, under Heinrich Himmler, consigned thousands of evangelical Christians to the ovens along with Jews, Slavs, Gypsies, and other "undesirables."

The Things of God

Aleksandr Solzhenitsyn, who recently returned to his native Russia to try to serve as a spokesman for morality and Christian values, once described his experiences as a child when the Bolshevik Revolution was still going on. At that time, he says, millions of Russians were being slaughtered. The streets ran red with blood, and anyone who disagreed with the ideals of the Revolution was either persecuted, reformed, or killed. At one point, the writer overheard two old peasants talking about what was going on, and their words stuck with him. He didn't grasp their meaning at first, but years later he knew what they meant.

"It is because we have forgotten God. That is why all this is happening to us," they said. "We have forgotten God!" In spite of his advanced education and his experiences both as a writer and a dissident—which led to his being sentenced to eight years in a prison camp for "reindoctrination"—Solzhenitsyn has said that he will never forget the wisdom of those simple peasants. When men turned their back on heaven in search of alien gods, they unleashed darkness and damnation upon the earth.

But surely we must see that a lot of the terror, violence, and self-destruction of our age is taking place because we are making the same mistakes. What is the separation of church and state but the proscription of God. And what are the nostrums of "diversity" and "tolerance" and "change" but a rejection of the Christian principles upon which this nation was founded. The crises of our age have come precisely because we have forgotten God and turned—like the Greeks, the Romans, the new intellectuals of the French Enlightenment, the people of Nazi Germany, and the Soviets—to an alien god of our own creation.

The recompense for our self-serving alienation takes many forms. We all recognize the social price being paid by society. But there is more. There are storms of many kinds that can only be seen as warnings to our age. The earthquakes that struck Northridge, California, and other communities on the northern edge of Los Angeles in early 1994 caught everyone by surprise. Emergency-planning officials claimed they were prepared for any emergency, but they were not ready for this one. The fault that blasted the San Fernando Valley on the morning of January 17 did not exist according to the best geological charts. It was beyond the realm of science, but it happened nevertheless.

Houses slid off their foundations, buildings collapsed and burned, and in some of the images that flashed across our television screens it was clear that the only things left standing in many places near the epicenter were the trees. What an awesome symbol. When the things of man collapse, only the things of God remain. Watching the events on television news, I was struck by the fact that the epicenter of the blast, in Northridge, Chatsworth, and Canoga Park, was an area where some seventy studios, suppliers, and distributors of pornography were housed. Every one of those businesses was seriously damaged, and the headquarters of the largest, VCA Pictures, was totally demolished. One insider took a look at the aftermath and told reporters, "It's put the fear of God in them. I'm telling you, it's enough to give you an attack of religion."

The Other America

The deterioration of moral, economic, and religious vitality in contemporary culture has been a slow and withering process. It would be hard to pinpoint a precise starting point, but the 1920s is a good rough estimate. The real atrophy, however, began in the 1960s and has been gathering momentum for the past thirty years.

It is clear today that there are forces of darkness in the world. We live with constant fear, and the implications of our national apostasy are dire and undeniable. Many people, especially under the age of thirty, do not believe that the world was ever a better place. But there are still some who remember what it was like before things began to change. While browsing my local newspaper, I happened across a letter from one of them published by Ann Landers in her syndicated column. The writer referred to a previous column in which Ms. Landers had expressed doubt that anyone would want to go back to "the good old days," and especially to the Depression era, regardless how good our memories may be.

"Well, you're wrong," said the letter writer. "I would." Then she went on to explain. "Money was scarce, and times were hard, but when things got tough, we did without and cut back on our lifestyle. We didn't look to government to make up the difference. People with food stamps weren't buying junk food or trading them for cash to buy cigarettes and beer. Churches administered help to those in need, and the homeless were taken care of by relatives.

"Schoolchildren," she continued, "learned because it was expected of them. They didn't have their education sugar-coated or made fun. Teachers were respected, not insulted and beaten up. The courses were geared to life. I mean reading and writing and arithmetic, not entertainment. You didn't worry that kids in your child's school might turn up with a handgun or a knife or cocaine.

"If you couldn't afford medical treatment," she said, "there were county hospitals. Many fine doctors learned a lot about patient care in those places. Men took off their hats when the flag passed by, and children were taught to stand at attention. Everybody knew all the words to the national anthem and 'America the Beautiful.'"

The writer also remembers, "The Sabbath was for church and other religious observances, not for football on TV or 'getting away from it all.' Holidays were observed on the day the event occurred and not moved around to give people a three-day weekend." And the letter concludes with this important assessment: "The big difference is that most people aren't as honest or as noble or as hard-working as they used to be, and that bothers me. I'm afraid it's going to get worse before it gets better." The letter was signed "A relic in Washington."[5]

What has happened to America is that we have forgotten God. When faith no longer informs our actions and gives direction to the hopes and dreams of the nation, things fall apart. This is the lesson we must learn. This is also the principal crisis that we must remedy.

In a Heritage Foundation address in the summer of 1992, Russell Kirk struck a similar chord with his concluding remarks: "Fundamentally, our society's affliction is the decay of religious belief. If a culture is to survive and flourish, it must not be severed from the religious vision out of which it arose. The high necessity of reflective men and women, then, is to labor for the restoration of religious teachings as a credible body of doctrine."

11

Devaluing of Human Life

JANET Adkins was the first. The fifty-four-year-old Portland woman was struggling with Alzheimer's disease when Dr. Jack Kevorkian rigged up a "suicide machine" to help take her out of her misery. Murder charges were filed, but on December 13, 1990, a Michigan judge dismissed the case, claiming that state laws do not prohibit assisted suicide. But the problem did not stop there.

In 1991, Sherry Miller, age forty-three, called on Kevorkian to end her battle with multiple sclerosis; and Marjorie Wantz, age fifty-eight, took the same option due to severe pelvic pain. A few months later, in 1992, Kevorkian participated in the suicides of

Susan Williams, Lois F. Hawes, Catherine A. Andreyev, Marguerite Tate, and Marcella Lawrence. In response to the growing number of lawsuits, court challenges, and injunctions placed against the physician, now known as Dr. Death, the governor of Michigan signed a temporary ban on assisted suicides.

But by January 1993, Kevorkian was back to work. Jack Elmer Miller was the first, followed by Stanley Ball, Mary Biernat, Elaine Goldbaum, Hugh Gale, Jonathon Grenz, and Martha Ruwart. These were just the spring collection. After the death of cancer patient Ron Mansur on May 16, a Michigan judge lifted the governor's ban on assisted suicides and ruled that all such restrictions were unconstitutional. But in June the Michigan Court of Appeals ordered that the ban remain while the justices considered the case.

In late summer, on August 2, 1993, Dr. Death added to his growing list of clients Thomas Hyde, a thirty year old from Novi, Michigan, who was suffering from Lou Gehrig's disease. And two weeks later Kevorkian was charged by the state's prosecutor with assisting in Hyde's suicide. But the doctor was undeterred. He helped dispatch Donald O'Keefe in September, Merian Frederick in October, and Dr. Ali Khalili in November. In December a judge dismissed charges against Kevorkian in O'Keefe's death and declared any ban on the suicide doctor's activities unconstitutional.

Finally, in early 1994, judges dismissed the state's charges against Kevorkian in the deaths of Khalili and Frederick, and on May 2, 1994, Kevorkian was acquitted by a Michigan jury of all charges in the death of Thomas Hyde. Before the television cameras, the physician and his attorney said they had driven a stake through the heart of the opposition. From this point, not only would Kevorkian be absolved of the murders of twenty people, but he would be free to continue his practice, dealing death without restriction. And doctors all over America would now be free to begin assisting their patients to take their own lives.

Birth of the Death Industry

Within hours of the jury's verdict in the Hyde case, Derek Humphry, founder and former head of the Hemlock Society and author of the 1993 best-seller *Final Exit*, announced that his organization, ERGO, was releasing a new set of "Safeguards and Guidelines for Physician-Assisted Suicide." Humphry's books and articles offer justification for suicide along with detailed instructions on how to carry it off, with or without help.

From now on, he told the media, ERGO would be working with lawyers, physicians, mental-health professionals, and patients' rights advocates to provide criteria for assisting people in taking their own lives. "Dr. Kevorkian's welcome acquittal in a Michigan court and the upcoming citizens' initiative election in Oregon in November," said Humphry, "make these safeguards essential."[1] Then the author handed out a list of ten tips for physicians and others who want to get involved. Jack Kevorkian and the courts of Michigan had set a new precedent, and Derek Humphry, of all people, was there to offer ethical standards for the death industry.

But the death industry goes back much, much further than that. One fatal stop on the way was the decision of the United States Supreme Court in 1973 that legalized abortion on demand. Since Norma McCorvey won her suit against District Attorney Henry Wade and the courts of Dallas County, Texas, in the case now known as *Roe v. Wade*, 30 million unborn babies have been killed by abortions in this nation.

Today more than 30 percent of all pregnancies end in abortion, and a growing number of women are now having their second, third, and fourth abortions. According to Dr. Richard Glasow of the National Right to Life Committee in Washington, D.C., "The steadily increasing repeat rate and the continued enormous annual number of abortions indicate that increasingly abortion is being used as a method of birth control."[2]

A Legacy of Despair

It is not an easy number to recite—31,460,374 legal abortions between January 1, 1973, and January 1, 1994. Today the average is more than 1.6 million abortions per year, 4,383 abortions per day, 182 abortions per hour, and 3 abortions per minute, every day of the year. Every 20 seconds an unborn child is murdered in the womb of its mother.

When Mother Teresa of Calcutta spoke at the National Prayer Breakfast in Washington, D.C., on February 3, 1994, she addressed a distinguished crowd of civic, political, and religious leaders, among whom was the president of the United States and the First Lady. She spoke about peace and love and the importance of prayer, but she also addressed some of the fundamental problems in this nation today.

"I feel that the greatest destroyer of peace today is abortion," she said, "because it is a war against the child, a direct killing of the innocent child, murder by the mother herself. And if we accept that a mother can kill even her own child, how can we tell other people not to kill one another?" Jesus gave his own life for us, she told her audience. We must also be willing to love until it hurts. "So, the mother who is thinking of abortion should be helped to love, that is, to give until it hurts her plans, or her free time, to respect the life of her child. The father of that child . . . must also give until it hurts."

Although her remarks were destined to be almost completely ignored by the national news media, the aging sister of mercy tried to offer a compassionate Christian perspective on this deeply divisive issue. "By abortion," she said, "the mother does not learn to love, but kills even her own child to solve her problems. And, by abortion, the father is told that he does not have to take any responsibility at all for the child that he has brought into the world. That father is likely to put other women into the same trouble. So abortion just leads to more abortion." And then she said, "Any country that accepts abortion is not teaching its people to love, but to use any violence to get what they want. This is why the greatest destroyer of peace and love is abortion."

Later in her remarks, she said, "The child is God's gift to the family. Each child is created in the image and likeness of God for greater things—to love and be loved." And then in her most passionate plea Mother Teresa said, "Please don't kill the child. I want the child. Please give me the child. I am willing to accept any child who would be aborted and to give that child to a married couple who will love the child and be loved by the child." She said the children's home in Calcutta, India, had already saved three thousand children from abortion.

The secular media ignored her remarks; they weren't politically correct. The women's movement ignored the remarks because they denied a woman's right to control her own body. The reigning politically elite ignored Mother Teresa's words of truth just as they have ignored the words of Elizabeth Cady Stanton, an early heroine of the women's movement, who said, "It is degrading to women that we should treat our children as property to be disposed of as we see fit." Another heroine of the women's movement, Susan B. Anthony, said, "I deplore the horrible crime of child murder. . . . No matter what the motive, love of ease, or a desire to save from suffering the unborn innocent, the woman is awfully guilty who commits the deed."

Life without Love

As tortured as the debate regarding abortion and euthanasia has become over the past two decades, these are by no means the only problems that should concern us. These are not the only issues that influence our attitudes and behavior. Loss of respect for human life does not begin or end with abortion; rather, the sanctity of life involves every aspect of our lives. The love of a mother for her child, the love of a husband for his wife, and the way members of society regard one another all declare our feelings about the value of life.

Beginning with the rise of relativistic thinking in the 1960s, a large segment of the American culture apparently decided they could trade responsibility and genuine commitment for sensual self-indulgence and self-gratification. Church and state, marriage and family, and many of our most sacred traditional values came under attack. The moral underpinnings of society were discarded in the name of personal freedom and self-actualization. But contrary to the promises of society's liberators, life did not become better for many people. Instead, it became even more meaningless and empty. And patterns of sociology were set in motion then that have subsequently robbed many people's lives of meaning and purpose.

The consequences of the self-serving decisions of the young and restless today have brought about the disasters of AIDS, venereal disease, unwanted pregnancy, illegitimacy, multiple abortions, abuse, death, violent crime, and much of the deep emotional turmoil that is the natural result of profligate living. The entire record of human history confirms that despair and disaster are the natural consequences of irresponsible self-indulgence. Immorality and hedonism contribute to the death of nations; yet a number of Americans want to ignore that dark reality.

Sex in marriage was meant to be a private and protected relationship centered on a lifetime commitment of love. The sixties, however, and the culture of "freedom at any cost" separated sex from marriage. Marriage was unnecessary and love became lust. Commitment was only as enduring as passion would allow; and generations of young women who would give anything for real love sacrificed virtue for passion. Looking for love in all the wrong places, they began settling for tawdry flirtations and barroom romances, which could only leave them broken and in despair.

Many young women today, deprived of their spiritual moorings and traditional values, throw themselves into careers and casual sex, and spend their lifetimes alone. Feminism preys on the weak and lonely ones, telling them they are victims of society and of men. They no longer recognize that it is the corrupt values and their own poor choices that have brought them despair. And the number of teenagers being sucked into this destructive pathology has reached epidemic proportions. Each day in America, 2,795 teenage girls get pregnant. That is a 500 percent increase since 1966. Each day in America 1,106 teenage girls have abortions, which is an 1,100 percent increase since 1966. And some 4,219 teenagers contract a sexually transmitted disease—an increase of 335 percent since 1966.

A statement from the Children's Defense Fund (CDF), reported in the 1994 edition of the *Index of Leading Cultural Indicators,* says that every sixty-four seconds a baby is born to a teenage mother in this country. "Five minutes later, a baby will have been born to a teenager who already has a child. Ten hours later, by the time this person perhaps returns home from work, more than 560 babies will have been born to teenagers in America. Adolescent pregnancy, which for too many young people begins or perpetuates a cycle of poverty, remains a crisis in America."

The Sanctity of Family

As the sanctity of life fades into oblivion in this nation, attachments that were once the foundation of culture are disappearing. Marriage is no longer a secure bond. For many, marriage is just a way of expressing affection that has no lasting significance. Marriage vows are not meant to be binding oaths before the God of Creation who ordained the sacred rite of marriage. Rather, couples make up their own vows using song lyrics, poems, and even gag lines to suit the whims of the moment. And that's about how long many of these marriages last—a moment. Vows are easily broken when the thrill fades away.

Half of all first and second marriages in America end in divorce. The idea of three, four, and five marriages—once a sure sign of debauchery reserved for movie stars and celebrities—is becoming common in suburbia. Living together has become the lifestyle of choice for the majority of young couples today, despite all the evidence that shows that couples who cohabit are less likely to stay together than those who choose marriage.

Perhaps the saddest statistic of divorce, and one that is often overlooked, is that nearly 60 percent of all first and second divorces involve children under the age of eighteen. Each year more than a million children become the innocent victims of divorce. Lawyers and counselors once suggested that the effects of divorce on children were about as serious as the common cold. But now they know that is not the case. Myron Magnet writes:

> *Contrary to the longstanding received opinion that children recover quickly from divorce and flourish in families of almost any shape, these changes have harrowed and damaged kids. Though of course many single-parent families work very well, lovingly nurturing children fully capable of happiness and success—and though everyone knows intact families that exemplify Franz*

Kafka's dictum that the middle-class family is the closest thing to hell on earth—in general, children from single-parent families have more trouble than children from two-parent families.[3]

Study after study shows that children in single-parent homes are more likely to suffer from poverty than kids from two-parent families. Single-parent households have less than one-third the median per capita income of two-parent households; and half of these are well below the poverty line. But as Myron Magnet also reports, "Growing up in a single-parent family puts its mark not just on a child's external economic circumstances but on his or her innermost psyche as well."

A nationwide study for the National Center for Health Statistics showed that children from single-parent homes were 200 percent more likely than children from two-parent homes to have emotional and behavioral problems. And fully 80 percent of all adolescents hospitalized for psychiatric and emotional problems come from single-parent homes.

Further Complications

At one time, specialists believed that the problems for children of divorce would be solved when the parents remarry, but the evidence shows that children with stepparents fare no better than those from single-parent homes. In fact, in many cases, stepfamilies suffer even greater trauma than single-parent families. In her analysis of troubled families, Barbara Dafoe Whitehead referred to the studies of Dr. Nicholas Zill, who found that "stepfamilies disrupt established loyalties, create new uncertainties, provoke deep anxieties, and sometimes threaten a child's physical safety as well as emotional security."[4] New relationships bring out intense anger, jealousy, and bitterness. Children are seldom prepared for such emotions.

219

This does not mean, of course, that remarriage is not a good idea or that a stepfamily cannot succeed in our society. There are many examples where combined or blended families are doing very well; there is plenty of evidence to show that stepfathers and stepmothers do make life better for children of divorce. But there is simply no substitute for keeping the integrity of the original, bonded relationship of a father, mother, and children. Ironically, the furor over Dan Quayle's controversy with TV's Murphy Brown has done more to reinforce this view than anything in recent times. But the simple fact is that there is no substitute for an intact and properly functioning family for the well-being of adults and children alike.

Because of the prevalence of divorce and the breakup of the family, pathologies have been released upon American society that we had not experienced in this nation until recently. And thanks to the growth of the "working mom" phenomenon, along with the growth of day care and children left unattended for part of the day, masses of young people are neglected and placed at great risk by their parents. Over the protests of working mothers, it is clear that such children are not receiving the love and the devoted attention they require by nature. Violence, sexual abuse, promiscuity, and many others problems grow out of this situation.

Today we have a generation of children growing up "unbonded." This is a relatively new form of disturbance, but it describes the phenomenon in which children grow up with no sense of relationship or responsibility to other people. They have no allegiance to parents, no loyalty to friends, no concept of right or wrong, and they become social misfits and ultimately a menace to society. Unbonded children have never had their share of love. They have never been the focus of affection and adulation with their mothers and fathers. They grow up in "warehouses for kids" while their parents are somewhere else, trying to keep up a "lifestyle."

And, in turn, these are the kids who turn to tobacco and alcohol at an early age. They are the teenagers who turn to drugs and heavy-metal music and easy sex. They are the young people who find guns and violence stimulating. They are the targets of gangs, cults, and others who prey on the young. They are easy targets for exploitation, from sexual abuse to drug addiction and street crime. Corruption of the young is one of the most shocking results of the lifestyle choices of parents today.

Children who grow up without bonding to a mother, a father, or at least one other human being will have no respect for authority. They demonstrate their anger and aggression in school. They are the kids who are always in trouble. When teachers try to make them behave, they lash out in anger. They have no attention span, frequently no verbal skills, and no desire to communicate. They believe that life is about exploitation and abuse, and they quickly learn how to get what they want by intimidation.

Unbonded children don't trust their teachers any more than they trust their mothers. They do not trust employers, managers, the police, or any other type of authority. And if they should happen to get married, their marriages almost always end in tragedy. At one time there were a few of these people in every society, people who grew up in very disturbed backgrounds. Today, however, the pathologies in average American homes, along with the manifest abuse inherent in the nationwide day-care system, have escalated this phenomenon beyond imagination. No community in America is untouched by its effects.

Juvenile gangs in almost every American city today are a direct expression of this problem. An enormous percentage of our young people are growing up emotionally disturbed because they have decided that life is cruel and meaningless. Life has no value for them, so they recite the old line, "Live fast, love hard, and die young!" But sadly, there are no beautiful memories for these young people. For them, life has lost its value and meaning.

Twilight of the Gods

A few years ago, CDF statistics reported that approximately 135,000 children bring guns to school each day. Ten children die of gunshot each day, and six teenagers commit suicide each day: That is a 300 percent increase since 1966. There has been a great increase in metal detectors and police guards in our schools, but the problems don't end there. The typical suicide death in this country is no longer an older male, depressed about finances or other personal problems. Today the most likely victim of suicide is a teenager who has decided life is not worth living.

The changes in the American culture are dangerous, and they affect every aspect of life—not just in the schools but in our homes, workplaces, and public places. The Bible teaches that all life is sacred, but that lesson is hardly considered anymore. Theologian Carl Henry has said that we are living in "the twilight of a great civilization." In addition to the wholesale murder of the unborn, we are witnessing violence and insurrection in our city streets, warfare in the churches and schools, and even cosmic disturbances in the world around us. There seems to be a revolution of all the seen and unseen forces of nature. We are confronted daily by evidence of the deepest cultural decline in modern history. Every day the world grows ever more dangerous. Every day we discover new monsters in the basement.

A storm of controversy broke out in early 1994 when it was discovered that nuclear researchers had used "human guinea pigs" for radiation experiments. With the approval of fetal tissue research, medical experiments are now using the vital organs of preborn infants that only hours earlier were declared nonhuman blobs of tissue. The life inside the womb is not human; but once outside the womb, it becomes a source of living human organs. What are the moral and scientific consequences of harvesting unborn babies for the sake of science? And what must such a process do to the human soul?

In some places flesh and viscera of aborted children are already being used to make collagen creams and ointments to retard facial wrinkling. And researchers in England known as "womb robbers" have said they are prepared to extract eggs from aborted female fetuses to implant into the wombs of women who have no eggs of their own. That plan was stopped by an act of Parliament, but we have to wonder what monsters such an immoral misuse of science would create. For the first time in history we would have children born to mothers who have never been born. Surely the sorcerer's apprentice has gone mad.

Moral Object Lessons

In the latter days of the Roman Empire, we can see a similar disregard for human life. When burdensome regulations and taxes made manufacturing, trade, and even common labor unprofitable, individuals were locked into hereditary trades and vocations for life, and their sons and daughters could have no vocational mobility at all. Eventually children came to be seen as a needless burden; so infanticide, which was forbidden by penalty of death in the glory days of Rome, suddenly became a convenient expedient. Abortion, strangulation of infants, and exposure to the elements were widespread practices in the closing centuries of the empire. In some cases, children were sold into slavery or prostitution. But almost no one could afford the luxury of bearing and raising children any longer. No one wanted the additional responsibility of caring for the young when life was so tenuous and pointless.

This was only one manifestation of the Roman devaluing of human life. Eusebius, the Christian historian who wrote during the fourth century, says that on some days Emperor Diocletian ordered as many as a hundred men, women, and little children slaughtered in the arena, and he adds, "There was not one filthy, dissolute act of which he was innocent."[5] In *The Roman Way*, Edith Hamilton describes the terrors that drew the crowds:

> *How savage the Roman nature was which the Roman law controlled is seen written large in Rome's favorite amusements, too familiar to need more than a cursory mention: wild beast hunts—so-called, the hunting place was the arena; naval battles for which the circus was flooded by means of hidden canals; and, most usual and best loved by the people, the gladiators, when the great amphitheatre was packed close tier upon tier, all Rome there to see human beings by the tens and hundreds killing each other, to give the victor in a contest the signal for death and eagerly watch the upraised dagger plunge into the helpless body and the blood spurt forth.*[6]

Hamilton then adds that the citizens of Rome, at all levels, seemed to require these awful spectacles to purge some dark menace within their nature. She says, "That was Rome's dearest delight and her unique contribution to the sport of the world. . . . Everywhere else Rome went the bloody games followed, and all the time they grew more bloody and more extravagant. . . . Of how many human beings met their death in these ways no estimate at all can be made." The spectacle of the circuses was not a redemptive experience for the crowds in the latter days of the empire; and the wanton destruction of human life wounded something in the spirit of the Romans.

As rivers of blood flowed over a period of decades and even

centuries, the people began to see what terrible butchery they were capable of carrying out. Some, perhaps only a few, were horrified by the depths to which they had sunk to satisfy their terrible desires. In time, their spirits grew weak, and their vitality was wounded by the experience.

Where Will It End?

Doctors in our county hospitals today are worried about the epidemic of violence in America. What they have found is that only a fraction of the real violence is ever reported. Thousands of shootings, stabbings, and beatings go unreported. Tribes of wild savages roam the streets day and night just looking for someone to hurt. Life has lost its value in much of the nation, and the prognosis is not good. The emergency-room staff at Boston City Hospital have estimated that they save seven wounded teens for every one that dies. The lucky ones, according to one physician, spend the rest of their lives paralyzed or carrying around colostomy bags.

Are we becoming desensitized to the suffering around us? Do we still find these things shocking? And does anyone still believe that government social programs will provide the way back to sanity? In Dartmouth, Massachusetts, two sixteen-year-olds and a fifteen-year-old burst into a classroom and murdered another youth in front of a high school class. When their sixteen-year-old victim fell dead, the attackers laughed and gave each other high fives. There was no remorse, no guilt, and no fear.

In some places outlaws like these are considered heroes. They are the heroes and role models for a new class of urban guerrillas growing up all around us. At about the same time this incident took place, two teenage boys in Pasadena, California, murdered three girls in a posh suburban home—to settle an argument.

Later, the boys told police they couldn't even remember what the argument was about.

Black, white; rich, poor; male, female; there is no apparent difference anymore. Forty years after the *Brown v. Board of Education* decision, which kicked off the civil rights movement, we have indeed achieved equality in America: the equality of the total self-destruction of a culture. Thirty years after the Supreme Court's decision in *Roe v. Wade,* the life of the unborn child has no meaning and no value to the majority of Americans. In a survey conducted in 1994 by the Republican Party, abortion was ranked dead last among the issues listed by voters as matters of concern. Mothers kill their young, parents leave their young for others to raise, and the nation is shocked when its children turn to violence, rage, and murder to solve their problems. For the young, life has lost its value.

But the cheapening of human life does not start with mass murder. It does not begin with gang violence and drive-by shootings. The cheapening of human life begins when a society loses respect for the cultural and moral foundations that give life meaning.

CONCLUSION

12

The Enduring Challenge

AFTER exploring some of the parallels between the ancient civilizations and our own, what conclusions can we draw about our prospects for the future?

We have seen that societies in decline undergo a number of critical changes and they endure many emotional struggles involving basic beliefs and practices. Nations that are dying are plagued by lawlessness and economic insolvency. We observed how governments begin to prey on the citizens through increased taxation and bureaucratic regulations, and we saw that the growth of bureaucracy is a sign of a disordered society. Education fails, historic cultural foundations are weakened, and important traditions are discarded. Then, along with a rise in materialism and self-centeredness, there is a rapid increase in immorality and a general loss of respect for human life. And along with the loss of traditional values, the decay of religious belief is a clear indication of greater troubles yet to come.

When the quality of life begins to deteriorate and when peace and order become impossible to maintain, these nations enter a period of self-indulgence, exploitation, and political opportunism, which leads inevitably to chaos and anarchy. Nations thus weakened frequently become victims of barbarians, both from inside and outside their own borders; and some kind of final humiliation generally comes through war, invasion, or plunder of their national treasures.

In these days of the new world order, we seem to be approaching just such a time of cultural dysfunction. The signs of decay are already quite clear. The federal government, the United Nations, and the empire builders of the world tell us they are searching for a "new paradigm" for society. The White House has called for a new "politics of meaning." And with no apparent grasp of the consequences of their words, some of our leaders are saying they want to "redefine what it means to be Americans in this century."

The whole world can see that the United States is going through a time of troubles. We see it in the headlines and on the evening news. While the White House and Congress experiment with domestic policy and institutional reforms, and while the State Department struggles with peacekeeping abroad, the people of this nation are engaged in a bitter debate over basic values—what has come to be known as the "culture war." It is a battle over fundamental beliefs and moral convictions, and the result of this ongoing struggle has been a dangerous polarization of society between the Right and the Left. Few Americans are left in the middle anymore. And in virtually every way, we are a nation divided.

As I worked on this book, I had the sense that there is a bigger picture in all of this that could only be detected after digging around long enough in the debris of the past. What seemed to shout at me from the pages of the great literature was a sense of momentum and purpose in the march of time.

Looking Backward

The context and the requirements of the condition known as civilization were first discovered by the peoples who settled in the valley of the Nile more than six thousand years ago. These Semitic tribes developed agriculture, industry, language, and some of the first religious observances. They learned how to manufacture goods for sale, and, significantly, they learned how to dry papyrus and to make *biblos,* or books. They colonized much of North Africa, and their commercial settlement in the Levant, called Byblos, became a trading center that interacted with the indigenous cultures.

Egypt was a major influence in the ancient Mediterranean, and its armies and merchant fleets stimulated new forms of learning and development wherever they stopped. When the Hebrews were still a nomadic nation in their seemingly aimless search for Canaan, they knew of the majesty of the pharaohs. And when they were eventually made slaves in Egypt, the Jews gained from the experience not only a higher level of culture and sophistication but a new sense of identity and purpose as a nation. The exodus from Egypt remains a pivotal moment for the Jewish people and a central element of the religion of Judaism.

But the destiny of mankind was not to remain isolated in the Nile delta. Greek culture was already rising to a higher level than the pharaohs ever achieved. Alexander the Great introduced marvels to Egypt that the people of the Nile had never seen or even imagined. He brought great treasures, wise and learned scholars such as Aristotle, a new uniformity of language that would endure for more than seven hundred years, and an acculturation of science, art, and philosophy that would become the dominant features of what we now recognize as the classical world.

The Romans, as Edith Hamilton has said, were a cruder, more practical people, driven by visions of wealth and glory. First they conquered the Greeks and the Phoenicians, and they profited immensely from the learning and the luxury of those cultures. Then they conquered Egypt, Africa, Syria, Anatolia, the eastern parts of Europe, and every land and people from Rome to Hadrian's Wall in the north of Britain. They claimed whatever they wanted and wasted millions of lives in the process. But what they gave back was even greater. They carried their knowledge of civilization to every land and people.

The Hebrew people were transformed and reformed countless times over more than four thousand years. Through many trials and tribulations, the nation was being prepared for the moment in history for which it had been created. In that remarkable moment in which the gospel was first preached in Judea and began to influence the lives and actions of the men and women of that vital era, civilization was forever changed. No theory, no ideology, no "ism" of our time can deny that essential fact of history. In three short years, Jesus the Messiah changed everything forever, and after him nothing would ever be the same.

The repeated ruin of Jerusalem by the Egyptians, Babylonians, Assyrians, and Romans looms large in the Old Testament prophets—each devastation served as a reprimand and as a refinement of the people. But the most remarkable fact is that, despite

constant defeat, captivity, and humiliation, the Jews always returned to the land, and they never lost their identity as a race or
as a "chosen people."

God's Plan for History

Clearly there was a purpose in history that was beyond human
invention. When the people of Israel were lifted up, it was to
fulfill the prophetic decrees; and when they were brought down,
it was to accomplish another stage of history. When the nation
was finally destroyed by the Romans under Titus, it was because
their sojourn in Judea was finished. The dispersion of the Jews to
every corner of the world was no accident of history: It was a
dramatic statement that God had an even bolder plan for his
people.

The best way to get the message of God's intervention in
human destiny to the ends of the earth, and the best way to
spread the word that the Messiah had come with a plan of
redemption and renewal, was to send every man, woman, and
child who had crossed paths with the Savior into the world. And
that is precisely what happened. God salted civilization with his
presence. And when the nation was restored miraculously after
more than fifteen centuries—when the times of the Gentiles
were at last fulfilled—it could only be seen as the handiwork of
God.

What we see happening in Israel today is the preparation for
the next great stage in the fulfillment of God's plan for history.
In his marvelous work *The History of the Jews,* Paul Johnson says
that as early as the mid–seventeenth century ethnic Jews were
beginning to migrate back to Palestine. They were so few and so
unremarkable at first they were hardly noticed. But in time their
numbers increased until, by the late nineteenth century, it was

clear that the "Great Return" prophesied by the Scriptures had begun.

Local violence and intensifying political debate within Palestine seized the attention of the world, until the British Empire was finally drawn into the dispute. In 1917, Lord Balfour wrote his famous letter to Lord Rothschild, the leading financier of the day and an ardent Zionist, in which he offered the support of Great Britain in the effort to establish a national homeland for the Jews in Palestine. In 1921, the British colonial secretary, Winston Churchill, created the nation of Transjordan as part of a resettlement program for the Arabs. And in 1948, the United Nations created the modern state of Israel. Today we are witnessing the final stages of this remarkable fulfillment.

Now that Yasser Arafat has his Palestinian state just a half hour's drive from the heart of Jerusalem, we have to wonder what surprises may be in store for us in the months ahead. Politicians and pundits are convinced that peace has come. Equal opportunity is now available to everyone in Palestine, and the future is theirs to control. But if we have learned anything in two thousand years of history, it should be that peace in the Middle East is always premature. In any dispute between Arabs and Jews, nothing is ever certain.

It was less than two decades ago that President Jimmy Carter persuaded Israel's Menachem Begin and Egypt's Anwar Sadat to shake hands for the cameras. The Camp David accords led to an Arab-Israeli treaty, signed by Jewish and Egyptian leaders on March 26, 1979. The media hailed the event and proclaimed it a magnificent achievement of U.S. foreign policy. Begin and Sadat were named to receive the Nobel Peace Prize jointly in 1978, though many felt the award should rightfully have gone to Carter. Only months after Camp David, the heroes flew to Stockholm to be feted. Then things fell apart.

In January 1979, the pro-Western <u>Shah of Iran</u> was toppled by Iranian militants, and the whole idea of peace in the Middle East came into question. The radical Islamic leader <u>Ayatollah Ruhollah Khomeini</u> returned to Iran from exile in Paris and took control of the nation. In November of that year, Khomeini's followers seized the U.S. Embassy in Tehran, taking sixty-six hostages. One month later, the Soviet Union invaded Afghanistan. Soon riots and bombings broke out again in Beirut and Tel Aviv, and by October 1981, <u>Anwar Sadat</u> was dead, murdered on an airport runway by his own soldiers because he had betrayed the Arab cause.

Now, a decade and a half after the Camp David accords, another Democratic president has decided to put his stamp on international diplomacy by bringing the Arabs and Israelis together. In 1993, <u>President Clinton</u> flew Israel's <u>Prime Minister Yitzhak Rabin</u> and <u>PLO leader Yasser Arafat</u> to Washington to sign an accord. Then in early 1994, the Jews and Arabs agreed to a trade, land for peace, and Israel ceded important territory in Gaza and the West Bank for a Palestinian homeland.

Once again the world has declared peace in the Middle East. But haven't we been here before? Isn't there another shoe to drop? The ancient blood feud between Arabs and Israelis is deeper and more complex than anyone who is not implicated (or who has not lived in the middle of it for a long period of time) can ever hope to understand.

Convenient Political Solutions

In 1990, just four months before the Iraqi invasion of Kuwait, I participated in a series of interviews and cabinet-level briefings in Israel and Jordan with members of the various parties involved in these historic disputes. The occasion was a familiarization tour for authors and publishers arranged by Dan O'Neill of Mercy

Corps International, and during our stay, my colleagues and I were able to speak with and interview many remarkable people.

Among the leaders we spoke to were Crown Prince Hassan of Jordan, interviewed in the Royal Palace at Amman, and later a dozen members of the central committee of the PLO at their headquarters in the Jordanian capital. In Jerusalem we spoke candidly with the U.S. consul, Phil Wilcox, at his private residence, and with Dr. Yahoda Haim, who provided a detailed policy briefing at the Israeli Foreign Ministry.

We met with Father Elias Chacour, the renowned Palestinian Catholic priest, at his home in Galilee and with Dr. Joseph Alpher, a lecturer and policy analyst with one of the leading think tanks in the Middle East, the Jaffee Center for Strategic Studies in Tel Aviv. These, among many other interviews over an intensive two-week period, helped to confirm what many suspected all along—that the hostility and resolve of both sides are deep and irrational beyond belief. And while it would be wrong to stop trying, I also understood that peace will never come to the Middle East but by the grace of God.

I was touched deeply by many of the things I saw and heard from both Arabs and Jews. I think of the strange sort of anguish and bold optimism of young Jewish immigrants like Bob Lang, an American-born settler who manages the West Bank community at Efrat—raising a handsome young family, building a town, struggling for purpose and survival in the midst of incredible tensions. One can only guess at the emotions such a man must feel today in response to the deals being mandated by Washington and Jerusalem. And I wonder how they will deal with repercussions from the massacre of thirty Muslim worshipers at the Dome of the Rock by the extremist Baruch Goldstein, a settler from Efrat.

In our conversation, Hassan of Jordan said that the West will never fully understand the problems of the Middle East, since we perpetually overlook the human dimension in favor of convenient political solutions. He has made this point before, saying, "The region is crying out for a new initiative and a positive, more determined, approach to our problems, but all we receive is evasion, procrastination, and prevarication." While American diplomats stumble around in search of easy answers and political advantages for the West, they run the risk of provoking immensely greater disasters.

Hassan says, "The Middle East is liable to become a flash point for a global confrontation. It could easily ignite a conflagration of international violence." According to the crown prince, the questions on the lips of Arabs today are basic ones: Who am I? To whom do I belong? How shall I face the future? But these are questions with a long and complex history. They are questions from the deepest regions of the soul. Perhaps the best answer is to be found in Hassan's book *Search for Peace,* in which he writes, "It is a poor world that recognizes only power, not morality, in the conduct of public affairs."[1]

Surely this is the truth the people of our own country need to understand, not just in relation to the problems in the Middle East, but in dealing with our own apparent plunge into national decline. Moral issues always amount to more than merely political concerns. And power in itself is an inadequate justification when profound cultural issues are involved.

The Transformation

What I learned from my look at the history of this ancient theater of strife and discord was that from earliest times there has been a clear pattern of movement from the south, through the Levant, and up into Europe. It can be seen best on a map, by drawing large arrows to show clearly how civilization has moved from East to West, across Europe and Africa and on around the globe.

The idea expressed by Arnold Toynbee's metaphor of "the chariot of religion" seems especially appropriate. The march of civilization from one land to another over the long centuries is visible proof of a purpose and a plan in history. God had prepared the soil, planted the seeds, and brought forth a harvest that would go forth to fill the earth with the glory of his truth. When a civilization becomes exhausted or fails to live up to its divine challenge, the wheel of religion moves on, seeking another resting place.

Rome was a vital instrument in his hands, and the legions accelerated this process in a remarkable way. The soldiers and the officers who had come to faith in Jesus Christ traveled from Carthage to Britain and everywhere in between. They spoke the truth as they knew it, built churches, and encouraged missions and evangelism in some places that would not see a trained priest for centuries. This irony goes unnoticed by many, but the same armies that brought death and destruction, pillage and rape, from the North Sea to the Indian Ocean in the time of conquest, also supplied the missionaries who would spread the early seeds of faith throughout the known world in the times of consolidation and peace.

When Rome itself finally collapsed in the late fifth century, the church was already flourishing on its own, and it gained much more than it lost in the transfer of power from Rome to Constantinople. In the thousand years from the barbarian invasions to the fall of Byzantium, a vast network of preachers and teachers had been established throughout the world. Africa was a major center of Christian learning until the mid–seventh century; and England, France, Spain, the Netherlands, and dozens of German states were Christianized by the time of the Ottoman conquest. The fall of Constantinople in 1453 simply allowed the church to return to Rome, where the center of Catholic worship has remained to this day.

By that time there was a new vitality in art, philosophy, and science; and these things gave mankind the impulse to move beyond the simple and the ordinary, and to search for new and even more remarkable discoveries. Columbus, Magellan, da Gama, de Soto, Coronado, and Cortés were among the scores of adventurers who would seek for new lands where the Word of God could go forth.

Modern revisionists have tried to say that Christopher Columbus was motivated by greed and corruption. He was an "imperialist," they say. But the explorer made his purposes perfectly clear in his journals. In his *Book of Prophecies*, he writes:

> *At a very early age I began to sail upon the ocean. For more than forty years, I have sailed everywhere that people go.*
>
> *I prayed to the most merciful Lord about my heart's great desire, and He gave me the spirit and the intelligence for the task: seafaring, astronomy, geometry, arithmetic, skill in drafting spherical maps and placing correctly the cities, rivers, mountains and ports. I also studied cosmology, history, chronology and philosophy.*
>
> *It was the Lord who put into my mind (I would feel His hand upon me) to sail from here to the Indies.*

What motivated the great adventurer was his Christian faith. And the idea of seeking new lands where the Word of God could go forth was a mission placed in his mind, he says, by the Lord.

So the sweep of history continued, and the faith of Jesus Christ came ashore in the New World. In San Salvador in 1502, Columbus planted the standards of the sovereigns of Spain and the Holy Roman Church. Just over a hundred years later, when the first boatload of English Puritans landed in 1607, Captains Christopher Newport and John Smith planted the Christian flag at Cape Henry, Virginia, and founded the settlement at Jamestown. And when the *Mayflower* landed at Plymouth Rock in 1620, Myles Standish and John Alden placed a cross upon the beach to dedicate New England to the glory of God.

The Renaissance, the Reformation, the Holy Roman Empire, the Spanish Inquisition, and the religious wars in Europe added momentum and drama to the pageant of history. Art and science glorified the Creation and reflected honor upon the Creator, and the message of faith continued its march westward with the sun. Even defiance of the church in Italy, Germany, France, and England did not alter the purpose that was being accomplished. God's plan of history was not impeded in the least.

The sudden appearance of atheism and other heresies only forced the faithful to reexamine their beliefs, and from the Nicene Creed in 325 to the Westminster Confession of 1647, each council of the church reaffirmed the central authority of Scripture, the deity of Jesus Christ, the importance of the holy sacraments, and the hope of eternal life.

The philosophes of the Enlightenment claimed the Christian faith was divisive. But those who upheld the faith were agreed on the basic principles of belief. The only ones divided by them were those who hoped for another truth and another reality. The new humanism promoted another truth and another vision of God. They worshiped man instead of God, so they, like the pagans of Rome, naturally found the gospel intolerable. But the humanist ideology has fared no better than paganism, and today, faced by the imminent collapse of all our man-made institutions, that ancient heresy is in utter disarray.

240

The Footprints of God

The idea that came to my mind when I had considered this perspective on the past was simple, but it made a profound impression on me. I realized that if God controls the nations, lifting them up, carrying them forward, and then moving on to accomplish the next stage of growth and development, then the achievements and disappointments of history may be seen as the footprints of God. And, furthermore, I realized that God must also care for each man, woman, and child in a special way, and that the achievements and disappointments of our lives are also part of a bigger plan.

It has often been said that pain and sorrow are the stimulants of the soul. We make little place in our lives for notions about God when we are victorious and flushed with our own success; we find him essential when we hurt. But the lesson of history is that it all matters to God. He is building something bigger, bolder, more audacious than anything any of us can imagine. And if he has conspired with history to use the nations for the manifest glory of Jesus Christ and for the mission of redeeming the world for himself, then isn't it also clear that he is using my losses, sorrows, and disappointments—as well as my joys—for similar ends?

But once I come to this point, I must also ask myself: Am I where the God of history wants me to be? Am I available to him today, or am I caught up in the petty details of my daily routine, complaining about the way I wish it could be?

When I look at the canvas of history, I am struck at first by the unique differences between the nations and empires of the past. Each has a color and character of its own. But I am also struck by the incredible similarities. If there was not something synchronous and interconnected in the processes of history, I would expect them to be much less similar.

Finally, I am struck by the recurrence of ideas and idioms over the ages. From the long view I understand that the bitterness, divisiveness, and disagreement in history emanate from the same basic source of conflict. As we observed in part 2, it is the ancient battle of soul and reason—a war between the eternal verities and the temporal vanities of man.

Today, society is plagued by one more outbreak of violence against the eternal verities. Cultural relativism, being promoted in the public schools and institutions of higher learning, says that the traditional values of Western civilization are one-sided, bigoted, and destructive. Historical revisionism, the attempt to rewrite history in a way that is less objectionable to the humanist credo, is just one more expression of this view. The trend of political correctness is perhaps most destructive, since it promotes overt and hostile censorship. But it will be a short-lived phenomenon. Even its advocates recognize the inherent dangers of thought control.

In the ancient societies, as in the Enlightenment, we saw the frightening increase of social and political polarization. We witnessed the rise of immorality, a growing disrespect for human life (through torture, exposure, abortion, euthanasia, and even commercial exploitation of the unborn), and the decay of religious belief. Ultimately, all these symptoms are interrelated. They are all weapons in an arsenal of doubt as old as history itself—a battery of disbelief arrayed against the forces of heaven and evidence of the ancient desire to evict God from his rightful place in the world.

The Source of Truth

Carl Michalson wrote nearly fifty years ago that Jesus Christ is "the paradigm which forms the very possibility of an ultimately meaningful history."[2] I am convinced that the lessons of history confirm that fact. We are living in a time of crisis; people everywhere are desperate for hope. We long for relief from the nightmare of fear and uncertainty. In the end, the only reliable answer for a nation in distress is a return to the "hinge of history"

242

and the Source of Truth that makes life meaningful and tolerable. Can we do that? Can our society be renewed in time to stop the ravages of anarchy and decay?

It is only too clear now, as one journal after another reports on the disastrous effects of four decades of socialist programming, that welfare dependency has virtually destroyed the American Dream for entire generations of U.S. citizens. The most remarkable feature of American-style democracy—which every observer since the time of Tocqueville has detected—is the remarkable sense of self-reliance and independence manifested by the people of this country. What made the American experiment unique in the first place was the fact that men and women here had the right to succeed or to fail on their own, without the complicity of government. Charity, public assistance, and aid to the needy were available from the churches or from private organizations. The aim of assistance was not to foster dependency but to provide the means for a fresh start. In a free society, the goal is to keep people honest and productive.

Unfortunately, that is not what Washington offers the disadvantaged today. Government paternalism has robbed people of all classes of their initiative and self-respect. It has bound millions of Americans in self-imposed slavery. Failed social programs that have shackled poor people for more than thirty years can be traced, almost without exception, to Lyndon Johnson's "Great Society" schemes. Based on the belief that some people are inferior or unable to compete in society, welfare doctrine patronized the poor and the weak, paid them off, took large numbers out of the workforce, and, by rewarding and subsidizing bad habits, actually encouraged the worst kinds of behavior.

Our own government contributed to the loss of self-respect, loss of ambition, and the kind of "idle hands" the old maxim tells us are "the devil's workshop." And when the natural desire to better oneself was stripped away, whole neighborhoods and communities were forced into blight and hopelessness, along with a terrible loss of spiritual and moral values. And, of course, lawlessness and anger breed in such an environment—the root of the problems we face today in the inner cities.

In his book *The Passion of the Western Mind*, Richard Tarnas observes that it was the blossoming of Christianity in the final years of the Roman Empire that led to the development of the individual conscience, a sense of responsibility, and an understanding of the differences between the laws of men and the authority of God. These were remarkable developments in the world of ideas. These new concepts, as expressed so succinctly by Augustine and the early church fathers, contributed not only to the development of a more mature faith but to an overall sense of self-worth and personal integrity. Tarnas says:

> *In its moral teachings, Christianity brought to the pagan world a new sense of the sanctity of all human life, the spiritual value of the family, the spiritual superiority of self-denial over egoistic fulfillment, of unworldly holiness over worldly ambition, of gentleness and forgiveness over violence and retribution; a condemnation of murder, suicide, the killings of infants, the massacre of prisoners, the degradation of slaves, sexual licentiousness and prostitution, bloody circus spectacles—all in the new awareness of God's love of humanity, and the moral purity that love required in the human soul.*[3]

Unlike the love of the world they had known under pagan rule, Christian love was not merely the love of Venus or Eros but the love of Christ, best expressed through compassion, sacrifice, and, yes, suffering. Whereas Christian doctrines during the years of persecution may have lacked some of the intellectual rigor of the pagan philosophies that dominated religious culture at that time, the faith of Jesus Christ nevertheless appealed to a broader mass of people in a way and to a degree that the Greek ideas never could.

The appeal of the Christian faith was universal. Its principles were uplifting and ennobling. It taught men to love their neighbors. Among both high and low, the rise of Christianity brought a new sense of purpose that would help to carry society through its defeats to a new level of achievement. That would prove to be a very important mission for the future of mankind. Ironically, it was the great power of the Roman Empire that allowed all these ideas to flourish. Even while pagan society was becoming increasingly corrupt, Rome provided the vehicle for transporting the gospel of Jesus Christ throughout the world.

Until Constantine's conversion to Christianity, even the best Roman emperors were either ruthless and unprincipled or malicious and corrupt, and it was clear that the empire could not survive for long in such hands. But the Eastern Empire, founded by Constantine at Constantinople (the seat of what would become the Byzantine Empire), built on the principles of an emergent Christian faith, survived the Fall of Rome, and continued in power and splendor until 1453 when the capital at Constantinople was overrun by the Ottoman Turks.

When the West emerged from the Dark Ages, a new Renaissance of art and culture was bursting forth, first in Rome, then in France, Britain, and the rest of Europe. The rediscovery of classical ideas stirred an awakening of the imagination and a new vitality of civilization. The Renaissance and the Reformation, which followed in 1517, were to become the cultural vehicles that would transport the faith of Jesus Christ into Europe and beyond—to the very ends of the earth.

The Treadmill of Time

The assessment of the cycles and trends in history shades naturally into philosophy; and the discussion of changing political conditions invokes questions about the spiritual and psychological well-being of society. For the British scholar Northcote Parkinson it is only too clear that the rise and fall of nations has been much too regular and too predictable not to suggest some sort of interconnection, some driving force, some logical pattern that deserves thought and study. But are we prepared to accept the lessons of history that may come from such a study? Do Americans and Europeans in these late hours of the twentieth century have the nerve to venture an assessment of our social conditions, and are we willing to do whatever it takes to bring the nation back to health?

In 1861, shortly before his own death, Thomas Babbington Macaulay wrote to a friend in America, "Your republic will be fearfully plundered and laid waste by barbarians in the twentieth century as the Roman Empire was in the fifth, with this difference: that the Huns and Vandals will have been engendered within your own country, by your own institutions." Like Tocqueville, the famous scholar was an admirer of this country, and he hoped the nation would prosper as a beacon of sane policy and behavior. But he feared the dangers of egalitarianism and liberalism, and he sensed that liberty itself would one day become the very source of our own self-destruction.

Arnold Toynbee said that in the final restive hours of the great civilizations, saviors would emerge from the crowd with proposals that, if heeded, could halt the decline of culture and even bring revitalization. Each is a creature of the hour who rises to prominence, and either pulls off a stunning miracle or leads the nation to inevitable chaos and humiliation. For confirmation of this idea, simply consider the fortunes of men such as Robespierre, Napoléon, Hitler, Mussolini, or Hirohito. On the other hand, think of Idi Amin, Fidel Castro, the Ayatollah Khomeini, and Saddam Hussein. Heroes and despots rise to champion great causes and to lead nations either to victory or to ruin.

Winston Churchill was a hero lifted up by a propitious moment, a visionary who led Britain and the West through the peril of a war they could not win; the sheer force of one man's personality saved the day. Mikhail Gorbachev, *Time* magazine's Man of the Year and a hero to some, led his nation to ruin but, in the process of abject humiliation and collapse, allowed the embers of the empire to survive. And today in Russia a new vision of faith and hope is struggling to be born. But where does America stand on the treadmill of time?

Perhaps we have not yet reached the point of collapse. Perhaps we will not reach it for centuries to come. Egypt endured three major and thirty-two minor incarnations before finally disintegrating under the yoke of Rome. Greece had two major revivals, and Rome had three. Perhaps Western civilization is in for a renewal sparked by the challenges being mounted today in Japan and China or the reawakening of the great nations of Eastern Europe or the now-unified European Community.

Perhaps the North American Free Trade Agreement will bring us a new sense of vigor and expansion. Or maybe there will be a great spiritual awakening that will shake the continent of North America to its very foundations. In his classic study of the evolutions of political thought and the rise and fall of nations, Northcote Parkinson assesses the prospects for Western society and says:

> *There would seem to be cyclic fashions and an inherent law of change. Were we to accept the teaching of history we should conclude that the political units we now describe as nations are*

likely to repeat the political sequence through which most of them have passed. Some, it is true, are too small to experience all these things; and two, perhaps, of a federal pattern, may prove too large. For the rest we might be tempted to predict a continuance of the treadmill round, ending only with the end of civilisation itself; a finish not necessarily very remote. Such a prediction would, however, be unjustified. For, while the course of history may reveal a trend, it does not prove that the trend is inevitable. There are instances of a danger being avoided, provided only that the danger has been perceived.[4]

Arnold Toynbee's final category of leadership, and the last and best hope for mankind, is the "Savior Incarnate in a Man," and there is only one candidate for that job. The book of Revelation says that one day Jesus Christ will come to bring peace to mankind, with wise leadership and marvelous solutions for every problem. When he came the first time, Jesus told his disciples he had come to bring a sword that would separate the faithful from the unfaithful and the foolish from the wise.

But when he comes again, it will be to bring lasting peace. But first, there must be judgment. In the meantime, how will we survive the risks and challenges to national security? And how will we deal with the evidence of decline?

The Challenge of Survival

My own position is that the signs of the times are unmistakable, and it is vitally important that men and women of conviction first acknowledge the scope and the complexity of the challenges before us today and then react with all due haste. The motivation for this book is my firm conviction that there *is* still time and we *can* do something. But this nation will not escape the fate of empires by simply wishing or by waiting for government to pull us through. We must renew our personal commitment to those bedrock values that have sustained this nation since its foundation, and we must put aside everything that prevents us from holding firmly to those truths, whatever perils it may entail.

In the battle for survival, your voice matters, your opinion counts, your prayers are vitally important, and your personal involvement is essential. Every one of the problems we have reviewed in these pages can be dealt with and solved by persistent and concerned action by godly men and women. Lawlessness, economic insolvency, and bureaucratic interference in people's lives can be stopped. Sound political action, seasoned by prayer and loving engagement, can turn the tide and restore order to these issues. The kind of committed activism by Christians that draws forth the very power of heaven to our aid in dealing with these matters will make all the difference.

Parental involvement in education, school choice, and confrontation of liberal ideologies in the classrooms can help restore balance and probity in the schools; and a renewal of family values and the traditional customs and beliefs of this nation can help to uphold and renew our cultural integrity. If people will simply confront their fascination with possessions, fashions, and other manifestations of materialism, they will be able to recover the richness and the joy of personal relationships. From those foundations come the most important values and the most enduring kinds of renewal.

One of the lessons of history is that immorality is not the cause of national decline but a symptom of lost faith. When people lose faith in themselves, their country, and their God, they slide naturally into the bad habits that bring on corruption and decline. Loss of their love for God leads to loss of self-respect, and from there it is only a short step to loss of respect for human life and all the types of degradation and abuse we have witnessed in recent years. To restore our relationships, we must return to our "first love"—that is, to our faith in Jesus Christ and to the values and hopes upon which the Founding Fathers relied.

There are many ways that God may seize the attention of a people. He may send prophets, plagues, or perils that cannot be ignored. He may send storms or disasters that force men and women to open their eyes. He may send revival, or he may send judgment and some terrible type of destruction. But when the time known only to God is fulfilled, and when his patience with our apostasy has run its course, he will move.

Six hundred years before the birth of Christ, the prophet Jeremiah was chosen to be God's instrument. When the people of Israel fell away from their first love, the word of the Lord proclaimed, "Let not the wise man bask in his wisdom, nor the mighty man in his might, nor the rich man in his riches. Let them boast in this alone: That they truly know me, and understand that I am the Lord of justice and of righteousness whose love is steadfast." Later, through the prophet Ezekiel, the Lord declared, "I will set My glory among the nations; all the nations shall see My judgment which I have executed, and My hand which I have laid on them."

From these prophetic utterances we should see that the fortunes of empires rise and fall, not by the ambitions and fortunes of men, but by the will of the Lord. God's purpose is to make himself known to the nations and to draw all men, women, and children unto himself. So long as our works further the kingdom of his Christ, the nations will be lifted up and their banners will be extended. But when the nations turn their back upon him and when the hearts of men and women are hardened, then history moves on, with or without us.

As you consider these lessons from the past, I challenge you to recommit yourself to the divine reality that precedes and supersedes all our activities and plans. When any notion of art, science, education, law, or theology attempts to deny the role that God and the study of his nature have played in history, it only demonstrates the folly to which we are susceptible. We cannot escape the reality of God in the universe, no matter how hard we may try. He is as much a part of us as our own minds, and we are involved with him, one way or another, forever.

The hopes and dreams of mankind have hardly changed over the centuries. We seek today what men have always sought, and we are susceptible to the same sorts of peril. It is my hope that this study will have awakened some of you to that reality and that it may cause many others to gain a new vision for the renewal of our culture. God is not yet finished with America, but for the time being the fate of the nation is still in our hands.

I BELIEVE no one can read the history of our
country without realizing that the Good Book and
the spirit of the Savior have from the beginning
been our guiding geniuses. . . . Whether we look to
the first charter of Virginia . . . or to the Charter of
New England . . . or to the Charter of
Massachusetts Bay . . . or to the Fundamental
Orders of Connecticut . . . the same objective is
present: a Christian land governed by Christian
principles. . . .

I believe the entire Bill of Rights came into being
because of the knowledge our forefathers had of the
Bible and their belief in it: freedom of belief, of
expression, of assembly, of petition, the dignity of
the individual, the sanctity of the home, equal
justice under law, and the reservation of powers to
the people. . . .

I like to believe we are living today in the spirit of
the Christian religion. I like also to believe that as
long as we do so, no great harm can come to our
country.

Former Chief Justice Earl Warren,
addressing the annual prayer breakfast
of the International Council
of Christian Leadership, 1954

APPENDIX

Classical Studies on the Fate of Nations

OVER the past three hundred years, many important books have been written to examine the fate of great empires and to try to detect patterns of ascendancy and decline that might be visible to a skilled observer. Among the earliest to apply a systematic and scientific approach was the Italian philosopher-historian Giambattista Vico, who believed that history is the key to any theory of civilization.

Vico's writings, especially his treatise called *The New Science*, published in the mid-eighteenth century, stressed that human beings are creatures of history and that human nature (and behavior) can change over time. He disputed the conclusions of Descartes, Spinoza, and Hobbes, which proposed a naturalistic vitalism in human nature. Vico said that literature, art, religion, philosophy, politics, and economics are the interrelated disciplines of the mind that, when viewed together, provide the clues to understanding the spirit of a culture.

He also believed that great nations follow a predictable pattern of growth, maturity, and decline, very much as living organisms. They are born, mature, and inevitably die, and their contribution to history is determined by the level of their achievements in the arts and sciences. Vico's ideas, in turn, had a profound deal of influence on the German philosopher Oswald Spengler, whose *Decline of the West* stirred controversy when it first became widely known in this country after the stock-market crash of 1929.[1]

In this important work, Spengler tried to show that principles of evolutionism, which were being debated at that time, were at work on an even grander scale in history. Like Vico, Spengler believed that cultures go through life cycles—birth, youth, maturity, decline, and death. The First World War, he said, was evidence that Western civilization had already entered a period of pernicious decline. He also expressed the belief that the final stages of civilization would lead to a period of totalitarianism under a succession of caesars who would impose a new order on society in their effort to fend off "the hordes from the East."

Adolf Hitler was apparently influenced by these theories, and the cataclysm ignited by the Nazis over the next two decades gave Spengler's ideas of decline uncommon currency and weight. Ironically, it was the Nazis' will to power that would eventually lead to their overreaching militarism and the final chaotic collapse of the Third Reich. History would come to see the Führer's

Nazi Millennium as an empire driven to suicide by its own imperialistic ambitions.

In the most classic study of Roman civilization ever written, *The Decline and Fall of the Roman Empire* (published in 1776), the English historian Edward Gibbon compiled a detailed portrait of the civilizations of Rome and the Byzantine Empire over the thirteen centuries of their existence. Gibbon believed that the final collapse of Rome was made inevitable by the slow decay of classical learning and the loss of intellectual curiosity. He blamed both of these to some degree on the victory of Christianity over paganism and said in one famous line, "I have described the triumph of barbarism and religion."

Despite this view, however, Gibbon offers a very insightful and appealing description of the process by which the Christian religion entered Rome. Describing its spread from Judea to the ends of the known world, he admits that the Christian church was a vital part of the saga of Rome. For while the empire was in an advanced state of disarray, he writes, and as the government was being undermined by bitter internecine struggles, "a pure and humble religion gently insinuated itself into the minds of men, grew up in silence and obscurity, derived new vigor from opposition, and finally erected the triumphant banner of the Cross on the ruins of the Capitol." And so complete was the victory of the Christian faith over the various cults and pagan religions of the day that it has not diminished since that time.

"After a revolution of thirteen or fourteen centuries," Gibbon adds, "that religion is still professed by the nations of Europe, the most distinguished portion of human kind in arts and learning as well as in arms. By the industry and zeal of the Europeans it has been widely diffused to the most distant shores of Asia and Africa; and by the means of their colonies has been firmly established from Canada to Chili, in a world unknown to the ancients."[2]

By the sheer magnitude of the panorama painted by these authors, we should be able to gain a better understanding of the processes of change and development wrought by time. The historians of the eighteenth and nineteenth centuries add a unique sense of depth to our grasp of the ancient cultures.

The End of History

From this summary of three of the important early writers in the field, we come back to our own time and a flurry of new books and articles that take a very different approach. Most of the modern writers who have analyzed the state of culture have warned that the amount of time left for Western society to make its contribution to history may already be about over. In the book *The End of History and the Last Man,* Rand Corporation political analyst Francis Fukuyama provoked an avalanche of critical reactions with his observation that the struggle to establish a model of political stability in the world has finally been settled.

Since the Berlin Wall came down and the cold war ended in the fall of 1989, writes Fukuyama, it is now clear that the paradigm of "liberal democracy" embodied in the United States Constitution has triumphed over communism, state socialism, and the command economies of Eastern Europe. Liberal democracy, he says, has long since proved its superiority to traditional monarchy, and consequently the West has emerged victorious in the cold war.

The German philosopher G. W. Hegel (the father of dialectics) believed that "rights" were an *end* in themselves, and once the "rights of man" were secured by any society, the evolution of political systems would naturally cease. Historical events would continue, of course, but the strife between competing political ideologies would end. The ultimate system for government would be in place, and there would be no need for further political development. This is Fukuyama's meaning of the term "the End of History."

The "first man" in his metaphor lives a life, as in Thomas Hobbes's famous description, that is "solitary, poor, nasty, brutish and short." Society's first men are proud, nationalistic, and aggressive, and the mission of post–cold war society must be to bring forth a "last man," which is the author's model of society when it has successfully vanquished pride, nationalism, greed, parochial biases, and militarism in favor of a new attitude of benevolence based on some sort of fusion of humanistic spirituality and political maturity.[3]

The counter to this book, *The End of the Twentieth Century and the End of the Modern Age,* was written by the Hungarian historian John Lukacs as a rebuttal to Fukuyama's argument. Lukacs does not believe that communism was ever a major threat to the West; neither were any other political ideologies. And the risk for America today is not socialism but nationalism. Nationalism, he stresses, was Hitler's illness, and it is a perennial temptation of republican democracies.

For all intents and purposes, Lukacs says, America's power, prestige, and presence in the world are finished. Though its influence may continue for some time, the "American Century" has come to a premature end, and America's authority as a source of culture and political convictions is on a rapid downhill slide. What lies ahead, he predicts, is a time of troubles that will threaten the very foundations of the modern nation.[4]

The Character of Culture

These and other recent works offer a variety of perspectives on the problems of our age, and most of them raise some fairly complex questions about the prospects for Western civilization. No doubt such questions are prompted in part by the auspicious moment of history in which we find ourselves. In this decade leading up to the end of the twentieth century and the unfolding of the third millennium of the Christian era, we sense the burden of history upon us as never before.

As we look toward the coming century, many would question whether America can even be considered an empire in the sense of Egypt, Carthage, Greece, or Rome. While the United States has great territory and wealth, and has established enviable standards in every aspect of culture, industry, government, and military power, our form of diplomacy has never been intentionally empire minded or imperialistic. Or has it?

Journalist David Halberstam, in his book *The Next Century,* certainly agrees that the American Century is over. America has been a nation needlessly burdened by "the myth of empire" for quite some time, he says, and the incivility and corruption of post–Watergate America is just an indication of the dishonesty and the flawed assumptions of our political leaders.[5] American arrogance and insensitivity to the views and values of other cultures is in itself a form of imperialism. Citing with apparent approval the isolationist views of Senator Robert A. Taft, Halberstam says that America has become hardened, led by men with no respect for the truth.

When Halberstam thinks of noble virtues, such as the drive for excellence and the sense of personal obligation, he thinks first of Japan and industry leaders like Kazuo Inamori, a tycoon with a Zen-like fascination for work. He is a man who builds factories first in his mind and manages with mystical grace. But when Halberstam thinks of America, he thinks of affluence, decadence, overly high consumption, and overly high expectations. The face he sees in America's mirror is the very image of decline.[6]

More recently, when Professor Samuel P. Huntington published his controversial essay on "The Clash of Civilizations" in the influential journal *Foreign Affairs* in mid-1993, he expressed concern that the hardening of the global community into several distinct racial and social enclaves was setting the world up for an imminent war of cultures—a clash of civilizations. "With the end of the Cold War," he says, "international politics moves out of its Western phase, and its centerpiece becomes the interaction between the West and non-Western civilizations and among non-Western civilizations."

Conceding that the great rise of transportation and immigration in this century has made it harder to define civilizations on the basis of geography, race, or culture alone, Huntington says that modern civilizations are still the broadest level of social and ideological identification of a people and the hardening of these structures is setting us up for imminent global conflict. He writes:

> *First, differences among civilizations are not only real; they are basic. Civilizations are differentiated from each other by history, language, culture, tradition, and, most important, religion. The people of different civilizations have different views on the relations between God and man, the individual and the group, the citizen and the state, parents and children, husband and wife, as well as differing views of the relative importance of rights and responsibilities, liberty and authority, equality, and hierarchy. These differences are the products of centuries. They will not disappear. They are far more fundamental than differences among political ideologies and political regimes. Differences do not necessarily mean conflict, and conflict does not necessarily mean violence. Over the centuries, however, differences among*

261

civilizations have generated the most prolonged and most violent conflicts.[7]

In modern times, Huntington says, we tend to think of nations as the key actors in global affairs. But in reality, individual nations have only been dominant players in global strategy for the last few centuries. Throughout the greater part of history, the focus has been on civilizations, and these have a vital legacy. "Civilizations are dynamic," he says, "they rise and fall; they divide and merge. And, as any student of history knows, civilizations disappear and are buried in the sands of time."[8] What Huntington specifically fears is a confrontation between the Christian West, the Islamic Middle East, and a newly energized Far East under some form of resurgent Confucianism—in other words, a war of religious fundamentalisms on a global scale.

It is true that history does reveal the destructive potential of religious fanaticism. During the first three centuries of the modern age, tens of thousands of Christians were brutally murdered because of their faith. During the Spanish Inquisition, thousands of heretics and infidels were "purified" by flame and by sword. In Iran and Arabia, in Indonesia, Pakistan, and India, as well as in Bosnia, we have witnessed the kinds of wars and rivalries generated by militant fundamentalism and the reactions to it. But is Huntington correct in his view? Is an increase in religious devotion the greatest concern for civilization?

The Great Civilizations

262

To better understand the nature of cultural decline and to help us recognize the kinds of forces that we will find in the rise and fall of empires, it will be helpful to identify a few of the earliest civilizations of antiquity and then to examine briefly some of the criteria by which civilizations are studied. To begin with, the term *civilization* generally designates a state of development in society in which there is a high level of cultural and technological achievement and a complex social and political structure.

Alfred North Whitehead defined a *great civilization* as any society committed to truth, beauty, adventure, art, and peace. The British archaeologist V. Gordon Childe defined civilization in terms of several kinds of practical inventions that he believed helped to transform cultures into civilizations. Among these were development of an alphabet and writing, metallurgy, standard units of measure, mathematics, monumental architecture, commercial vitality, a class of artisans, agricultural irrigation, strategies for storage and barter of surplus production, and the use of the plow.

Scholars today are less inclined to limit themselves to such rigid categories. Most modern researchers prefer to examine the kinds of social structures present within the culture. One of the first things they would look for would be evidence of a class system, probably based on the ownership of property and control of the sources of labor and production. Second, they would expect to find some form of political and religious hierarchy that is not only compatible with the culture but that contributes to the social and spiritual development of the population. And they would also expect to find evidence of a systematic division of labor and a workforce that includes farmers, laborers, builders, craftsmen, merchants, soldiers, and political advisers, as well as a ruling class.

The ancient Mediterranean societies are the ones best-known to history, and due in part to the massive amount of research and analysis that has been devoted to them, they are also the civilizations most easily defined. Oswald Spengler listed only eight great civilizations in his writings. However, when the English historian Arnold Toynbee published his *Study of History* (in twelve volumes published between 1934 and 1972), he identified as many as thirty-five distinct civilizations and analyzed fully twenty-one of them. Of that original list, only six remain today.

Notes

Chapter 2

1. Bob Herbert, "Violence in the State of Denial," *New York Times,* 27 October 1993, A23.
2. Herbert, "Violence."
3. Charles Murray, "The Coming White Underclass," *Wall Street Journal,* 29 October 1993.
4. John Leo, "At a Cultural Crossroads," *U.S. News & World Report,* 20 December 1993, 14.
5. Charmaine C. Yoest, ed., *Free to Be Family: A Special Report* (Washington, D.C.: Family Research Council, 1992), 96ff.
6. R. Emmett Tyrrell, Jr., *American Spectator,* October 1993, 14.
7. Walter K. Olson, *The Litigation Explosion* (New York: E. P. Dutton, 1991), 339.
8. José Ortega y Gasset, *Mirabeau: An Essay on the Nature of Statesmanship* (Manila: Historical Conservation Society, 1975).
9. Russell Kirk, "Can Our Civilization Survive?" address presented to members of the Heritage Foundation, July 24, 1992.
10. Os Guinness, *The American Hour* (New York: Macmillan Free Press, 1993), 414.

Chapter 3

1. James Dale Davidson and Lord William Rees-Mogg, *The Great Reckoning,* rev. ed. (New York: Simon & Schuster, 1993), 13.
2. Paul Kennedy, *The Rise and Fall of the Great Powers* (New York: Vintage Books, 1989), 533.
3. Kennedy, *Rise and Fall,* 439.

Chapter 4

1. David Lambro, "Government Is Fastest Growing U.S. Industry," United Feature Syndicate, Inc., Washington, D.C., 17 March 1994.
2. June O'Neill and David O'Neill, *The Impact of a Health Insurance Mandate on Labor Costs and Employment: Empirical Evidence* (Washington, D.C.: Employment Policies Institute, September 1993).

3. Thomas Jefferson, The Declaration of Independence.
4. Figures reported annually by David Keating of the National Taxpayers Union, based on cumulative state, local, and federal taxes.
5. Russel Kirk, *Roots of American Order* (Washington, D.C.: Regnery Gateway, 1991), 129.
6. Michael I. Rostovtzeff, *The Social and Economic History of the Roman Empire* (Oxford: Oxford University Press, 1926), 453. Cited in Kirk, *Roots,* 130.
7. Kirk, *Roots,* 129.

Chapter 5
1. Donald Dudley, *The Civilization of Rome* (New York: Meridian, 1993), 238.
2. Diane Ravitch and Chester E. Finn, Jr., *What Do Our Seventeen Year Olds Know?* (New York: Harper & Row, 1987).
3. Thomas Sowell, "Indoctrinating the Children," *Forbes,* 1 February 1993, 65.
4. Sowell, "Indoctrinating."
5. Charles J. Sykes, "Opening Up the Public-School Gulag," *National Review,* July 20, 1992, 18.
6. Samuel L. Blumenfeld, *NEA: Trojan Horse in American Education* (Boise, Idaho: paradigm, 1984).
7. Samuel Francis, "Beam Us Out," *Chronicles,* April 1994, 11.
8. David Barton, *America: To Pray or Not to Pray?* (Aledo, Tex.: Wallbuilders Press, 1991).
9. Allan Bloom, *The Closing of the American Mind: How Higher Education Has Failed Democracy and Impoverished the Souls of Today's Students* (New York: Simon & Schuster, 1988), 26.
10. Dinesh D'Sousa, *Illiberal Education: The Politics of Sex and Race on Campus* (New York: Vintage, 1992), xiii.
11. Charles Sykes, *A Nation of Victims: The Decay of American Character* (New York: St. Martin's, 1992), 49.
12. Russell Kirk, *The Roots of American Order* (Washington, D.C.: Regnery Gateway, 1992), 462.
13. Bloom, *American Mind,* 165.

Chapter 6
1. Samuel Noah Eisenstadt, *The Decline of Empires* (Englewood Cliffs, N.J.: Prentice Hall, 1967), 2–3.
2. James Burnham, *The Suicide of the West* (Washington, D.C.: Regnery Gateway, 1985), 59.

3. Hubert H. Humphrey, in "Six Liberals Define Liberalism," *New York Times,* 19 April 1959, Magazine sec. 13.
4. Burnham, *Suicide,* 305.
5. Jean-François Revel, *Democracy against Itself: The Future of the Democratic Impulse,* trans. Roger Kaplan (New York: Macmillan Free Press, 1993), 258.
6. John A. Garraty and Peter Gay, eds., *The Columbia History of the World* (New York: Harper & Row, 1972), 1163.
7. Peter Collier and David Horowitz, *Destructive Generation: Second Thoughts about the Sixties* (New York: Summit Books, 1989), 177.
8. Collier and Horowitz, *Generation,* 15.
9. F. W. Brownlow, "Thoughts of Empire," *Chronicles,* February 1993, 16.
10. Alexis de Tocqueville, *Democracy in America,* trans. George Lawrence (New York: Harper & Row, 1969), 293.
11. Tocqueville, *Democracy,* 236.
12. Tocqueville, *Democracy,* 691.
13. Tony Judt, *Past Imperfect: French Intellectuals 1944–1956* (Berkeley: University of California Press, 1993).
14. Henri Peyre, "The Influence of Eighteenth-Century Ideas on the French Revolution," in *Intellectual Movements in Modern European History,* ed. Franklin L. Baumer (New York: Macmillan, 1965), 72ff.
15. Christopher Dawson, *Enquiries into Religion and Culture* (Freeport, N.Y.: Books for Libraries, 1968), 345.

Chapter 7

1. Geoffrey Bruun, *The Enlightened Despots* (New York: Holt, Reinhart & Winston, 1967), 25.
2. David Ogg, *Europe of the Ancien Régime: 1715–1783* (New York: Harper & Row, 1965), 350.
3. Thomas J. McCormick, *America's Half-Century* (Baltimore: Johns Hopkins University Press, 1989), 216ff.
4. Allan Bloom, *The Closing of the American Mind* (New York: Simon & Schuster, 1987), 382.
5. Bloom, *American Mind,* 382.
6. Jean-François Revel, *Democracy Against Itself,* trans. Roger Kaplan (New York: Macmillan Free Press, 1993), 92–93.
7. Heather S. Richardson, "The Politics of Virtue: A Strategy for Transforming the Culture," address to the Heritage Foundation, reprinted in *Policy Review,* fall 1991, 23.
8. Romans 8:21, NKJV.
9. Romans 8:23, TLB.

Chapter 8 Increase in Materialism

1. Anita Manning, "What's Pop Culture Teaching Our Kids? Parents Fear Reign of Sex and Violence," *USA Today,* 16 March 1992, 1D.
2. Michael Lewis, "Moby Malls," *Worth,* October 1993.
3. Charles Colson with Ellen Santilli Vaughn, *Against the Night: Living in the New Dark Ages* (Ann Arbor, Mich.: Servant Publications, 1989), 67.
4. John W. Wright, ed., *The Universal Almanac 1993* (Kansas City, Mo.: Andrews & McMeel), 1992.
5. Charmaine C. Yoest, ed., *Free to Be Family: A Special Report* (Washington, D.C.: Family Research Council, 1992), 19.
6. Amitai Etzioni, *The Spirit of Community: Rights, Responsibilities and the Communitarian Agenda* (New York: Crown Publishers, 1993); cited in *Utne Reader,* May/June 1993, 53.
7. Etzioni, *Utne Reader,* 54.
8. Livy, preface to bk.I, *The History of Rome from Its Foundation,* trans. Aubrey de Selincourt (Baltimore: Penguin, 1967).
9. Polybius, *The Histories,* trans. W. R. Paton (Cambridge: Harvard University Press, 1960).
10. James Q. Wilson, *The Moral Sense* (New York: Macmillan Free Press, 1993), x.
11. Salvian, *On the Government of God,* trans. Eva M. Sanford (New York: Columbia University Press, 1930).
12. Robert Wuthnow, "Pious Materialism: How Americans View Faith and Money," *Christian Century,* 3 March 1993, 238ff.
13. Os Guinness, *The American Hour* (New York: Macmillan Free Press, 1993), 398.
14. Guinness, *The American Hour,* 398.
15. Guinness, *The American Hour,* 363.

Chapter 9 Rise in Immorality

1. Charles Doe, "Navy to Expel 24 Academy Midshipmen," UPI Newswire, 28 April 1994.
2. Daniel Patrick Moynihan, "Defining Deviancy Down," *American Scholar,* winter 1993, 17.
3. Charles Krauthammer, "Defining Deviancy Up: The New Assault on Bourgeois Life," *New Republic,* 22 November 1993, 20ff.
4. James Q. Wilson, *The Moral Sense* (New York: Free Press, 1993), ix.
5. Joe Klein, "How about a Swift Kick?" *Newsweek,* 26 July 1993, 30.
6. Carl F. H. Henry, *Christian Countermoves in a Decadent Culture* (Portland, Oreg.: Multnomah, 1986), 9.
7. Dr. Dobson's newsletter, Focus on the Family, January 1994.

8. Erwin Lutzer, *Exploding the Myths that Could Destroy America* (Chicago: Moody, 1986), 47.

9. Herbert Marcuse, *Counter-Revolution and Revolt* (New York: Beacon Press, 1972), 17.

10. Marcuse, *Counter-Revolution,* 127.

11. Catherine Edwards, *The Politics of Immorality in Ancient Rome* (London: Cambridge University Press, 1993), 50.

12. Procopius, *The Secret History,* trans. C. A. Williamson (New York: Penguin, 1981), 120ff.

13. John Silber, *Straight Shooting: What's Wrong with America and How to Fix It* (New York: Harper & Row, 1989), xv.

14. Paul Johnson, *Intellectuals* (New York: Harper & Row, 1988), 342.

15. Jacques Ellul, *The Betrayal of the West* (New York: Seabury Press, 1978), 196.

16. 2 Chronicles 16:9, TLB.

Chapter 10

1. Susan Cyre, "Fallout Escalates over 'Goddess' Sophia Worship," *Christianity Today,* 4 April 1994, 74.

2. Joseph A. Harriss, "The Gospel according to Marx," *Reader's Digest,* February 1993, 68.

3. Anita Manning, "New Age Looks to the East," *USA Today,* 22 February 1990, 1D.

4. Manning, "New Age."

5. Ann Landers column, Creators Syndicate, 26 April 1994.

Chapter 11

1. Associated Press Wire Service Report, 3 May 1994.

2. Richard D. Glasow, Ph.D., "Abortion Statistics Paint Grim Picture: Part I," *National Right to Life News,* 30 March 1994, 17.

3. Myron Magnet, "The American Family, 1992," *Fortune,* 10 August 1992, p. 43.

4. Barbara Dafoe Whitehead, "Dan Quayle Was right," *Atlantic Monthly,* April 1993, 71.

5. Eusebius, *History of the Church from Christ to Constantine,* trans. G. A. Williamson (New York: Dorset Press, 1965), 334ff.

6. Edith Hamilton, *The Roman Way* (1984; reprint New York: Book of the Month Club, 1991), 194.

Conclusion

1. Hassan bin Talal, *Search for Peace* (London: Macmillan, 1984), 4ff., 131.

2. Carl Michalson, *The Hinge of History: An Existential Approach to the Christian Faith* (New York: Scribner's, 1959), 240.

3. Richard Tarnas, *The Passion of the Western Mind: Understanding the Ideas That Have Shaped Our World View* (New York: Ballantine, 1993), 117.

4. C. Northcote Parkinson, *Evolution of Political Thought* (Boston: Houghton Mifflin, 1958), 304.

5. Jeremiah 9:23-24, TLB.

6. Ezekiel 39:21, NKJV.

Appendix

1. Spengler's work in German first appeared in 1918, near the end of the First World War; the English edition, in two volumes, first appeared in 1932.

2. Edward Gibbon, *The Decline and Fall of the Roman Empire,* vol. I (New York: E. P. Dutton, 1978), 430.

3. Francis Fukuyama, *The End of History and the Last Man* (New York: Avon, 1992).

4. John Lukacs, *The End of the Twentieth Century and the End of the Modern Age* (New York: Ticknor & Fields, 1993), 272f.

5. David Halberstam, *The Next Century* (New York: Avon, 1992), 16.

6. Halberstam, *Century,* 88ff., 99.

7. Samuel P. Huntington, "The Clash of Civilizations?" *Foreign Affairs,* vol. 72, no. 3, summer 1993, 24–25.

8. Huntington, "Clash," 24.

SELECTIVE BIBLIOGRAPHY

Anchor, Robert. *The Enlightenment Tradition.* Berkeley: University of California Press, 1967.

Barton, David. *America: To Pray or Not to Pray?* Aledo, Tex.: Wallbuilders Press, 1991.

Bennett, William J. *Index of Leading Cultural Indicators.* New York: Simon & Schuster, 1994.

Bentley-Taylor, David. *Augustine: Wayward Genius.* Grand Rapids: Baker, 1980.

Berlin, Isaiah. *The Crooked Timber of Humanity: Chapters in the History of Ideas.* New York: Knopf, 1991.

Beus, J. G. de. *The Future of the West.* New York: Harper & Bros., 1953.

Bloom, Allan. *The Closing of the American Mind.* New York: Simon & Schuster, 1987.

———. *Giant and Dwarfs: Essays, 1960–1990.* New York: Simon & Schuster, 1990.

Boorstin, Daniel J. *The Discoverers: A History of Man's Search to Know His World and Himself.* New York: Random House, 1983.

Botsford, George Willis. *A Sourcebook of Ancient History.* New York: Macmillan, 1913.

Breasted, James Henry. *The Conquest of Civilization.* New York: Harper & Bros., 1926.

Bruun, Geoffrey. *The Enlightened Despots.* New York: Holt, Reinhart & Winston, 1967.

Burnham, James. *The Suicide of the West.* Washington, D.C.: Regnery Gateway, 1985.

Bush, Vannevar. *Science Is Not Enough.* New York: Morrow, 1967.

Butterfield, Herbert. *Christianity and History.* London: Bell, 1950.

Cameron, Averil. *The Mediterranean World in Late Antiquity, A.D. 395–600.* London: Routledge, 1993.

Clive, Geoffrey. *The Romantic Enlightenment.* New York: Meridian, 1960.

Clough, Shepard B. *The Rise and Fall of Civilization.* New York: Columbia University Press, 1951.

Collier, Peter, and David Horowitz. *Destructive Generation: Second Thoughts about the Sixties.* New York: Summit Books, 1989.

Colson, Charles, with Ellen Santilli Vaughn. *Against the Night: Living in the New Dark Ages.* Ann Arbor, Mich.: Servant, 1989.

D'Sousa, Dinesh. *Illiberal Education: The Politics of Race and Sex on Campus.* New York: Random House, 1991.

Davidson, James Dale, and Lord William Rees-Mogg. *The Great Reckoning.* Rev. ed. New York: Simon & Schuster, 1993.

Dawson, Christopher. *Enquiries into Religion and Culture.* Freeport, N.Y.: Books for Libraries, 1968.

Dudley, Donald R. *The Civilization of Rome.* New York: Meridian, 1993.

Durant, Will, and Ariel Durant. *The Lessons of History.* New York: Simon & Schuster, 1968.

Eddy, George Sherwood. *God in History.* New York: Association Press, 1947.

Edwards, Catherine. *The Politics of Immorality in Ancient Rome.* London: Cambridge University Press, 1993.

Ehrenberg, Victor. *Man, State, and Deity.* London: Methuen & Co., 1974.

Eisenstadt, Samuel Noah. *The Decline of Empires.* Englewood Cliffs, N.J.: Prentice Hall, 1967.

Ellul, Jacques. *The Betrayal of the West.* New York: Seabury Press, 1978.

Fukuyama, Francis. *The End of History and the Last Man.* New York: Avon, 1992.

Garraty, John A., and Peter Gay, eds. *The Columbia History of the World.* New York: Harper & Row, 1972.

Gay, Peter. *The Enlightenment: The Rise of Modern Paganism.* New York: Knopf, 1967.

Gibbon, Edward. *The Decline and Fall of the Roman Empire.* New York: E. P. Dutton, 1978.

Grant, Michael. *The Ancient Mediterranean.* New York: Meridian, 1969.

———. *The Climax of Rome.* Boston: Little Brown, 1968.

Grousset, René. *The Sum of History.* Translated by A. & H. Temple. Westport, Conn.: Hyperion, 1979.

Guinness, Os. *The American Hour.* New York: Macmillan Free Press, 1993.

———. *The Dust of Death: A Critique of the Counter Culture.* Downers Grove, Ill.: InterVarsity, 1973.

Halberstam, David. *The Next Century.* New York: Avon, 1992.

Hamilton, Edith. *The Greek Way.* New York: Norton, 1983; New York: Book of the Month Club, 1991.

———. *The Roman Way.* New York: Norton, 1984; Book of the Month Club edition, 1991.

———. *Witness to the Truth: Christ & His Interpreters.* New York: Norton, 1957.

Hayek, F. A. *The Fatal Conceit: The Errors of Socialism.* Chicago: University of Chicago Press, 1988.

Haywood, Richard Mansfield. *The Myth of Rome's Fall.* New York: T. Y. Crowell, 1958.

Heilbroner, Robert L. *The Future as History.* New York: Harper & Row, 1960.

Henry, Carl F. H. *Christian Countermoves in a Decadent Culture.* Portland, Oreg.: Multnomah, 1986.

———. *Twilight of a Great Civilization: The Drift toward Neo-Paganism.* Wheaton, Ill.: Crossway, 1988.

Hine, Thomas. *Facing Tomorrow.* New York: Knopf, 1991.

Joad, C. E. M. *Decadence: A Philosophical Inquiry.* London: Faber & Faber, 1959.

Johnson, Paul. *A History of the Jews.* New York: Harper & Row, 1987.

———. *Intellectuals.* New York: Harper & Row, 1988.

———. *Modern Times.* New York: Harper & Row, 1983.

Jones, E. Michael. *Degenerate Moderns: Modernity as Rationalized Sexual Misbehavior.* San Francisco: Ignatius Press, 1993.

Jones, Tom B. *In the Twilight of Antiquity.* Minneapolis: University of Minnesota Press, 1978.

Judt, Tony. *Past Imperfect: French Intellectuals, 1944–1956.* Berkeley: University of California Press, 1993.

Kagan, Donald. *Decline & Fall of the Roman Empire: Why Did It Collapse?* Lexington, Mass.: D. C. Heath, 1962.

Katz, Solomon. *The Decline of Rome and the Rise of Mediaeval Europe.* Ithaca, N.Y.: Cornell University Press, 1955.

Kennedy, D. James, with J. Nelson Black. *Character & Destiny: A Nation in Search of Its Soul.* Grand Rapids: Zondervan, 1994.

Kennedy, Paul. *The Rise and Fall of the Great Powers: Economic Change and Military Conflict from 1500 to 2000.* New York: Vintage Books, 1989.

Kirk, Russell. *Enemies of the Permanent Things.* New Rochelle, N.Y.: Arlington House, 1969.

———. *The Roots of American Order.* Washington, D.C.: Regnery Gateway, 1991.

Koestler, Arthur. *The Ghost in the Machine.* New York: Macmillan, 1968.

Kristol, Irving. *On the Democratic Idea in America.* New York: Harper & Row, 1972.

Lukacs, John. *The End of the Twentieth Century and the End of the Modern Age.* New York: Ticknor & Fields, 1993.

Lutzer, Erwin. *Exploding the Myths That Will Destroy America.* Chicago: Moody Press, 1986.

MacMullen, Ramsey. *Corruption and the Decline of Rome.* New Haven, Conn.: Yale University Press, 1988.

Mansfield, Harvey C., Jr. *America's Constitutional Soul.* Baltimore: Johns Hopkins University Press, 1991.

Manuel, Frank E. *The Age of Reason.* Ithaca, N.Y.: Cornell University Press, 1961.

Marcuse, Herbert. *Counter-Revolution and Revolt.* New York: Beacon Press, 1972.

McCormick, Thomas J. *America's Half-Century.* Baltimore: Johns Hopkins University Press, 1989.

McNeill, William. *The Rise of the West.* Chicago: University of Chicago Press, 1963.

Merkley, Paul. *The Greek and Hebrew Origins of Our Idea of History.* New York: Edwin Mellen, 1987.

Michalson, Carl. *The Hinge of History: An Existential Approach to the Christian Faith.* New York: Scribner's, 1959.

Mora, Gonzalo Fernández de la. *Egalitarian Envy: The Political Foundations of Social Justice.* Translated by Antonio T. de Nicolás. New York: Paragon House, 1987.

Muggeridge, Malcolm. *The End of Christendom.* Grand Rapids: Eerdmans, 1983.

Nisbet, Robert. *The Present Age: Progress and Anarchy in Modern America.* New York: Harper & Row, 1988.

Nye, Joseph S., Jr. *Bound to Lead: The Changing Nature of American Power.* New York: Harper/Collins, 1990.

Ogg, David. *Europe of the Ancien Régime: 1715–1783.* New York: Harper & Row, 1965.

Olson, Walter K. *The Litigation Explosion.* New York: E. P. Dutton, 1991.

Ortega y Gasset, José. *The Revolt of the Masses.* New York: Norton, 1957.

Parkinson, C. Northcote. *The Evolution of Political Thought.* Boston: Houghton Mifflin, 1959.

Pelikan, Jaroslav. *The Excellent Empire: The Fall of Rome and the Triumph of the Church.* San Francisco: Harper & Row, 1987.

Peyre, Henri. "The Influence of Eighteenth-Century Ideas on the French Revolution." In *Intellectual Movements in Modern European History.* Edited by Franklin L. Baumer. New York: Macmillan, 1965.

Powys, John Cooper. *The Meaning of Culture.* New York: Norton, 1929.

Procopius. *The Secret History.* Translated by C. A. Williamson. New York: Penguin, 1981.

Revel, Jean-François. *Democracy against Itself: The Future of the Democratic Impulse.* Translated by Roger Kaplan. New York: Macmillan Free Press, 1993.

Roberts, Craig, and Karen LaFollette. *Meltdown inside the Soviet Economy.* Washington, D.C.: Cato Institute, 1990.

Rostovtzeff, Michael I. *Social and Economic History of the Roman Empire.* Oxford: Oxford University Press, 1926.

Sartre, Jean-Paul. *What Is Literature?* Translated by Bernard Frechtman. New York: Philosophical Library, 1949.

Schaeffer, Francis A. *How Should We Then Live?* Wheaton, Ill.: Crossway, 1989.

Shirer, William L. *The Rise and Fall of the Third Reich.* New York: Simon & Schuster, 1959.

Siegfried, André. *Nations Have Souls.* Translated by Edward Fitzgerald. New York: G. P. Putnam's Sons, 1952.

Silber, John. *Straight Shooting: What's Wrong with America and How to Fix It.* New York: Harper & Row, 1989.

Solzhenitsyn, Aleksandr. *A World Split Apart: Commencement Address Delivered at Harvard University, June 6, 1978.* New York: Harper & Row, 1978.

Soren, David, et al. *Carthage. Uncovering the Mysteries and Splendors of Ancient Tunisia.* New York: Simon & Schuster, 1990.

Spengler, Oswald. *The Decline of the West.* New York: Knopf, 1937.

———. *Man and Technics.* London: Allen & Unwin, 1931.

Starr, Chester G. *The Roman Empire, 27 B.C.–A.D. 476: A Study in Survival.* New York: Oxford University Press, 1982.

Sykes, Charles J. *A Nation of Victims: The Decay of the American Character.* New York: St. Martin's, 1992.

Talal, HRH Hassan bin. *Search for Peace.* London: Macmillan, 1984.

Tarnas, Richard. *The Passion of the Western Mind: Understanding the Ideas That Have Shaped Our World View.* New York: Ballantine, 1993.

Tenney, Merrill C. *New Testament Times.* Grand Rapids: Eerdmans, 1965.

Tocqueville, Alexis de. *Democracy in America.* Translated by George Lawrence. New York: Harper & Row, 1969.

Toynbee, Arnold J. *Civilization on Trial.* New York: Oxford University Press, 1948.

———. *A Study of History.* Abridged by D. C. Somervell. London: Oxford University Press, 1946.

———. *A Study of History.* Rev. ed. with Jane Caplan. London: Oxford University Press, 1972.

Toynbee, Arnold, and Abraham Shallit, eds. *The Crucible of Christianity: Judaism, Hellenism and the Historical Background to the Christian Faith.* London: Thames and Hudson, 1969.

Weiss, John. *Conservatism in Europe, 1770–1945: Traditionalism, Reaction and Counter-Revoluton.* New York: Harcourt Brace Jovanovich, 1977.

Willey, Basil. "The Touch of Cold Philosophy." In *Intellectual Movements in Modern European History.* Edited by Franklin L. Baumer. New York: Macmillan, 1965.

Wilson, James Q. *The Moral Sense.* New York: Macmillan Free Press, 1993.

CLASSICAL SOURCES

Eusebius. *History of the Church from Christ to Constantine.* Translated by G. A. Williamson. New York: Dorset Press, 1965.

Herodotus. *The Persian Wars.* In *Greek and Roman Historians.* Translated by George Rawlinson, edited by C. A. Robinson, Jr. New York: Holt, 1957.

Josephus. *The Works of Josephus: Complete and Unabridged.* Translated by William Whiston. Pearson, Mass.: Hendrickson, 1987.

Lactantius. *A Source-Book of Ancient History.* Botsford, George Willis, and Lillie Shaw Botsford. New York: Macmillan, 1913.

Marcus Aurelius. *Meditations.* Translated by A. S. L. Farquharson. New York: Dutton, 1961.

Plato. *The Republic.* Translated by Allan Bloom. New York: Harper/Collins, 1968.

Pliny the Elder. *Natural History.* Translated by H. Rackham. Cambridge: Harvard University Press, 1962.

Plutarch. *Lives of the Noble Greeks and Romans.* Edited by Charles Eliot. Harvard Classics edition. New York: P. F. Collier & Son, 1909.

Polybius. *The Histories.* Translated by W. R. Paton. Cambridge: Harvard University Press, 1960.

Robinson, C. A., ed. *Selections from Greek and Roman Historians.* New York: Holt, Reinhart & Winston, 1957.

Salvian. *On the Government of God.* Translated by Eva M. Sanford. New York: Columbia University Press, 1930.

Suetonius. *The Lives of the Twelve Caesars,* with introduction by Joseph Gavorse. New York: The Modern Library, 1931.

Tacitus. *A Source-Book of Ancient History.* Botsford, George Willis, and Lillie Shaw Botsford. New York: Macmillan, 1913.

REFERENCE

Draper, Edythe, ed. *The Almanac of the Christian World.* Wheaton, Ill.: Tyndale House, 1990.

Wright, John W., ed. *The Universal Almanac 1994.* Kansas City, Mo.: Andrews & McMeel, 1994.

INDEX

A

abortion 110, 165–166, 213–216, 223, 226
American culture 21, 26, 29, 39, 91, 109–110, 112, 122, 141, 147, 150, 154–156, 166, 168, 175–176, 187, 222
American economy 116
American family 28, 87, 157–160, 215, 217, 218–221
American legal system 10, 20–21, 26, 30–32, 177
   history of 31–32
   Judicial misconduct 30
American value system 35
ancient Egypt 37, 64–65, 144, 186, 204, 231, 247, 260
ancient Greece 3, 35–36, 115, 122, 143, 144, 161, 186, 205, 207, 247, 260
apostle Paul 144–145
art 36, 135, 185, 240, 245, 257

B

baby boomers 156, 203
baby busters 156
Bader-Ginsburg, Ruth 180
behaviorism 90
Bennett, Wm. J. 5, 7
Berlin Wall 47
Bloom, Allan 77, 137–138
Blum, Harold F. 3
Bolshevik Revolution 207
Bolsheviks 66, 81

Bonaparte, Napoléon 119, 130, 247
bonding 220–221
Bretton Woods Conference (July 1944) 51
British Empire 50, 111, 234, 238, 245
Burke, Edmund 14
Burnham, James 103–105

C

Carthage 3, 37, 115, 162–166, 186, 238, 260
childhood 158–159, 177, 220
civilization 229, 231, 238, 247, 263
Closing of the American Mind, The 137
Columbus, Christopher 239
communism 8
Cult of Reason 95–96, 102, 132
cultural relativism 242
Cultural relativity 89–90
Cultural Revolution 74–75
culture 145–146, 230

D

Davidson, James Dale 44–47
death industry 213
deconstruction 117
deconstructionism 123, 133–135, 138, 168, 176, 185
Derrida, Jacques 134
Descartes 93
deTocqueville, Alexis 69, 112–116, 243, 246

Dewey, John 84–86
discipline 37
divorce 218
    American family 220
    effects on children 218– 219

E
earthquakes 2, 208
education 35, 98–99, 106,
    178–179, 209, 222, 229, 249
    American 77–78
    curricula 79
    early American 86
    of the Roman Empire 74
    violence in schools 76, 222, 225
educational standards 90
educators in America 75
Elders, Dr. Joycelyn 22, 181–182
Empress Theodora 189
Enlightenment 81, 93, 97, 102,
    111, 113, 116–117, 119–123,
    126–127, 139, 142–145, 161,
    194, 196, 205, 208, 240, 242
entertainment 186
European Community 43, 46, 112,
    247
European economic policy 52
existentialism 117, 138

F
Fay, Michael 5
federalism 116
Feuerbach, Ludwig 205 - 206
five-hundred-year cycles 47
footprints of God 240–241
Founding Fathers 14, 250
France 50, 85, 112, 115, 116, 119,
    143, 186, 240, 245
free market 50
free-market system 61
French Revolution 93, 117, 120,
    126, 128, 132

G Ginsburg 180
Gospel of Thomas 204
government spending 55, 61
Great Britain 143
Great Depression 55, 209
Great Reckoning, The 44

H
health care reform 54, 60, 116
Heritage Foundation 5–6, 61, 210
Hine, Thomas 11–12
Hitler 81, 247, 256
Hobbes, Thomas 93, 118, 259
humanism 31, 90, 99, 121, 123,
    139, 144–145, 168, 179, 205,
    240, 259
Humphry, Derek 213

I
idolatry 204
illegitimacy 25, 87, 157, 216, 217
illiteracy 76
income tax 51–53, 62
Israel 233

J
Japanese industry 45
Japanese stock market 43, 45
Jefferson, Thomas 62– 63, 132
Jesus Seminar 203–204
Judicial activism 21, 32

K
Kennedy, Paul 48– 49
Kevorkian, Dr. Jack 211–213
Keynes, John Maynard 52 .
Kirk, Russell 7, 39, 91, 112, 210

L
Lenin, Vladimir 8, 205
Lerner, Michael 154

liberalism 102–104, 108, 123, 179, 249
Locke, John 93, 95–96, 118
Lonely Crowd, The 153

M
Mann, Horace 84–85
Marcuse, Herbert 184–185, 194
Marx, Karl 205–206
McCormick, Thomas J. 136
media 23, 27, 35, 80, 149–150, 160, 176, 214–215
entertainment 186
metanoia 197
Middle East 234–237
money 151, 167
moral deficiency 174
morality 107, 168–169, 176–177, 183, 193, 207, 216, 249
moral relativism 133, 184
mores 113, 114, 186
Mother Teresa 214–215
music 109, 149, 185–186
as entertainment 160
videos 109, 149

N
National Education Association 78–80, 82–83, 85
Naval Academy 174–175
neoclassical age 94, 97, 116
Nero 190–192
New Age 33, 202, 205
New York Stock Exchange 41, 43

P
Palestine 234
phenomenology 134
philosophes 81, 93, 132, 139–140, 143, 194, 240

political correctness 79–81, 83, 88–89, 102, 103, 180
public schools 87

R
Radical Right 82
raison d'être 107, 122
Rees-Mogg, Lord Wm. 44–47
relativity 92 - 93, 103, 121, 177, 179
religion 107, 121, 155, 160, 167, 169, 178, 180, 184, 238, 257
religious right 182
Rise and Fall of the Great Powers, The 48
Robespierre, Maximilien 129–130, 246
Roman Empire 33, 36–37, 38, 50, 64–65, 67–68, 73–74, 80, 81, 110, 111, 115, 120, 122, 125–126, 132, 143, 144, 160, 163, 166, 186–192, 205, 207, 223–224, 232, 233, 238, 240, 244–245, 246, 247, 257, 260
Rousseau 93, 97, 119–120, 126

S
selfishness 154, 166, 168, 230
serial killers 23
shopping malls 152
sixties, the 32–33, 109, 117, 139, 141–143, 156, 177, 185, 209
socialism 60
Sophia 200
source of truth 97, 242–243
Soviet Union 21, 61, 66, 80, 168, 201, 205, 208
Spain 50, 115
statism 85
stock market crash 55
symptoms of decline 16

T
tabula rasa 96
Tanit 165–166
Ten Commandments 9, 92
Toynbee, Arnold J. 15, 143, 238, 246, 263, 184
trilateralism 46

U
United Nations Monetary and Financial Conference 51
U.S. economy 44, 47, 63

V
values 134

violence 9, 225
violence in schools 76, 222, 225

W
welfare 13, 25, 27, 50, 54, 56, 62
Western culture 14
Western democracy 59, 201
World Council of Churches 201
world economy
   future prospects 45
World Parliament of Religions 199

Z
zero-sum hypothesis 49